Preserving the Built Heritage:
Tools for Implementation

Salzburg Seminar books

address global,

contemporary issues

in the arts, education,

business, law,

government, and science.

Preserving the Built Heritage

Tools for Implementation

J. Mark Schuster

with John de Monchaux
and Charles A. Riley II, editors

Salzburg Seminar
Published by University Press of New England
Hanover and London

Salzburg Seminar

Published by University Press of New England, Hanover, NH 03755

© 1997 by Salzburg Seminar
Printed in the United States of America

5 4 3 2 1

CIP data appear at the end of the book

Contents

Olin Robison
Preface   vii

I.   The Tools of Government Action

1. John de Monchaux and J. Mark Schuster
Five Things to Do   3

2. Stefano Bianca
Direct Government Involvement in Architectural Heritage
Management: Legitimation, Limits, and Opportunities
of Ownership and Operation   13

3. David Throsby
Making Preservation Happen: The Pros and Cons of Regulation   32

4. J. Mark Schuster
Inciting Preservation   49

5. John J. Costonis
The Redefinition of Property Rights as a Tool for
Historic Preservation   81

6. J. Mark Schuster
Information as a Tool of Preservation Action   100

7. J. Mark Schuster
Choosing the Right Tool(s) for the Task   124

II.   Partnerships for Action

8. Charles A. Riley II
When Public Meets Private   157

9. Lester Borley
Presentation, Promotion, Persuasion, and Partnerships: The
Creative Uses of Information and the Role of National Trusts   164

10. Dasha Havel
Preservation and Partnerships in Emerging Market Economies   184

Appendixes

Katherine Mangle
A. Annotated Bibliography   203

B. A Guide to Preservation Resources Online   208

C. Organizations Involved in the Conservation of the
Built Heritage   213

The Salzburg Seminar   219

Participants   221

Contributors   225

Index   229

Preface   *Olin Robison*

Throughout its fifty-year history, the Salzburg Seminar has consistently and consciously devoted its attention to the dynamic and delicate interface between cultural issues and public policy. Historic preservation is one area that brings this interface into particularly high relief, since preservation issues cut across so many interests and jurisdictions and involve such a wide variety of actors—politicians, civil servants, architects, and art conservationists, as well as a broad range of corporations, foundations, and nongovernmental organizations. Perhaps the very fact that the Salzburg Seminar's own home, the eighteenth century, late baroque castle, Schloss Leopoldskron, is in itself a case study in preservation, has prompted the Seminar to devote a series of sessions over the years to historic preservation themes. The most recent of these was Session 332: "Preserving the National Heritage: Policies, Partnerships, and Actions," convened in December 1995. This particular session grew out of the recognition that traditional approaches to preservation are inadequate to meet the current challenges of cultural stewardship. It was framed in large part to investigate why these approaches have become inadequate and to identify innovative options for government, corporate, and private involvement.

The Salzburg Seminar assembled a distinguished international faculty for Session 332, representing a remarkable spectrum of professional and geographic backgrounds. The roster of lecturers from the United States, Switzerland, the United Kingdom, Australia, the Czech Republic, and Austria included experts from the fields of architecture, urban planning, law, and cultural economics, as well as representatives of public and private historic preservation institutions. The noteworthy group of Fellows was equally diverse in geographic and professional terms. Fifty-one Fellows from thirty-one countries attended the session, with 45 percent coming from Eastern Europe, 21 percent from Northeast Asia, 14 percent from Western Europe, 12 percent from North America, and 8 percent from Africa. The professional background of participants was highly representative of many disciplines relating to the fields of historic preservation; many Fellows held senior government positions in heritage departments and ministries. The private sector was well-represented by architects, landscape architects, planners, conservation consultants, and numerous members of nonprofit preservation organizations. Scholars from a variety of academic fields, including art history, cultural anthropology, cultural history, urban planning, tourism planning, and architecture, rounded out the eclectic array of faculty and Fellows assembled for a week at Schloss Leopoldskron. The panoply of preservation activities in which we were engaged ranged from preserving the old cities of Cairo, Mostar, Jerusalem, Dubrovnik, Sanaa,

Nazareth, and Jeddah to preserving Hindu temples in Rajastan, bronze-age burial mounds in Hungary, archaeological sites in Zimbabwe, townscapes in the Northeast of the United States, early modern architectural sites in Estonia, industrial architectural sites in Transylvania, Swahili architecture in Mombassa, temples in Nepal, and ancient ruins in Tajikistan.

This striking diversity sparked an exceptionally lively and engaging debate on various philosophical and practical approaches to historic preservation in both the participants' respective countries and also within the broader global context. We were pleased by the positive results of gathering a group so diverse, and tremendously gratified by the unique spirit of dedication to the international cause of historic preservation that permeated the session. Participants particularly relished the opportunity to discuss the preservation of the built environment as an issue of public policy in surroundings so eminently relevant to and reflective of the topic at hand. The issue truly came to life in the Schloss—as evidenced not only by the provocative lectures and plenary discussions, but also by the large number of informal presentations given by the Fellows during the course of the week on a wide range of topics including Preservation in the Former Yugoslavia: Mostar and Dubrovnik; An Integrated Approach to Total Landscape Management and its Potential for the Preservation of National Heritage; New Lessons from an Old City—Jerusalem; A Decade of Conservation in India; The Role of Museums in Historic Preservation; Historic Preservation in Jeddah; Conservation of the Old City of Sanaa and the Old City of Yemen; World Monuments Watch Site Nominations; Emergency Preparedness and Historical Preservation; The Beginnings of Industrial Architecture in Transylvania; The State of Historic Preservation in Hungary; Partnerships in Europe; The State of Historic Preservation in the Czech Republic; Preservation in Africa; Macedonian Cultural Heritage in the Ohrid Region; Historical Preservation in Tibet; National Dress of the Tajik People; and Three Tools for the Upgrading of the Historical Quarter of Cairo.

This book attempts to capture the intellectual essence of the session, its focus on preservation as an issue of public policy, and its underlying premise that there is a need to strengthen public action with respect to preservation. Readers should know that this session was less a technical investigation of good conservation practices and much more a critical analysis of preservation policies in a variety of settings and a conscious search for new ways to render preservation policies more effective. The inherent difficulty of this approach was of course the complexity of backgrounds and situations in the participants' respective countries. The conceptual framework of the session allowed for a systematic investigation of the issues by focusing on the modes of intervention or the taxonomy of "tools"—as they were frequently referred to during the course of the week—that governments may select from when designing and implementing heritage preservation programs. It became apparent during the course of the week that the effectiveness and applicability of the modes of government intervention depended greatly on the existing set of variables in each country. The most significant of these variables were held to be the particular property to be preserved; the existing level of trust and distrust in government action; the level of government involved—national, state, or local; the amount of resources available; the stability of the respective legal, political, or economic system; and the presence or absence of compelling moral incentives to protect and preserve a site. While faculty and Fellows acknowledged some difficulties in developing a common vocabulary for preservation during the course of the week, a remarkable sense of cohesion and a strong shared concern for the preservation of the world heritage permeated the session and led to the formation of new formal and informal international partnerships for preservation.

We could not have undertaken this project without generous support from the J. Paul Getty Trust, the Samuel H. Kress Foundation, and an anonymous donor, whose support for the Salzburg Seminar's sessions on the arts has been unwavering. Other supporters of the session and its Fellows were The Rockefeller Foundation, the Provost's Fund for the Humanities, Arts and Social Sciences at the Massachusetts Institute of Technology, The Florence and John Schumann Foundation, and the United States Information Agency.

Finally, I want to express my appreciation on behalf of the Salzburg Seminar to the co-chairs of Session 332, John de Monchaux and J. Mark Schuster, both professors in the Department of Urban Studies and Planning of the Massachusetts Institute of Technology, whose ideas, expertise, creativity, enthusiasm, and general leadership gave this session, and this book, life. Thanks, too, to Susanna Fox, Program Director, Kim Thorton, Program Assistant, and all of the staff of the Salzburg Seminar for their assistance in bringing this session to fruition. I also want to thank Dr. Charles A. Riley II, the editor of both of the Seminar's arts books, for his fine work in shepherding this volume, and with him, Tom McFarland and the Seminar's friends and colleagues at the University Press of New England.

December 1996

I

The Tools of Government Action

1   John de Monchaux and
                                                   J. Mark Schuster

Five Things to Do

This book was born in discussions that took place at the 332nd session of the
Salzburg Seminar, "Preserving the National Heritage: Policies, Partnerships,
and Actions," which took place in Salzburg, Austria, in December 1995. At
that time seventy or so Fellows, faculty members, and observers, who shared a
deep and practical concern for the preservation and sustainable use of heritage
resources, considered the evolving role of the state in preserving that heritage,
particularly in the new democracies of Central and Eastern Europe.

Gathered together from over thirty countries, we found that despite our
considerable differences we shared a number of common values: an informed
affection for the buildings, historic settings and landscapes, and other heritage
resources inherited from the past; a deep concern about the physical and institutional resources available to preserve—and sensibly use—these resources; a
growing anxiety about ill-considered public and private attitudes towards the
heritage; and a determination to strengthen government policies and actions
with respect to the heritage. That determination—to strengthen government
policies and actions—became the focus for the Seminar as well as for the current volume. Nevertheless, the other three concerns were never far removed
from our debates; indeed, they emerge repeatedly in this volume as realities
that constantly need to be addressed in preservation. Moreover, we recognized
that state action is increasingly mediated through intermediary institutions as
well as through private action. Thus, the emergence of new partnerships in
heritage preservation became another ancillary focus of our attention.

In this volume we take a rather unusual perspective on heritage preservation, one that, as far as we are aware, is not yet fully represented in preservation literature. We adopt what has been termed by Lester Salamon and Christopher Hood, among others, a "tools approach" to government action.[1] This
approach focuses on the generic tools that can be found in the state's toolbox of
possible actions; by highlighting the attributes of these tools it illuminates new

3

ways to approach preservation action as well as the hazards of ill-conceived action plans.

This volume is unique, we believe, in that it systematically applies the tools approach to a particular sector of government action: historic preservation. Much of the literature on government tools, by contrast, focuses on a particular tool—such as regulation or tax incentives—or discusses tools generally without reference to a particular application. Here we attempt the much more difficult task of exploring the implications of each tool for the preservation of the built heritage. Because we are treading relatively untilled ground, much of what we say will be tentative and preliminary, but we believe that the following chapters demonstrate conclusively that the tools approach yields considerable leverage and an understanding of preservation action that will well reward further research along these lines.

This is not to suggest that the literature on historic preservation has neglected a discussion of the tools of state action—some excellent work is beginning to highlight the substantial differences in the use of tools across countries—but that the discussion has not been as complete or as systematic as we would like.

Hood makes a point of emphasizing that the tools approach to studying state action is a "deliberately one-eyed approach."[2] By this he means that it focuses on attributes of state action that have not normally been the focus of attention, while leaving other, more familiar attributes in the background. We chose to pursue this one-eyed nature of our inquiry even further by inviting a faculty from fields outside of or tangential to historic preservation to contribute to both the Seminar and this volume. Accordingly, the chapters that follow look at the tools of state action in preservation through the eyes of an economist, a lawyer, a public policy analyst, and two directors of major nonprofit organizations, as well as through the eyes of architects and city planners. Thus, in this book we ask you, the reader, in Hood's words, "to look at government in one rather particular and unfamiliar way—as a set of basic tools or instruments which have to be continually drawn upon, combined in varying mixes and applied to the . . . tasks which modern government is (or feels) called upon to undertake."[3] In this way, we hope to offer a fresh perspective to the debate on appropriate modes of preservation action.

Five Tools

In the Department of Urban Studies and Planning at the Massachusetts Institute of Technology, we annually teach a course on the implementation of urban design policy. In that course we argue that there are five and only five things that governments can do—five distinct tools that they can use—to implement their urban design policies, including their policies vis-à-vis the preservation of the built heritage. (We also believe that these are the only tools available to the state in *any* area of government intervention, but defending that claim goes well beyond the bounds of this volume.) Thus, we propose that governments can preserve the built heritage with five generic tools, and that a city, state, or national government will choose from this menu of tools, or modes of intervention, when it designs a program of action with which it hopes to implement its policies.

These five tools of government action—ordered from the heaviest to the lightest government intervention, but also, interestingly, from the most familiar to the least familiar—are the following:

- *Ownership and Operation.* The state might choose to implement policy through direct provision, in this case by owning and operating heritage resources.
- *Regulation.* Alternatively, the state might choose to regulate the actions of other actors, particularly those private individuals or institutional entities that own and occupy heritage resources.
- *Incentives (and disincentives).* The state might provide incentives or disincentives designed to bring the actions of other actors with respect to heritage resources into line with a desired policy.
- *Establishment, allocation, and enforcement of property rights.* The state can establish, allocate, and enforce the property rights of individual parties as these affect the preservation and use of heritage resources.
- *Information.* Finally, the state can collect and distribute information intended to influence the actions of others who might be engaged in the preservation or use of the built heritage.

We contend that one can usefully map onto these five tools all programmatic actions of the state with respect to the heritage. Not that we will find many examples of pure tools in use; rather, we will find that tools are combined for the best results in particular circumstances. Nevertheless, these five tools are the fundamental building blocks with which the government implements heritage policy, and in order to select the best tool in any particular context, one must understand the attributes of each.

We explore the choice among the five tools more fully in Chapter 7, after examining each individually in the next five chapters. These chapters explain each tool as a discrete mode of government intervention. We hope to make clear the circumstances in which each mode of intervention is best used, alone or in combination, to achieve a desired policy outcome. Tool choice is, of course, constrained in the world of action by politics, economics, and preexisting social relationships and institutional structures. While we do not wish to diminish the influence of these real-world constraints on action, we have elected to postpone a discussion of these constraints until the latter half of Chapter 7, so that we can lay out the full realm of possibilities for action before limiting that realm.

Five Messages

For us, an absolutely critical aspect of each of these tools is that each tool would send a particular message if the state adopted it as part of any program of action. In an era when new models of the state are rapidly evolving, we are paying more attention to the relationships between the state and other sectors of society, and recognizing that those relationships can and should be harnessed to promote the public good. Thus, paying attention to the implicit message being sent by the state through each of the generic tools seems particularly important.

These fundamental messages might be characterized as follows:

Ownership and Operation	"The state will do X."
Regulation	"You must (or must not) do X."
Incentives/Disincentives	"If you do X, the state will do Y."
Property Rights	"You have a right to do X, and the state will enforce that right."
Information	"You should do X," or "You need to know Y in order to do X."

Each of these messages implies a very different relationship between the state and those whose actions it is trying to affect. The underlying message must be appropriate to a particular set of circumstances in a particular place and, accordingly, must inform the choice to be made among the various tools. We will do well to keep these messages in mind as we explore the rich toolbox that is already available and consider the new combinations of tools that are constantly being invented to preserve the built environment.

On the Number Five

When we suggest to our students at MIT that there are only five distinguishable modes of government intervention, no more and no fewer, their immediate reaction is that we must be wrong. Surely there must be a sixth that neither of us has thought of. Doesn't the state do many more than five sorts of things?

Our response is not to defend the number five. In fact, we offer a prize for the student who convinces us that there is a sixth mode, a possibility to which we return in Chapter 7. But, so far, our response has been to reiterate the point once made by an American cultural icon, Yogi Berra, a former baseball player for the New York Yankees. It is said that he once went into a pizza parlor and, after ordering his pizza, was asked, "Mr. Berra, would you like your pizza cut into six slices or twelve?" "Oh, six," he replied, "I couldn't possibly eat twelve."

For us, there is a powerful lesson in this story about the leverage one achieves through categorization, and in this sense the current volume is simply an attempt to leverage understanding through categorization. At one end of the analytic spectrum, all government action might be lumped into one category, but that one category is no help in teasing out the nuances of how a government might act. At the other extreme, every individual government program might be thought of as a different form of government action, but this extreme disaggregation also offers little analytical leverage. What does help is a relatively small number of categories, small enough to be remembered, but large enough to capture the most important differences, small enough to obscure minor variations across tools, but large enough to promote thinking about expanding the variety of tools used.

For us, five is just about right. (But our offer of a prize for a sixth still stands.)

Why This Approach?

We believe that a tools approach to preserving the heritage is apt and timely for a number of reasons. For every nation, preserving the national heritage involves a wide variety of actors: governments, private interests, and, increasingly, the nonprofit or private institutions of civil society. Preservation issues affect many different interests, which may, or may not, share an underlying concern for the heritage. But an approach that articulates government actions in terms of this variety of interests and motives has a greater potential to succeed than one that relies on the traditional base of government ownership and operation alone.

All governments want to lighten their curatorial burden for the heritage, particularly the built heritage. For some this desire was brought on by recent fundamental changes in their political and economic settings. Other governments, such as our own (Australia and the United States), are realizing that public resources for state intervention in cultural matters are increasingly limited. In all cases the responsibility for cultural stewardship must be spread more evenly over a broader set of shoulders including individuals, the private sector, nongovernmental organizations, and other nonprofit institutions. A tools approach, we hope, shifts attention towards the means whereby private resources and market forces can be better engaged in this challenge.

In many parts of the world, the cultural heritage of a nation or region is increasingly seen as a resource in programs for economic development. The World Bank, for example, has recently insisted that explicit attention be given to cultural constraints and opportunities. If economic development programs are carried out with sensitivity to cultural issues, with deep technical competence, and with a concern for long-term economic sustainability, they will have the potential to serve both economic and preservation goals. Inevitably, economic development policy and programs rely heavily on competitive incentives, a workable regulatory framework, deal making, and high-quality information. If such economic programs are to be married to the thoughtful preservation and use of the built heritage, then policy based on congruent modes of intervention is likely to produce better results.

Salamon gives a further reason for this approach in the introduction to his book on the tools of government action.[4] He argues, from an American perspective that we believe applies generally, that a tools approach is a necessary—and overdue—complement to policy analysis that heretofore has focused only on the relationship of policy to outcome. The tools approach, which seeks to understand the relationship of the "technology" of public action to its effectiveness, may better explain the successes and failures of government action than earlier research that does not explicitly address the tools of implementation. Hood gives additional arguments for a "tool-kit perspective" in *The Tools of Government*.[5] He points out that having a sense of the basic tools available to government helps us both make sense of the complexity of modern government and better match the policy to be accomplished with the tool for that job.

A tools approach is also useful for an important analytical reason: it facilitates a cross-national comparison of intervention strategies. Having a fixed template to superimpose on each country's modes of intervention brings important differences into high relief and may identify alternative possibilities. There are few consistent frameworks that have been developed within this field of analysis to foster comparison, and so it is rather difficult, with the current documentation, even to construct a reliable picture of most countries' forms of intervention.

Robert Stipe, a well-known American writer on historic preservation, has pointed out that there are many misconceptions about what approaches other countries take.[6] He argues that though different countries clearly emphasize different combinations of tools, national preservation programs are remarkable more for their similarities than for their differences. In the sense that they draw on the same menu of five possibilities (and on all parts of that menu) he is absolutely correct. As we shall see, the United States, for example, relies more heavily on indirect (particularly tax-based) incentives than do other countries. With a framework built around a generic set of tools, one can see these differences more clearly and speculate on their importance.

The mixed quality of the comparative literature suggests another caution: just because a country uses a particular tool does not mean that that tool has been particularly effective (or more effective than other tools might have been). Thus, we have made no attempt to catalog the use of the various tools country by country. Indeed, the literature is neither complete enough nor structured enough to allow a complete comparative catalog. The task of completing a truly comparative description of government interventions deserves and awaits further research attention.

In the end, the analysis of government action through a consideration of the tools at its disposal is a device to give coherence to an otherwise bewildering panoply of programs and policies, rather than a device to explain the relationships between policy, action, and results. Our focus in this volume is unapologetically on the former, though in Part II we raise some of the issues that would be important in a full consideration of the latter.

The Case for Government Intervention

The authors of this volume share a common belief that governments must intervene to preserve the heritage, though we might disagree about the appropriate boundaries of that intervention. Though a debate on this issue would lie beyond the scope of this volume, we would like to take a moment to suggest why government intervention in the preservation and sustainable use of the heritage remains a necessary activity in a world increasingly dependent on the marketplace for initiative and investment.

Many of the central arguments for government intervention are economic. A number of them have to do with economic efficiency. If the market for historic buildings and spaces is not capable of sustaining these places, public intervention may be needed. Markets tend to account for the private benefits, not the social benefits, of consumption. Whenever social benefits exceed private benefits, a good will be under-produced unless extra-market influences can be brought to bear in the marketplace. Because markets are usually unable to foster "spillover effects"—in this case economic benefits that accrue to others because of an individual's actions to conserve a historic place—a case for public encouragement of the individual's activity can be made. An allied argument is the need to foster what might be called the "interstitial benefits," whereby the quality of the public realm as a whole can be greater than the sum of its parts, provided that private conservation action is externally stimulated and coordinated. One might argue, too, that governments need to exercise responsibility for the intergenerational benefits to be derived from the preservation of historic places. The market has no ready mechanism to do this. A final efficiency argument is based on the recognition of "option demand." To maintain the option of having a future choice to consume a good or service for which there is no current market demand, we must rely on extra-market forces.

The second family of economic arguments for government involvement has to do with equity. Markets often encounter geographic realities that threaten private support of a historic setting, they may neglect the cultural interests and legacies of minority groups, and they may bar access to historic places with price barriers. All of these cases warrant government intervention.

But notice how easy it is to slip into the vocabulary of economics to describe the "value" and "worth" of government intervention in historic preservation. There are other, cogent reasons for a government to pay attention to the preservation of the built environment. Among the most important are educational reasons. We believe that society should have at its disposal physical manifestations of its history, aspirations, successes, and tragedies, and should present and interpret those physical resources. These societal values—note again how hard it is to avoid the concepts and vocabulary of economics despite our best intentions—differ, we believe, from purely economic motivations.

Finally, there are political motivations, by which we mean motivations of the body politic, rather than politically strategic motivations. By one analysis, the state will further those goals that more than a majority of its citizens call it to support, whatever the basis of that support.

Though the authors of this volume generally believe the arguments for government intervention to be convincing, they also believe that government needs to act more adroitly to preserve the built heritage, both in using its own resources and in engaging the much greater resource of private and institutional action. A careful consideration of the tools of government action serves that need. Our overall intention is to help train better designers of new preservation policies and programs and better users of current policies and programs. It is to these tasks that we now turn.

The Structure of This Volume

In preparing for the Salzburg Seminar, we found the management guide produced for the International Symposium on World Heritage Towns in Quebec to be particularly useful.[7] This guide speaks to town governments faced with the challenge of safeguarding historic urban places in a time of change. Using a tools approach, though less formally than this volume does, it provided us with a number of ideas, including a useful inventory of tasks that must be performed, by the private, the public, or the nonprofit sector, to accomplish preservation objectives. This list of tasks, which can be applied equally to individual buildings, ensembles, public spaces, or to any other form of heritage resource, included identification, protection, conservation, restoration, renovation, maintenance, and revitalization. To this list of tasks we would add the animation and sustained use of these resources.

Our structure for the Seminar, as well as for this book, was to ask each author to imagine how a government would cause each task to be performed by using, in turn, each of the tools it possesses. Thus, Stefano Bianca addresses a government's ability to undertake these tasks directly with its own resources through ownership and operation; David Throsby examines the basis for a government's capacity to regulate and require private action that would accomplish one or more of these tasks; J. Mark Schuster looks at a government's ability to provide incentives, through grants, tax relief, and other inducements, that would motivate others to undertake these tasks; John Costonis assesses government's ability to define and allocate property rights to perform one or more of these tasks; and, finally, Schuster looks at government-provided information designed to influence private and public support of these tasks. In concluding the first part of this volume, Schuster then reflects on each of these contributions by looking at factors involved in the choice of the appropriate tool or tools for the preservation tasks at hand. In Part II, after an introduction by Charles Riley, we bring together two important contributions by Lester Borley and by Dasha Havel that demonstrate the nature and nurture of the partnerships among nongovernmental organizations, the private sector, and governments, which arise of necessity in the use of these tools.

Because we made the choice to limit the Seminar sessions to a consideration of the built heritage, the examples we use address the particular problems of the built heritage. By continuing that focus in this volume, we intend to keep this material coherent rather than to belittle the importance of government policy and action vis-à-vis all types of heritage resources. As Lester Borley points out later in this volume, it is increasingly clear that one needs to adopt an all-encompassing definition of the cultural heritage in order to do a responsible job at preserving any of its elements.

Notes

1. Lester Salamon, ed., *Beyond Privatization: The Tools of Government Action* (Washington, D.C.: The Urban Institute Press, 1989); and Christopher C. Hood, *The Tools of Government* (Chatham, N.J.: Chatham House Publishers, 1986).
2. Hood, *The Tools of Government*, xi.
3. Hood, *The Tools of Government*, xi.
4. Salamon, *Beyond Privatization*, chap. 1.
5. Hood, *The Tools of Government*, 7–9.
6. Robert E. Stipe, "Introduction," in Anthony Dale, *Volume I: France, Great Britain, Ireland, The Netherlands, and Denmark*, Historic Preservation in Foreign Countries, ed. Robert E. Stipe (Washington, D.C.: United States Committee of the International Council on Monuments and Sites, 1982), 2–4.
7. International Symposium on World Heritage Towns, *Safeguarding Historic Urban Ensembles in a Time of Change: A Management Guide* (Quebec: Organization of World Heritage Towns, 1991).

References

Hood, Christopher C. *The Tools of Government*. Chatham, N.J.: Chatham House Publishers, 1986.

International Symposium on World Heritage Towns. *Safeguarding Historic Urban Ensembles in a Time of Change: A Management Guide*. Quebec: Organization of World Heritage Towns, 1991.

Salamon, Lester, ed. *Beyond Privatization: The Tools of Government Action*. Washington, D.C.: The Urban Institute Press, 1989.

Stipe, Robert E., series ed. Historic Preservation in Foreign Countries, later retitled Historic Preservation in Other Countries. Washington, D.C.: United States Committee of the International Council on Monuments and Sites, various dates. Volumes in the series include:

> Dale, Anthony. *Volume I: France, Great Britain, Ireland, The Netherlands, and Denmark*. 1982.
> Will, Margaret Thomas. *Volume II: Federal Republic of Germany, Switzerland, and Austria*. 1984.
> Gleye, Paul H., and Waldemar Szczerba. *Volume III: Poland*. 1989.
> Leimenstoll, Jo Ramsay. *Volume IV: Turkey*. 1989.

Direct Government Involvement in Architectural Heritage Management: Legitimation, Limits, and Opportunities of Ownership and Operation

As the author of the first chapter on the "five tools," I thought I might take advantage of this privilege by sharing with you a few rather philosophical thoughts that may shed light on the wider context of this volume—even at the risk of opening up a number of complex and possibly confusing issues. But then, as we are all aware, the complexity of heritage preservation is the very matter of this volume. So please bear with me as I venture into some fundamental questions about the meaning of conservation before addressing my main topic, the ownership and operation of heritage assets by government institutions.

Why Conservation? Why Government Involvement?

Why do we need to preserve the architectural heritage at all, and why should governments have a responsibility in this process? To convinced conservationists such questions may sound surprising. Yet, seen from a wider historic and cultural viewpoint, preservation in the form we know it today is a relatively young phenomenon, rooted in needs and concepts that emerged in nineteenth-century Europe. Preservation in our modern sense was almost never an issue in pre-industrial and non-European civilizations as long as those civilizations were held together by the forces of a living "tradition," that is, the powerful social practice of daily life, rooted in shared spiritual convictions.

13

Although restrained by their adherence to shared values and collective modes of behavior, traditional societies were often light-hearted, if not reckless, in dealing with the material heritage of their own cultures or with that of their predecessors. They had limited consciousness of history in the academic sense of the term, and little sense of managing an architectural patrimony for later generations. Deeply immersed in their own cultural system, and held together by strong social and spiritual bonds, traditional societies did not develop the critical distance that characterizes later, more scientific approaches to the heritage, including archaeology and art history. Old traditions were based not on abstract theories but on practiced faith, and thus spontaneously took concrete form in a range of natural variations, which reflected the personal imprint of those who articulated them, while maintaining an underlying coherence.

Based on this cultural self-assurance, traditional civilizations renovated, changed, or replaced earlier buildings with full confidence in the improvement they were making and with no apparent feeling of cultural loss. A perfect illustration of this attitude is the recurrent transformation of many European churches through various historic periods, a centuries-long process of evolution within the same Christian tradition—which sometimes confronts modern conservationists with the difficult decision of exactly which historic layer to preserve. Things become even more complicated when different cultures and traditions overlap in the same place. Greek and Roman columns were commonly used, for example, in the construction of Christian basilicas and Muslim mosques—a very pragmatic attitude towards architectural heritage, to say the least. Looking at the complex growth process of historic cities such as Rome, Split, or Damascus, to mention just a few, would offer another array of interesting case studies and insights. There one could observe, for instance, how Roman amphitheaters were turned into medieval housing compounds, how former palaces defined the layout of complete neighborhoods, and how an Hellenistic agora was transformed into the first monumental mosque of Islam.

Without digressing much further, let me just make the point that the richness and variety of many preindustrial historic cities we admire today result from a seemingly incoherent, if not careless, attitude to the past. While there may be a coherence in terms of shared values or a consistent genius loci, there is no strict uniformity of style. Countless incremental interventions, carried out over many generations, have produced the complexity and the depth of historic patterns that fascinate the modern eye. Though the contrasts, if not contradictions, among such individual interventions may puzzle us today, certain social and environmental constraints kept them within a compatible range of variation. The single elements blend into a well-orchestrated symphony of distinct, but correlated architectural forms. All of us cherish the qualities embodied in such historic products and agree that the various layers of past interventions must be preserved to the fullest possible extent. When judged in our own terms of preservation, though, we have to admit that the very genesis of this accumulated heritage was fundamentally anti-historic and nonscientific.

Here we face a paradoxical situation, because modern concepts of restoration and preservation are based on a deep-rooted change of paradigms that resulted, on the one hand, in the disruption of traditional (organic) cultural growth processes, and, on the other hand, in the need for conservation to safeguard the inherited patrimony and transmit it to future generations. Preservation is thus the consequence of a process of alienation, in which certain members of a society no longer recognize their deeper values and motivations in its material culture. Preservation can thus substitute for a living tradition, though it lacks the power of procreation and may no longer be able to engage the society as a whole.

This major change of paradigms began in the so-called Enlightenment of the late eighteenth century, and gained full momentum towards the middle of the nineteenth century, when age-old values, social structures, and production processes underwent a massive change. Indeed, the nineteenth century generated a break unlike any other in the history of human civilization. Secularization, industrialization, and the growth of modern sciences and technology, combined with the emergence of national ideologies and complex bureaucratic systems, fundamentally changed the definition of culture and corresponding lifestyles. The changes continue as we enter the second phase of the industrial revolution, in which information starts driving the sciences and related cultural development mechanisms. The gradual replacement of knowledge and practiced values by abstract and often dogmatic sciences—or by the impact of an omnipresent information system—has not only produced a certain spiritual vacuum in our daily reality, it has also weakened our natural cultural bonds with both the past and the future. As a result of this erosion, diverging attitudes have emerged: dismissive or nostalgic with regard to the past, and utopian or defensive with regard to the future. Meanwhile, a new material culture grew explosively over the past 150 years in the "developed" part of the world, but one could argue that cultural wealth, speaking in a more spiritual sense, hardly increased and was even diminished by this process.

It is therefore no surprise to observe that modern civilization, in spite of all its achievements, is still in quest of deeper values and meaning. Looking at architecture as an expression of contemporary trends, one can easily follow this search in the stylistic developments of the last 150 years. There are good reasons to interpret the nineteenth-century revivals of historic styles (and the restoration concept that went with them) as deliberate attempts to reproduce lost values in somewhat artificial (if not superficial) form. The early twentieth-century modernist movement, in turn, was a legitimate reaction to this disguise, insisting on honesty and truthfulness with regard to function and to the new industrial production processes, but unable to provide a lasting cultural identity and a deeper sense of truth. Moreover, modernism, particularly its urbanistic concepts, often proved destructive to the built environment and the cultural heritage.

Today we witness another revivalist trend, as postmodern architecture tries to restore the connections with history and compensate for the bleak environment produced by the sweeping propagation of the modern style. Future generations will have to judge whether this attempt succeeded in producing valid cultural expressions. I realize that many of my architect colleagues may not entirely concur with this interpretation, but I feel that this is the broad background against which we have to see modern preservation efforts. The massive change that characterizes modern civilization since the late nineteenth century, in conjunction with the possibility that societies have lost touch with their essential values, are the main reasons we call for the preservation of the built cultural heritage today.

Though this analysis in many ways justifies and enhances it, institutionalized preservation does have certain conceptual pitfalls. One of them is that cultural heritage might now be perceived as a frozen substance, no longer subject to a natural evolution; another is the fact that the sudden break in traditions (defined as the continuous flow of values and practices) has created an artificial divide between ancient and modern, and between conservation and development. Indeed, conservation is on the verge of becoming a science of its own, detached from the daily concerns of society. The divide might well be further accentuated when governmental and administrative structures transform preservation into an institutional task, since this tends to eliminate more spontaneous and personalized cultural initiatives. One may deplore this situation, but it is the modern context in which preservation has to operate. Being aware of the inherent ideological shortcomings of the institutional preservation approach may help us overcome them in our practical work. One way to achieve this, as I will argue below, is to see conservation as part of wider development processes, bringing in social and economic forces to support heritage survival, while at the same time introducing a cultural dimension into current development concepts, which tend to be far too limited when they exclude social and cultural values.

We can now return to my initial question and give a better justification for preservation and for the government's role in it. Monuments embody collective and timeless values that the present is no longer able to reproduce and that, therefore, need to be considered irreplaceable resources.[1] More than mere repositories of past traditions, they contain the seeds of potential future developments, which may grow through the creative efforts of later generations. By transmitting their messages across time, heritage assets can root contemporary societies, give them a sense of place and continuity, and validate their deeper aspirations. Admittedly, such cultural and spiritual messages can be interpreted differently in different periods and by different viewers—in fact, history is full of examples of creative misunderstandings—yet it is still important to have a permanent reference point. Thus, present society has an eminent need, if not a duty, to preserve and to transmit the essential part of its patrimony to future generations; governments, as legitimate representatives of society, must act as responsible custodians and supreme managers of their cultural patrimony. To perform this duty well, the state must set up the right strategies, balanced between development and conservation, to incite, coordinate, and implement the necessary conservation actions, and to defend these actions against the interests of individuals who value outcomes that conflict with a broader public interest.

As the primary responsible agents of cultural heritage management, governments are, in a way, the owners of their cultural patrimony, but they can choose how best to exert and implement this power. This range of action is defined by two extremes: on the one hand, using only the state's moral authority to stimulate, enable, and force (if necessary) the individual or collective owners of cultural heritage properties to preserve them according to clear guidelines or rules, based on inventories of the existing patrimony; on the other hand, to own and operate the majority of buildings and spaces deemed worthy of preservation. In reality, of course, these two extremes contain a wide range of intermediate situations. The choice depends on local traditions and political systems, as well as on which forms of intervention will prove the most effective. I shall return to an explicit consideration of state ownership and operation of heritage properties after discussing some more practical problems of heritage management, which, as we will see, strongly influence the desirable mode of intervention and the required institutional back-up.

The Scope and the Potential Conflicts of Heritage Management

Acknowledging the value of the heritage, surveying it, and inventorying it are the first steps towards effective preservation. Today, it is most often the government, through national, provincial (state), or local agencies, that ensures that this task is undertaken comprehensively and consistently, though in many countries nongovernmental, nonprofit organizations are playing an increasing role in preservation.[2] As soon as one starts thinking through the actual applications and possible consequences of this process, one inevitably runs into the problem of priorities: as total preservation is clearly impossible, cultural heritage assets must be ranked in relative importance and conservation projects must be assessed according to actual social and economic feasibility. In other words, what is it that *should* and *can* be preserved?

Obviously, the range of what can be regarded as "national heritage" is enormous, and the way in which individual heritage items can be cared for differs from case to case, as I will discuss in a moment. To mention just a few major categories, there are, for instance:

- Environmental assets, such as virgin landscapes, natural park reserves, agriculturally cultivated areas, and manmade natural environments.
- Landmark monuments of unique historic and/or architectural importance, which may have survived as archaeological vestiges, ruins, complete structures, or still operating buildings.
- Minor monuments, which may not be unique, but which testify to the spirit of a period or establish the context for a major monument.
- Ensembles of monuments, which, through their setting and their interrelationship with the adjacent spaces, provide a relevant testimony to the past.
- Complete historic urban fabrics, which, through their layout, street system, housing patterns, and composite civic structures grown over many centuries, embody the complex patterns of life of earlier generations.
- Movable artifacts, which may or may not have been related to specific buildings, including objects of daily use that incorporate the traditions of their own culture or of different civilizations.

Glancing through this short list of preservation assets, you will immediately realize that only small parts of it can be treated in an archaeological or museal way, that is, by physically isolating the heritage object from its original context and creating a protected environment around it. Today, the increasing need for preservation tends to expand the limits of "heritage," to the extent that preservation necessarily overlaps, and sometimes conflicts with, more mundane development concerns and solid commercial interests.

Take the example of a protected landscape. It must be consistently cultivated to retain its character; it must produce the basic agricultural income required for those involved in its upkeep, if not for larger segments of the population; it must accommodate residents and accept recreational uses connected with tourism, it must cope with appropriate road construction, and water and electricity supply; and so on. All of these activities necessarily call for certain compromises with regard to conservation, yet without them conservation may not even be possible.

Or take the example of a historic city. While it may be relatively easy to deal with key monuments, such as a cathedral or a town hall, the situation becomes much more complex once you consider them in a physical and socioeconomic context comprised of roads, busy public open spaces, historic houses, and traditional commercial or industrial facilities, and try to imagine all the activities and support structures needed to maintain these heritage resources as part of a living environment. Furthermore, problems of private use and ownership arise, which cannot always be resolved by direct government intervention. All of these complications have to be tackled if the overriding objective is to maintain the viability of the historic city, which implies allowing for a measured, natural evolution. Restoration of single monuments without conserving or rehabilitating their historical environment and without supporting the vital social and economic forces that sustain them would make little sense and would eventually deprive the historic substance of its nutrients.

What I want to emphasize with these examples is that there is not *one* rigid method of conservation, but a range of distinct modes of intervention. These modes are correlated to a number of criteria, such as the uniqueness of the structure, its meaning for the society (or for certain groups in the society), its context, its physical condition, its past, present, and potential functions, its ownership, and, not least, the financial resources that can be mobilized for its conservation and maintenance. These factors will determine the most appropriate type of intervention for each case, which may range from archaeological preservation at one extreme to substitution or redevelopment at the other, with possibilities such as partial renovation or adaptive re-use in between.

In short, conservation policy, to be successful, cannot be conceived in the abstract. It must take into account and integrate as much as possible society's current aspirations and living patterns. It must find appropriate uses for restored or converted structures in order to keep them alive—except, of course, in the case of archaeological monuments or museal conservation. It must allow for proper maintenance, and it must, above all, be financially affordable. Conservation should be considered not a separate discipline, but an integral part of more comprehensive environmental planning and economic development—although a very special part, as it deals with highly sensitive resources which cannot be replicated, and therefore depends on distinct rules and regulations. Experience shows that unless it is included in an overall development framework, conservation policy will be difficult to implement or will lose its *raison d'être*. For without such a proactive approach, the heritage to be preserved may be partly gone once conservation measures are ready to be applied. Integrated procedures are therefore mandatory, though certain compromises and trade-offs will have to be made as planners negotiate between divergent objectives and constraints.

The Government's Role in Promoting Integrated Conservation

Having traced a broad picture of general conservation issues and their implications, I return to the question of what should or could be the government's role in this field. I contend that the government's involvement has to take place simultaneously on three main planes: (1) legislation that provides legal protection of the common good represented by the cultural heritage against short-sighted private interests; (2) an overall strategy that includes heritage concerns in social, economic, and physical development plans at national, regional, and local levels; and (3) actual ownership and operation of important sites and monuments that cannot be sustained by the private sector, either because private demand for these resources does not exist, or because the private sector is unable to deal with specific conservation cases.

The government's role as a responsible custodian of national or universal heritage is perhaps best reflected by the first plane of intervention, that is, by legal provisions that define the degree of protection extended to key sites and monuments. While we probably agree that the government is morally obligated to provide this legal protection on behalf of society, we also know the limits of such protection. To work, laws must be enforced, and enforcement is only realistic in carefully selected, highly important cases and for clearly defined structures or spaces. Extending blanket legal protection to large areas or composite structures in daily use is certainly justified as a matter of principle, but such protection can only be fully applied if the actual users are committed to it. Furthermore, especially in Western countries, legal protection may often conflict with private development rights and raise compensation issues, which in many cases necessitate acquisition by the government and therefore require public funds, which are usually limited. Finally, by itself, legal protection is no guarantee for preservation, since without proper use, management, and maintenance, a building or a landscape may deteriorate and eventually lose its qualities or its substance.

Efficient legal protection is therefore indispensable but not sufficient. Furthermore, legal provisions can be effective only if they are backed by strong group solidarity. People must perceive a clear interest in abiding by the rules of protection; they must be able to identify with the protected heritage elements and their underlying values. To this end, legal measures should be issued and managed by the institutional representatives of the groups most directly concerned. While overall protection at the national level may be useful, the subsidiarity principle—allocating direct responsibility to the lowest possible institutional level—may also have its role to play, ensuring a more tangible interrelation between the society and its heritage.

The second plane of government action, which is a complement to legislation, is development guidance at national, municipal, and community levels. Often this task is overlooked under the assumption that conservation and development are two separate issues, pursued by different and unrelated authorities. Nothing could be more fatal for the preservation of the national heritage. As mentioned before, preservation, if conceived in a comprehensive and realistic manner, overlaps by necessity with the full spectrum of development activities, such as infrastructure provision, traffic planning, housing provision, social facilities planning, economic development of private sector commercial activities, tourism development, and so on. Unless heritage management is part of an overall development process that can be shaped to respect and sustain historic features in part to benefit that development process, preservation will remain a marginal, erratic operation with a limited chance of success.

Accordingly, conservation concerns and actions must be a part of every development instrument, such as national and regional development plans, urban land use plans, community and neighborhood investments, and the like. In the case of important historic cities, it is often appropriate to define and delimit districts through special legislation and to establish a local development authority under the umbrella of the municipality or of the national government. Within district boundaries, this authority can pursue, in a largely autonomous manner, the planning, conservation, and daily management of this more delicate urban nucleus, giving a high priority to the rehabilitation of the historic fabric. Such specialized agencies have been successfully implemented not only in Europe, but also in places such as Tunisia, Morocco, and Syria. Whether or not autonomous districts of this type can be established, there is an array of different tools to control development that require minimal or no direct investment by the government, but provide substantial stimulation and guidance. These instruments are presented in the other chapters of Part I of this volume and include, for instance, economic incentives such as grants, tax exemptions, soft loans, and transfers of development rights. These tools must be used consistently and aggressively, as the architectural heritage cannot be replaced once it has slipped beyond a certain degree of disrepair.

The third plane of government action, actual ownership and operation of architectural heritage, raises certain questions. To what extent can the government afford the acquisition of large heritage estates and land holdings? Is ownership and operation by the state the only or the best solution to ensure the survival of the patrimony? How effective is this method in terms of managing limited financial resources? These questions, of course, do not fully apply to those governments that are the sole and only landowners because private ownership has been abolished or has not existed for long periods of time. There, the main issue is whether the government, while already owning all cultural heritage assets (among all the other holdings), can appropriately operate and maintain this stock.

In the remainder of this chapter, I would like to concentrate on the more critical case, where government has to secure the survival of heritage elements in a free market context, which can expose protected structures to the pressures of private sector development. Here, while the acquisition of important heritage elements by the public sector may often be the most obvious solution, it also carries the risk of absorbing large amounts of public funds, and should therefore be used very selectively, in order to maximize each investment. Indeed, public sector ownership and operation does not have to focus exclusively on historic buildings to assist the cause of conservation. One tends to forget the benefits that can be derived from the ownership and management of public open spaces. Practically all governments, irrespective of their political system, own the public street network, the major squares attached to it, and generally also the related public facilities, as well as the development rights for infrastructure systems in historic areas. This ownership not only amounts to a considerable share of land (15 to 20 percent of the total surface), it also allows strategic actions to be undertaken. Carefully implemented, such actions can result in the upgrading of an historic area as a whole, through the stimulating impact channeled through these land holdings, which could be compared to the fibers of an urban fabric. Poorly implemented, the improvement of vehicular access and infrastructure can also have highly destructive effects on an historic city, either directly or by fueling speculative trends. Government, therefore, has a major stake in the development of historic areas; even if it does not own individual historic buildings itself, it can create favorable conditions for conservation to be undertaken by private owners.

Government investment in public land holdings and networks can provide an inducement for others to improve their heritage properties, thereby increasing their financial value; that increase in value can then, at least in part, be captured by the government for reinvestment in the heritage. By cunning management of the increased value, the government may be able to create the funds needed for investment in the heritage, either through subsidies, or by acquiring, restoring, and possibly selling dilapidated buildings. However, initial investments in the public realm, such as improving streets and public open spaces or making the inner city more accessible with new feeder roads (a delicate operation to be handled with great care), tend to create disparities by adding value to adjacent buildings while depreciating buildings and land that do not directly benefit from these public investments. Government administrations, therefore, have to make sure that mechanisms for balancing these added values with their attendant added costs are in place before embarking on such operations. This derivative instrument of public ownership and operation is yet to be acknowledged and implemented.

In addition to managing current public properties, the authorities may decide to own and operate important components of the national heritage that do not normally belong to the public domain. This may occur, for instance, if monuments of national importance are in private ownership, but the owners do not have the means to conserve the building. As long as privately owned heritage components can be properly used and maintained, the government may not need to intervene (except in cases where public access for reasons of unique artistic value or educational merit is mandatory). But once public funds or external donor funds become the only way for a monument to survive, government ownership and operation may be necessary to sustain the moral ownership of collective values. As a rule, such investments should be reserved for key monuments only and for cases that cannot be resolved by any other means, in order to save precious public funds, which may produce wider conservation benefits if spent in an indirect manner.

Different Modes of Ownership and Operation

The whole question of public versus private ownership and how both sectors should interact is becoming an increasingly important topic in discussions on heritage preservation. Conservation policies must be able to cope with a variety of property conditions according to the ideological position each government adopts with respect to real estate holdings and related urban management policies. In this section, I will attempt to characterize in a few words four typical cases, focusing on the complex situation of conservation in the urban context, while acknowledging the shortcomings of any such generalization.

Western Europe

Most Western European countries have managed to retain a sizable portion of the cultural heritage embedded in their historic cities. An ancient tradition of civic pride and, in many cases, good community management and an appreciation of the public common good, have contributed to their preservation of relatively intact historic cities. However, European cities underwent a strong transformation in the second half of the nineteenth century, with the advent of new modes of vehicular traffic and the introduction of the boulevard concept. They were menaced again by World War II, as well as by the forceful urban redevelopment concepts of modernism. These concepts were particularly virulent from the fifties to the seventies, but were soon balanced by more comprehensive urban conservation concepts developed as a reaction to this threat. While physical change has since been better held in check, important social changes have occurred as historic city centers have become the main targets of increasing cultural tourism, and as the growing postindustrial service industries have discovered the advantages of an inner-city location for business, as did the upper class for residence. The resulting "gentrification" has created problems of its own, but it has provided the means for an economic regeneration of the old cities and for corresponding restoration and rehabilitation projects. Many European city administrations must be credited for the technical skill with which they managed this physical renewal, preventing major structural changes in the urban fabric, and establishing a productive interaction between private and public sector interventions. Italy and France led the way in developing the topological and morphological methods through which the urban fabric around protected key monuments could be appraised and rehabilitated.[3]

United States and Canada

In the United States and Canada, private property rights are so predominant that government ownership and operation of landmark buildings is quite limited, and historic buildings, where they exist, often suffer from the impact of a radically changed environment, with corresponding problems of scale and texture. The government is forced to catch up, so to speak, with commercial interests and development, trying to enforce preservation by laws and regulation, or to convince private foundations, private nonprofit organizations, or private owners to take an active part in it. Thus, preservation in these countries depends largely on whether it can be turned into a profitable enterprise or encouraged by tax incentives and subsidies. The government also receives considerable tax income from successful development in the private sector, particularly from property tax at the local level, which would allow it to invest in relevant conservation actions, but the speculative pressures in a deregulated market are such that soaring land prices often prevent direct ownership and operation. In such cases, alternative measures such as the governmentally sanctioned transfer of development rights are needed to beat the market with its own arms.

Formerly Communist Countries

In many formerly communist countries, the situation is radically different from either of the previous cases, since in many instances the government was, has become, or still is the owner of major portions of real estate, even if the land has been leased for the construction of private houses and facilities.[4] Yet, until very recently, there was no entrepreneurial tradition, either in the (almost nonexistent) private sector or in the public sector. A heavily centralized bureaucracy, although set up to facilitate implementation, often burdened conservation, as it ignored potential driving forces such as community commitment and personal motivation.

Since the fall of communism, government land ownership in many countries still represents a huge dormant asset, which increases in value as privatization gains momentum. For the future, much will depend on how this vast real estate asset is managed, how the possible sale of government-owned land is linked to precise development and conservation rules, and whether an appropriate portion of the realized financial gain is set aside to be re-invested in heritage management and environmental improvement.

Muslim Countries

For the developing world, I will limit myself to the case of historic cities in Muslim countries. While many of these cities can muster an architectural heritage as important as that of their European counterparts, the socioeconomic conditions, and, equally important, the prevailing attitude to conservation, are very different. The stability of many of these traditional cities stemmed from strong social cohesion based on tribal bonds and practices as well as from inbuilt, largely self-regulatory, governance mechanisms, usually without highly formalized civic institutions. While Islam gave high priority to the private domain, individuals were constrained by internalized concepts of public good, maintained and enforced by the consensus of the respected leaders of the society.

Western governance systems and their different values abruptly introduced in the colonial period and, paradoxically, reinforced after independence, dismantled this traditional system and led to a breakdown of traditional urban management. Corollary problems such as the departure of the bourgeoisie from the old cities, the demographic pressures generated by the ruralization of the historic center, the change in production systems, and the low economic force of the present population have contributed to this decay.

Government actions in this context have oscillated between two extremes. Rich countries with highly centralized administrative structures have tended to expropriate private land holdings and to pursue wholesale redevelopment of historic districts (as in many places in Saudi Arabia). Poor countries have tended to ignore the historic core and to give priority to the development of "modern" districts. This meant leaving the architectural patrimony to its own fate, while the private sector, bereft of proper guidance and incentives, exploited the historic urban fabric, putting short term benefits before long-term preservation and cultural continuity.[5] Even where legal protection of the heritage exists, it has little meaning in societies that tend to rely on a web of personalized bonds and authorities, rather than on formal civic institutions.

This alarming situation, which exists in many Third World countries, demonstrates that the fundamental problem in urban conservation may be not the choice between public sector or private sector predominance, but rather the establishment of urban management policies and community development models that can sustain the rehabilitation and regeneration of historic cities as a whole. Obviously this can best be achieved by the close cooperation of the private and public sectors, a cooperation based on shared values, clear mutual obligations, and agreed-upon development tools and mechanisms.

Mixed Ownership and Operation Schemes

This quick overview of different approaches to urban conservation shows that exclusive government ownership and operation, even where feasible, may not be desirable, as it neglects the potential forces of personal care and group solidarity. At the same time, however, unrestricted private ownership and operation may conflict with collective values and ignore corresponding heritage concerns, unless social or moral constraints provide internal checks and balances.

Clearly, too, the failure of state ownership, at the one extreme, does not necessarily mean that swinging to the opposite extreme will resolve the problem. The shortcomings of a totalitarian government bureaucracy cannot be redeemed by shifting to total deregulation, nor can the excesses of the free market be cured by giving exclusive priority to state intervention. Accordingly, in the following section, I will review certain basic modes of connecting public concerns with private initiatives, either by relinquishing part of the government's authority to nongovernmental or private entities or by imposing a guiding framework for private investment.

Sudden changes in political systems can produce situations in which governments inherit all of a society's architectural heritage assets, without being able to sustain or to manage them. In this case, the outright sale of this property, attaching conditions with regard to future use and maintenance, may be one option. Another, less risky, possibility is lease arrangements, whereby the government retains ownership and defines the mode of rehabilitation, but leaves it to the private operator—preferably a nongovernmental nonprofit organization committed to the cause of conservation—to manage the building in ways that benefit the community, to provide public access, and to generate at least the income needed for maintenance, if not more for reinvestment in cultural projects. According to the importance of the building, the nature of its desirable reuse, and the finances of the lessee, the rent may be nominal (especially if the building requires an up-front investment by the leasing party), or it may generate an income, which the municipality can use to fund the upkeep of monuments that are restricted in use and economic potential. In the case of irretrievably ruined buildings of no major archaeological importance, the municipality may lease the plot to a private investor with the contractual obligation to rebuild it (maintaining certain topological and volumetric constraints) and to use it in a manner consistent with its historic context. When such operations are linked with the improvement of public infrastructure and public open spaces, the municipality can benefit from the value added through growing rental income and to some extent amortize its investment in the improvement of the historic area.

A reciprocal model, based on predominant private ownership, would be the establishment of national or municipal trusts created to increase the public's control over essential heritage components. Such trusts can benefit from donations or legacies of private owners who want to give their landmark buildings to the public (or who cannot fulfill their maintenance obligation), but they can also acquire buildings actively with the help of charitable organizations, dedicated lottery revenues, or other specially allocated government resources. A private donor might in some cases retain a life-long right of personal use or attach certain conditions to the property's donation, which must, however, not prevent its conservation. In some cases, a national or communal government institution may want to bestow its moral authority to the trust but not be involved in the daily management of its portfolio. It may then find a committed nongovernmental organization to manage the trust's affairs in the public interest, while actively searching for private funding, funding that a fully governmental institution is not normally able to tap.

The historic precedent for the public role of trusts and foundations is a model rooted in the governance tradition of Muslim societies. I am referring to the *waqf* system, which could best be described as a religious endowment. In the Islamic tradition, spiritual and mundane concerns are strongly interwoven, as exemplified by the function of the mosque as the central community facility and by the close relation between religious, commercial, educational, and recreational facilities in any traditional Muslim city center. The public domain, therefore, benefited from the religiously motivated donations of rulers and rich private individuals who wanted to be remembered for their good deeds or to redeem themselves for less commendable deeds in other realms. Donations would consist not only of mosques and social welfare buildings, but also of shops, houses, fields, and the like, all intended to sustain community facilities, to pay employees, or to ensure perpetual support of the needy. Operated over centuries and managed by the respected leaders of individual communities, the *awqaf* (plural of *waqf*) constituted a comprehensive, citywide welfare and heritage management system directly serving society and yet not subject to governmental authority—protected, in fact, against the whims of greedy rulers. A *waqf* could also be constituted as a private family foundation, ensuring housing or income for future generations. The *awqaf* of each city gradually accumulated large real estate holdings—up to 30 percent and more in most historic Muslim towns—and could theoretically finance the maintenance of the main public buildings and monuments on a continuous basis. The drawback of this system was its inherent lack of flexibility, which in a certain way froze all its land holdings and made it difficult to react to circumstances not foreseen at the time of the donation.

Over the last fifty years, with the rise of national governments and Western administrative systems, many *waqf* properties have been "nationalized" or handed over to the central government. The question now is how can the existing assets best be used in the interest of both positive community development and good heritage management, acknowledging that modern conditions may require revised approaches. The *waqf* model, if properly reformed, may be a good model for a semigovernmental heritage management institution, fueled by private contributions and anchored in the old customs and traditions of Muslim societies.

The urban development corporation is another model for public/private co-operation. It is used to redevelop urban problem areas where former land uses (often industrial) are no longer viable, but where location suggests good economic potential once new development parameters are established and implemented by government agencies and private investors working in concert. This model, also adopted for the reconstruction of war-torn cities such as Beirut, may be adjusted to the more specific conditions of historic city centers, combining the improvement of living conditions with the conservation of the physical fabric. One of the major problems will be how to harness speculative forces and powerful private investors to serve the public good. Recently, a proposal for the creation of "Historic Area Development Corporations" (HADC) has been put forward at a World Bank conference, suggesting that HADCs could be established in historic cities by a single piece of special legislation, which would "surmount the many obstacles that presently impede any decisive action for the conservation and revitalization of historic cities in many parts of the world."[6]

The HADC, as a public/private partnership under a management representative of (or responsible to) all interests involved, would ensure that costs and benefits would be shared equitably. The corporation could be set up as a limited liability company with existing landowners (and possibly tenants) becoming shareholders following an agreed-upon ratio. Private investors could obtain shares by injecting capital, while the government, holding all public land assets including streets, squares, vacant land, and social facilities, would initiate and facilitate urban revitalization. Depending on the circumstances, as a major incentive, infrastructure improvement could be financed either by the government or by the HADC itself. The creation of a HADC would ensure that added values would be captured and reinvested in urban rehabilitation.

Conclusions

Let me conclude this chapter by summarizing the rationale, the limitations, and the opportunities of government intervention. No more words are needed, I think, concerning the justification for the government to intervene in preservation matters in its role as a custodian of cultural heritage. This intervention should, as much as possible, consist of steering both development and conservation concerns. When direct government interventions in preservation projects are necessary, they should not stifle, but encourage associated private initiatives, since the government—for reasons of predominantly private ownership, limited financial resources, and costly maintenance—will never be able to deal with the whole spectrum of conservation. Indirect types of intervention, if properly implemented, often give the government more leverage than do direct ownership and operation.

There are certain pitfalls to heritage ownership and operation by the government. Bureaucratic systems—and a governmental heritage administration is no exception—are prone to inertia, may have little or no initiative, and may lack the motivation of directly concerned players. Only leadership by strong, well trained, and committed individuals can counterbalance the potential deficiencies of the system. Therefore, we must look for opportunities in which government institutions can be most efficient in heritage management. Governments should do what they can do best: coordinate the others involved in conservation and development and ensure that their investments contribute to overall goals. They should not be ashamed to act in an entrepreneurial manner, using all the means and tools they can harness in the interest of appropriate, efficient, and, if possible, self-sustaining conservation projects. Only by combining their moral authority with inventive market mechanisms will they have a chance to preserve the essential parts of their national heritage.

Lack of funds is a recurring complaint in conservation, and in certain poverty-struck areas it imposes the seemingly inevitable choice between development and conservation priorities. This fatal polarity is somewhat misleading, as it implies an incompatible dichotomy between cultural continuity and the upgrading of living conditions, a dichotomy which often depends on imported models of "development" that are alien to and untenable in many local conditions. In many "poor" countries, hidden resources are never mobilized, while scarce public funds are often spent on facilities, equipment, and conveniences that may satisfy the needs of a minority, but do not contribute much to meaningful social and cultural development. By deciding on the right priorities, establishing an appropriate institutional set-up, providing the right incentives, and harnessing existing resources, modest as they may be, conservation and development can be made to work hand in hand.

Governments have a key role to play in this process by setting the goals, creating the tools, and encouraging concerned community groups, interested nongovernmental organizations, and committed individuals to become active players within a shared framework of mutual obligations and benefits. Development and heritage management both require critical choices all along the way, and unless such decisions are endorsed and supported by their future users, projects may not be socially and economically sustainable, leaving an even heavier burden to the government.

Finally, coming back to my introductory theme, I want to emphasize that salvaging the physical shell of past cultures and civilizations, though commendable, may prove meaningless if it is not supported by parallel efforts to encourage a living culture that can creatively relate to the physical heritage. In computer terms, the software is at least as important as the hardware. Good heritage management requires that the material heritage be validated by nonmaterial values and by meaningful use of historic structures. In today's context, the active use of heritage assets can provide more than valuable inspiration to individuals; by strengthening the specific local identity of places, it can offset the creeping uniformity of our industrial and postindustrial urban environment.

Notes

1. Analogies between nonrenewable ecological resources and corresponding cultural resources were drawn more than twenty years ago in Ernst Basler and Stefano Bianca, *Zivilisation im Umbruch: zur Erhaltung und Gestaltung des menschlichen Lenbensraums* (Stuttgart: Huber, 1974).

2. In a world where modern communication facilities have abolished distances and frontiers, a new international dimension of heritage management has also emerged. There are unique monuments that have a universal value, which transcends the boundaries of individual nations while the custodians of this heritage may not always have the means to preserve it. This is the raison d'être for the existence of organizations such as the United Nations Educational, Scientific, and Cultural Organization (UNESCO) and for comprehensive inventories such as the World Heritage List, which in turn can urge national governments to take care of their legacy and can assist them in their preservation or mobilize the help of bilateral donors. See Bernard M. Feilden and Jukka Jokiletho, *Management Guidelines for World Cultural Heritage Sites* (Rome: International Center for the Study of the Conservation and Restoration of Cultural Property [ICCROM], 1993).

3. Consider, for example, the case of Bologna as described in Donald Appleyard, ed., *The Conservation of European Cities* (Cambridge, Mass.: MIT Press, 1979); and Commune di Bologna and Ente Bolognese Manifestazioni Artistiche, *Bologna–Centro Storico* (Bologna: Alfa, 1970).

4. Good background material on the heritage situation in Eastern and Central European countries is to be found in Zbigniew Zuziak, ed., *Managing Historic Cities* (Cracow: International Cultural Centre, 1993).

5. For the case of Arab and Muslim historic cities see Stefano Bianca, *Urban Form in the Arab World—Past and Present* (Zurich: VdF editions, ET, forthcoming).

6. See Ismail Serageldin, "Revitalizing Historic Cities: Towards a Public-Private Partnership," pp. 337–63 in *Culture and Development in Africa, Proceedings of an International Conference Held at the World Bank, Washington, D.C., April 2–3, 1992,* ed. Ismail Serageldin and June Taboroff (Washington, D.C.: World Bank, 1994), 347.

References

Appleyard, Donald, ed. *The Conservation of European Cities.* Cambridge, Mass.: MIT Press, 1979.

Basler, Ernst, and Stefano Bianca. *Zivilisation im Umbruch: zur Erhaltung und Gestaltung des menschlichen Lenbensraums.* Stuttgart: Huber, 1974.

Bianca, Stefano. *Urban Form in the Arab World—Past and Present.* Zurich: VdF editions, ET, forthcoming.

Commune di Bologna and Ente Bolognese Manifestazioni Artistiche. *Bologna–Centro Storico.* Bologna: Alfa, 1970.

Feilden, Bernard M., and Jukka Jokiletho. *Management Guidelines for World Cultural Heritage Sites.* Rome: ICCROM, 1993.

Serageldin, Ismail. "Revitalizing Historic Cities: Towards a Public-Private Partnership." In *Culture and Development in Africa, Proceedings of an International Conference Held at the World Bank, Washington, D.C., April 2–3, 1992.* Ismail Serageldin and June Taboroff, eds. Washington, D.C.: World Bank, 1994, 337–63.

Zuziak, Zbigniew, ed. *Managing Historic Cities.* Cracow: International Cultural Centre, 1993.

3   David Throsby

Making Preservation Happen:
The Pros and Cons of Regulation

The term *regulation* is used in economics to denote almost any form of government intervention in market processes. Nowadays, in the world at large, it is more widely known via its antithesis, deregulation, by which is meant the withdrawal of government from the marketplace (with the corollary that the private sector moves in and market forces are allowed to operate more freely).

In more precise usage, however, regulation means something more specific than simply any form of government action; it denotes the use of measures that require or enforce certain behavior in firms or individuals.[1] In this interpretation, "regulation refers to sustained and focused control exercised by a public agency over activities that are valued by a community."[2]

Regulation in this sense connotes both a degree of certainty in the regulatory authority as to the goals to be achieved by its regulations, and the power of the authority to enforce those regulations. If a spectrum exists along which policy instruments lie, with persuasion at one end and coercion at the other, then regulation in the more precise sense clearly falls at the latter end of the range.

Regulation in general has long been a matter of interest in economics, from both normative and positive points of view. The theories of regulation that have been developed can be divided into ones that proceed from the point of view of the public interest and ones that proceed from private interests. Essentially, public interest theories express the need for collective intervention to remedy market failure. Regulation in its broader sense may be warranted to curb monopolization or imperfect competition in markets, to provide public goods, to correct for externalities, to pursue distributional justice, and so on. Regulation in its more specific sense can also be rationalized on such normative public interest grounds as providing means for society to pursue its collective goals. Private interest theories, by contrast, interpret the existing regulations in terms of self-seeking behavior by private individuals or firms. Such theories portray the regulatory process as being prone to "capture" by interest groups which can turn the process to their advantage.

The purpose of this chapter is to assess the advantages and disadvantages of regulation in forming and implementing urban heritage conservation policy.[3] Because this volume focuses on "tools" for government action, I will consider regulation only in the restricted sense noted above; that is, for my purposes, regulation involves control of behavior by directive means, imposed by a superior authority asserting the state's role to act when private behavior may not be in the public interest. The necessity of state action means that regulatory control will tend to be centralized rather than diffuse in its administration and enforcement.[4]

The layout of this chapter is as follows: In the next section I discuss the ways in which regulation can be applied to urban heritage protection, and in the following two sections I consider, respectively, the disadvantages and advantages of regulatory instruments in this context. I canvass some further issues in the third section, including questions of valuation, financing, and administration, and then end with some concluding remarks.

Applying Regulation in Urban Heritage Conservation

The conservation and preservation of the urban heritage can be construed in economic terms as a problem in the management of capital assets. These assets are both physical capital, that is, buildings, groups of structures, or other tangible investment goods, and cultural capital. The concept of cultural capital is not yet well developed in economics.[5] Nevertheless, we can define cultural capital in the context of urban heritage as comprising the capital value of a building, a collection of buildings, or more generally a place, that is additional to their value as purely physical structures, and that embodies the community's estimation of the value of the asset in terms of its social, historical, or cultural worth. The concept of cultural capital allows economists to reevaluate the wealth of a nation in terms of its cultural resources.

Cultural capital, like the physical capital in which it is contained, is subject to decay if neglected. Society must therefore decide how much investment is required to prevent the deterioration of cultural capital or to provide for its improvement. In applying investment appraisal methods to such investment decisions, the relevant methodology is social cost-benefit analysis, where a significant component of the benefits arise as public goods or externalities that are not accounted for in private decisions. The process of regulation in the context of urban heritage conservation can be construed as one of regulating the level and/or nature of the investment in this cultural capital.

In looking at the various types of regulation in use, one can draw a distinction between what might be called "hard" and "soft" regulation. Hard regulation comprises enforceable directives requiring certain behavior, implemented through legislation, and involving penalties for noncompliance. Soft regulation comprises unenforceable directives calling for certain behavior, implemented by agreement, and not involving penalties. Both types of regulation seek to change behavior, the first by involuntary means, the second by encouraging voluntary compliance. While most individuals would not normally think of the latter as regulation because of its voluntary, penalty-free nature, I believe discussing soft regulation under the general rubric of regulation helps to clarify the usefulness of regulation as a tool for preservation.

Hard Regulation

Many different types of hard regulation exist in the urban heritage context. We can draw the main ones together under four headings.

First, there is regulation relating to the existence of a building, a group of buildings, or a site embodying cultural capital. The most obvious example is the preservation or conservation order that prevents demolition of a structure. This sort of regulation may be imposed at the local level, or, in the case of buildings or other places of national significance, through some listing process that overrides the autonomy of the local authority.[6]

Second, there is regulation relating to the appearance, function, and/or use of heritage buildings and sites. Such regulations may restrict the use to which such structures can be put, or the way in which their use can be changed or adapted to modern conditions. In addition, regulations in this category may impinge on design, for example in relation to alteration, renovation, restoration, or addition.

Third, there is regulation relating to land use affecting heritage buildings and precincts. Such regulation may be imposed through zoning restrictions that limit the types of structures that may be erected and the types of activities that may be carried on in certain areas. Zoning constraints are a particularly important element in urban planning.

Finally, there is regulation affecting the process by which heritage decisions are made. A certain sequence of stages may have to be followed, for example, to reach a decision relating to use or reuse of a historic property. Such a sequence may require that expert assessment, community consultation, official review, or other steps be undertaken as part of the decision-making process under particular jurisdictions.

Soft Regulation

By soft regulation, I refer to the imposition of constraints on behavior through treaties, conventions, charters, guidelines, codes of practice, and other instruments that operate through agreement rather than coercion. Several such conventions exist at the international level, and accession to them imposes some obligations on national governments to adhere to their provisions. The principal international agreements relevant here are:

- The International Charter for the Conservation and Restoration of Monuments and Sites, Venice, 1966;
- The International Convention for the Protection of the World Cultural and Natural Heritage, UNESCO, 1982; and
- The International Charter for the Protection and Management of the Archaeological Heritage, Lausanne, 1990.

In addition, at the national and local levels in many countries, various guidelines exist for cultural preservation that fall into this category of soft regulation.

An example of this type of nondirective regulation is the Burra Charter, drawn up in a small town in South Australia in 1978 and ratified by the International Council on Monuments and Sites (ICOMOS) ten years later.[7] The Burra Charter defines conservation as all the processes of looking after a place so as to retain its cultural significance,[8] including maintenance, preservation, restoration, reconstruction, adaptation, or some combination of these. The Burra Charter expresses three basic beliefs:

- that the cultural significance of a place is embodied in its fabric, its contents and its setting, and in the associated documents;
- that the cultural significance of a place is best retained by identifying its significance and considering all the issues associated with its use and its future, and from those investigations developing a policy for its conservation; and
- that keeping records will facilitate the understanding and interpretation of places of cultural significance.

The charter provides a set of clearly articulated principles, procedures, and practices for approaching conservation work. A number of countries accept it as a code for voluntary regulation of conservation behavior and use it to guide the formulation of corresponding hard regulations, where relevant.

Problems with Regulation

To many economists, regulation is a dirty word—or at the very least somewhat unclean. Let us review the principal reasons why economists regard regulation with such distaste, in order to assess how relevant are its disadvantages to regulating urban heritage conservation. For these purposes, we can distinguish four main problem areas with regulation, as seen from an economic viewpoint.

Regulation Creates Inefficiency

In the economic model of the operation of market processes, the free interaction of demand and supply will lead, under certain assumptions, to a "socially optimal" outcome, one in which all participants are as well off as they can be, and no one can be made better off without making someone else worse off. In these circumstances, economists argue, regulation distorts the free working of the market, resulting in an outcome that must be less than socially optimal. This distorting effect of regulation creates the inefficiency; the intervention moves the market outcome away from the social equilibrium, and the resulting resource allocation is not as efficient as it would be without regulation.

The urban property market offers an illustration. In a free market, a certain number of properties might be bought and sold over a given time period, resulting in certain levels of satisfaction to buyers and profits to sellers in the market. Imposing a regulation that, for example, declares some buildings as historic, and hence unable to be sold, would create a technical inefficiency: buyers' satisfaction and sellers' profits would not be as high as they would otherwise have been.

This example also illustrates the limitation of this sort of analysis. The "social optimum" in this simple instance is defined as the welfare of only the immediate players in the market, whose position has clearly deteriorated as a result of the distorting effect of the regulation. However, a broader measure of social benefit, for example, one that incorporated external or public good benefits to the community at large through the designation of historic buildings, might lead to a different conclusion as to the social value of the outcome.

Regulation might be further considered inefficient because of its possibly arbitrary incidence when uniform standards are applied. Suppose that a grant of $1 million is to be provided to ten houses in a historic street to enable conservation work to be undertaken. A "uniform" approach might decree that the grant be divided equally among the recipients. Clearly, however, for some houses the $100,000 would be inadequate, whereas for those in better condition it might be excessive. A more efficient rule would allocate the sum so as to equalize the marginal benefits from conservation for each property. Again, it is apparent that an arbitrary solution creates inefficiency.

Regulation Is Costly

One can identify two main types of costs of regulation.[9] First, there are administrative costs involved in formulating standards and in monitoring and enforcing them, which are incurred by the public agency. Second, there are compliance costs, which are the expenditures firms and individuals must make in order to meet the regulatory requirements. Measuring these costs may be difficult, since firms and individuals might have made these expenditures anyway, and hence they cannot be attributed directly to regulation.

Intervention of any sort incurs costs, however, so one should attempt to assess regulation's relative cost by comparing it with other instruments. It is unclear whether the administrative and compliance costs of direct regulation are greater or less on average than for other forms of state intervention.

Regulation Offers No Incentive to Do Better

Although specifying minimum standards of behavior (backed up by effective enforcement) assures that those minima will be met, regulation generally provides no incentive for firms and individuals to do better. In the environmental area, for example, it has been observed that maximum pollution limits for industry invite firms to pollute up to that level, and do not encourage them to reduce their harmful emissions to lower levels than the specified maxima. The urban conservation context offers similar examples, such as setting maximum or minimum requirements for design standards, land or building usage, site coverage, and so on.

The Regulatory Process Can Be Captured

The idea that regulatory processes can be subverted to serve a private interest rather than the public good emerged during the 1960s and 1970s, prompted particularly by the work of George Stigler and others of the Chicago school. In the definitive article on this issue, Stigler suggested that as a rule, regulation is "acquired" by an industry, which then operates the regulatory process primarily for its own benefit.[10] Subsequently, capture theories of regulation have been extended to incorporate rent-seeking behavior on the part of self-interested firms and individuals.[11]

Urban conservation certainly offers possibilities for capture of the regulatory process. Perhaps the best examples come from the area of land use regulation; cases abound where zoning laws have been turned to private benefit through indirect or direct influence on the regulatory process.

The regulatory process may be captured not only by the regulated, but also by the regulators.[12] In the area of heritage protection, "expert" opinion and entrenched professional interest may on occasion weigh more heavily in deciding the desirable form and extent of regulation than the views of the community at large, resulting in regulations that serve the interests of those in power rather than of people in general. As Alan Peacock puts it, in some circumstances "the 'objective function' of those engaged in heritage provision will reflect the tastes and preferences of the public official rather than that of voters."[13]

Of course, capture theories apply to regulation in general, and not only to the specific sense of regulation being considered in this chapter. Thus, whether this potential disadvantage weighs more heavily against direct controls than, say, against subsidy programs, which may also be subverted to private benefit, depends at least partly on how easily the interested parties can manipulate the mechanics of implementation. This is essentially an empirical question.[14]

When Is Regulation Desirable?

The above catalogue of drawbacks to the tool of regulation appears to cast a long shadow over its possible use in urban heritage conservation. One can, however, identify several positive characteristics of regulation that may indicate its use in certain circumstances. I suggest that there are five situations in which the advantages of regulation may prove decisive in its favor.

When There Is an All-or-Nothing Choice

Problems of urban heritage preservation, perhaps more often than in other fields, present decision makers with all-or-nothing choices. A good example is the choice between preservation and demolition of a historic building. While preservation itself contains a series of further options (maintenance, restoration, alteration, and so on), the initial decision whether to retain the structure is a binary question. In such circumstances, instruments that allow gradations of behavior are inappropriate; the simplest way to preserve the building is to forbid its demolition. Of course, as always, such a regulation needs to be backed up with the power to monitor and enforce it.

When set in the context of a single building at a single point in time, the question of preservation is indeed an all-or-nothing matter. However, when the scope is widened to embrace more than one such choice, the decision is no longer all-or-nothing, but a matter of degree. Take the case of ecclesiastical architecture in Italy. Vatican City is the home of St. Peter's. There is only one such basilica in Italy, and its preservation is a matter of national and international significance. An order forbidding its demolition, enacted at the national level, is of the utmost importance. But although there is only one St. Peter's, there are many cathedrals in Italy, and from the national point of view there may be a decision as to how many cathedrals are worthy of preservation. Thus, an all-or-nothing choice in regard to one building becomes a question of degree in regard to a class of buildings. In Milan, which has one Duomo but many churches, preserving the Duomo through appropriate regulation is incontrovertible, but protecting all local churches is again a matter for decision. At the parish level, preserving the local church from demolition becomes once more an all-or-nothing choice for those affected, and regulation can again be used to achieve this end. In other words, whether a choice is all-or-nothing depends on its context. Nevertheless, within that context regulation is likely to be the best way to secure a desired outcome.

This discussion also raises questions of who benefits from preservation and who should pay for it, matters to which I return below.

When There Is a High Risk of Social Damage

Regulations have the advantage of being direct and deterministic in their outcome. In some circumstances in the area of urban heritage preservation, the social costs of individual action might be so high that it must be prohibited outright by regulation, rather than allowing market forces to determine a solution. Presumably some advertiser, for example, would be prepared to pay a large price to erect an illuminated sign on top of the Sydney Opera House, on the facade of Notre Dame, or on the roof of the Tower of London—perhaps even a price large enough to tempt the operators of these facilities to consider the offer. But the social cost of such action would be so great as to warrant prohibition by regulation, where other less stringent measures may conceivably fail. In effect, no price can be high enough to offset the social cost of such action, and hence a definitive regulation is appropriate to forbid such action entirely.

In the area of cultural tourism, there are many instances in which tourist use of sensitive sites entails such a high risk of damage that restriction of use by regulation is warranted. Such situations arise frequently in controlling the impact of tourists on the natural environment (wetlands, coral reefs, wilderness areas, and so on), but also exist in the cultural heritage area. In the urban context, the case of Venice springs readily to mind; there, certain types of regulation may be the most effective means of limiting damage to the urban fabric by excessive numbers of visitors.

Justification for the use of regulatory instruments under this heading need not be framed only in negative terms, that is, preventing or curbing action. Regulation may also be indicated when the immediate public benefits from some action are judged to be so great relative to their costs as to warrant that the action should be enforced rather than simply encouraged. An example might be the requirement to provide certain levels of public amenities in urban redevelopment schemes involving heritage properties or precincts. Such amenities might provide such a high level of public benefit relative to their cost that it is better to secure them through regulation than to hope that other, "softer" forms of intervention will yield the same result.

When There Is a Need for Certainty

The previous justification for regulation is a particular case of a more general advantage, namely the fact that regulation, provided it can be enforced, delivers outcomes with certainty. When the public interest is best served by a clear and predictable outcome, subject neither to negotiation, nor concession, nor special dealing, then regulation may be indicated. In designing safety standards that govern public access to buildings and sites, for example, it may be desirable to leave nothing to chance, but rather to ensure certain compliance through regulatory means.

When Short-Run Flexibility Is Required

Another advantage of regulations is that they may be invoked and removed relatively speedily. Direct controls may be a useful supplement to other measures, as in a system of charges for the continuing maintenance of acceptable environmental, conservation, or preservation conditions. Regulatory controls are useful because, compared to the difficulty of changing tax incentives or implementing other instruments, they can be introduced, enforced, and removed with relative ease. Some crises can be predicted at best only a short time before they occur, and it may be too costly, for example, to keep tax rates sufficiently high to prevent such emergencies at all times. Therefore, it may be less expensive to make temporary use of direct controls, despite any economic inefficiency that may be introduced by their use.[15]

In the field of urban conservation, temporary preservation orders show the flexibility of direct controls; they can be introduced at short notice to forestall the demolition of historic properties until some due process of consultation or consideration can be pursued.

When Other Instruments Are Not in Place

Circumstances may arise when instruments other than regulation may be preferable, but for one reason or another they are not available. In such situations, it may be necessary to resort to regulation as the chosen tool if the desired social outcomes are to be achieved.

Some examples may be drawn from the current problems facing economies in transition. In Central and Eastern European countries, many urban buildings have, over the last few years, been transferred to private ownership or have been "reprivatized" (handed back to their former private owners). Many of these buildings, individually or in combination with neighboring buildings, are of heritage value. Under state ownership, they were protected to some degree; under private ownership, a free-for-all may exist unless regulation can be introduced to prevent demolition or neglect in appropriate cases or to control reuse. In these circumstances, the withdrawal of one tool (direct government ownership) must be accompanied by the immediate introduction of another (an appropriate regulatory framework), if the desired social benefit is to be maintained or enhanced.

In countries with economies in transition and in developing countries, the infrastructure may not yet exist to support the use of more complex instruments for the implementation of heritage policy; hence authorities may have little choice but to rely on regulation, which may be simpler to impose and administer. Sophisticated taxation schemes or complicated proposals for trading in property rights to promote heritage preservation presupposes a sophistocated financial, legal, and administrative infrastructure, which may not exist yet in these countries, whereas straightforward regulatory devices are more easily implemented. In these circumstances, the use of regulation might be seen as temporary, a holding operation until conditions evolve that support other preferred policy instruments.

Some Further Issues

I turn now to several wider issues raised by the preceding discussion.

Valuation

If the issue of urban heritage preservation is framed as a problem of investment appraisal using a social cost-benefit analysis, as I have suggested above, the question of valuation of benefits arises. Much of what I have argued concerning the applicability of regulation relies on there being effective means of assessing the public interest. If regulations are to achieve the desired social objectives, the regulatory designers and implementers need some objective indication of the nature and extent of public benefit to be gained from alternative strategies.

Some progress has been made in developing methods for assessment of nonmarket benefits such as those derived from cultural preservation. For example, contingent valuation methods,[16] in which respondents in a survey or some other hypothetical decision context are asked about their willingness to pay for intangible qualities such as the public-good benefits of historic monuments and sites, offer some hope of gaining insight into community demand for such benefits. However, as Bruno Frey has pointed out, such studies are one step removed from the political realities of decision making, and may not be as useful as direct referenda on these questions.[17] Nevertheless, all such information can be seen as input to the process of regulatory design and a useful complement to wider attitudinal and other information on social valuation.[18]

An aspect of valuation that is particularly important in the heritage context is the long-term nature of the benefits provided by historic preservation. We who are alive today benefit from the enjoyment and use of buildings and sites that have been preserved as a result of decisions made by generations long since dead. We need to recognize that decisions we make now will affect future generations. If this responsibility is important to us, we will want to behave accordingly. But the issue of valuation is especially difficult in this context: if it is problematic to measure how much people living today benefit from preserving the national heritage, how much more problematic is it to impute a value on behalf of beneficiaries as yet unborn? Recent interest in notions of sustainability, in which the issue of intergenerational equity forms a core component, offers some hope of resolving the theoretical and empirical problems in this area.[19]

The issue of valuation also raises the question of taste. In the urban heritage field, matters of fashion and taste constantly arise. Can regulation be expected to reflect the public interest in this respect? This obviously is a difficult matter to resolve, depending as it does on subjective criteria, where opinions differ markedly and "experts" abound. Perhaps all that can be said is that decisions cannot be delayed indefinitely while differences of opinion are settled; someone has to take responsibility in the end. One hopes, at least, that processes are in place in regulatory design and implementation that ensure that the public interest is served through wide consultation and the best informed expertise, and that such processes are not subject to the imposition of quixotic, idiosyncratic, or ignorant opinions.[20]

Financing

A basic question in heritage preservation is: Who should pay? Regulation, as I noted above, imposes costs on individuals, firms, and governments. By enforcing certain behavior, regulation leads to costs that might not otherwise have arisen, and distributes those costs in ways that may or may not be equitable. How those costs are distributed offers a very specific answer to the question of who is to pay.

When property subject to heritage-related regulation is privately owned, the direct costs of complying with the regulation will fall, in some cases, squarely on the private owners, even though the regulation is intended to achieve some social purpose. For example, the listing of historic buildings may oblige owners of affected property to meet maintenance or renovation costs that they would not voluntarily have incurred. While these expenditures probably secure at least some private benefit for the owners (in improved amenity or in enhanced capital value of the property), a proportion of them could be attributed to the provision of a public benefit, and hence some contribution of public funds would be warranted. In other cases, public funding might be construed as partial or full compensation to private owners if the regulation, which has been imposed to secure some public benefit, has demonstrably lowered the owners' amenity or property values, or has prevented them from making more profitable use of their asset.

Such public contribution to the costs of regulation when property is privately owned and the financing of heritage protection of publicly owned buildings raise broader questions; we can consider them in terms of the theory of public goods with varying degrees of localness. Returning to the issue of Italian churches: Who enjoys the public-good benefits from preservation of these particular historic buildings and sites? The answer to this question determines in principle the appropriate franchise for the regulatory decision, and the appropriate sources for financing conservation activity. For instance, in regard to St. Peter's in Rome, the Duomo in Milan, and many other churches of historical significance in Italy, there is, as we have noted above, a national as well as a local interest in their preservation: people throughout Italy derive benefit from the existence of these buildings.

It is appropriate, then, that national regulation, and financing, be established to ensure that these buildings survive and that conservation is enabled. How far such national regulatory power extends (that is, how many buildings are protected) is a matter for political judgment at the national level, a decision that will be influenced as much by purely fiscal as by cultural considerations. In turn, at the provincial level, some buildings not regarded as significant enough to warrant national protection will nevertheless be judged worthy of regulatory control (and financing) at the lower level. A similar proposition might be put at successive levels, down to the most local (the local government area, the suburb, the village). In all cases the range of beneficiaries can be identified and the corresponding tax base for financing the provision of benefits can be determined; regulatory instruments applied at the appropriate level have their proper place.[21]

These considerations can also be extended upwards to the international level. Many historic monuments and sites throughout the world are of a significance that transcends national boundaries. In such cases, decisions to introduce regulatory control may properly be made by the international community. Of course, in these cases, national sovereignty issues come to the fore, and the influence of the international community may be limited to expressions of hope that countries will accede to and abide by treaties and conventions covering such situations (in particular, the World Heritage Convention mentioned earlier).[22] Nevertheless, there is some scope for voluntary international financial transfers in this area; as Dick Netzer notes:

People in rich countries do have an interest in heritage protection (in other countries), amply demonstrated by the substantial private and government support from rich countries in the case of catastrophic episodes, like the flooding in Venice in the 1960s. Poor countries and places can't and won't do enough to satisfy the demand for heritage protection from the richer countries.[23]

A further issue in the public financing of heritage protection relates to the growing demand for preservation, which arises partly because of increased awareness, partly as a result of past neglect, and partly because new "heritage" is constantly being added to the existing stock. Françoise Benhamou has pointed out that the increase in the demand for finance in the heritage area is both a consequence and a cause of regulation: a consequence because regulations covering listing of historic buildings and sites are constantly being extended, and a cause because to a certain extent the increased demand for funds prompts government into new regulation, for example, to share the financial burden between public and private sectors.[24]

Administrative Structures

When discussing the drawbacks of regulation, I noted the administrative costs of the regulatory process. It remains only to reiterate that there may be alternative ways to deliver regulation, and alternative ways to monitor and enforce it. In the real world of urban planning, delivery of regulatory services is frequently inefficient, expensive, disorganized, contradictory, and sometimes finally ineffectual. Such failures should not be taken necessarily as an indictment of regulation per se as a policy instrument, since in many cases these problems could be eliminated by better ways of doing things. Administrative structures may require radical rethinking, such as the suggestion made by Ismail Serageldin for establishing a Historic Area Development Corporation as a means of revitalizing historic cities.[25] Such a proposal could streamline the choice of policy instruments, allowing regulation to take its proper place alongside complementary measures. It has the added appeal of potentially contributing to a rationalization of the financing of heritage expenditures, with appropriate participation by all stakeholders, both public and private.

Conclusions

In this chapter, I have put the case for and against the use of direct controls in urban heritage preservation. What is the balance of the argument? It is not sensible to attempt a single or universal answer to this question, but I have certainly argued that, contrary to the first reaction of many economists, there is a convincing case for regulation in this area in certain circumstances. This argument derives from the evident need to assert the public interest over what, in many situations, are private property decisions. Policy formulation in this area should ideally require some understanding of the differences between individual and collective valuation of heritage benefits in specific cases, and some assessment of what the community (local, national, international) is prepared to pay for these benefits.

The possible capture of the regulatory process remains the greatest single threat to this conclusion, insofar as the entire process can be unraveled and the public interest seriously violated if the regulatory process is subverted. As I have noted, though, this threat is present to a greater or lesser degree with most policy tools, so it should not be seen as a problem specific to regulation.

Ultimately, an effective heritage policy strategy is unlikely to rely only on a single instrument, such as regulation, but is likely to contain a mix of tools, chosen for specific tasks. In this respect, urban heritage policy may be seen as similar, say, to environmental policy.[26] In the area of national heritage protection, the tool of regulation is likely to find an important place in that mix.

Notes

1. A distinction is sometimes made between social and economic regulation, where the former means protective regulation dealing with the vulnerability of individual citizens, while the latter connotes regulation addressing imperfections in the operations of markets. See, for example, Eugene Bardach, "Social Regulation as a Generic Policy Instrument," in *Beyond Privatization: the Tools of Government Action,* ed. Lester M. Salamon (Washington, D.C.: Urban Institute Press, 1989): 197–229. In this paper I am generally referring to both types of regulation.

2. Philip Selznick, "Focusing Organizational Research on Regulation," in *Regulatory Policy and the Social Sciences*, ed. Roger G. Noll (Berkeley: University of California Press, 1985): 363–67.

3. For a collection of recent papers on the economics of heritage, see the proceedings of the conference "Economic Perspectives of Cultural Heritage," Canizzaro, Italy, November 1995, published as Michael Hutter and Ilde Rizzo, eds., *Economic Perspectives of Cultural Heritage* (London: Macmillan, 1996). For a broader view of regulation in the cultural sector generally, see Emilio Giardina and Ilde Rizzo, "Regulation in the Cultural Sector," in *Cultural Economics and Cultural Policies*, ed. Alan Peacock and Ilde Rizzo (Dordrecht: Kluwer, 1994): 125–42.

4. This does not imply, however, only central government action; it simply suggests concentration of activity, whether at a local, state, national, or international level.

5. See further in Fikret Berkes and Carl Folke, "A Systems Perspective on the Interrelations Between Natural, Human-Made and Cultural Capital," *Ecological Economics* 5 (1992): 1–8; and David Throsby, *Linking Culture and Development Models: Towards a Workable Concept of Culturally Sustainable Development* (Paris: World Commission on Culture and Development, 1994).

6. For an extensive discussion in the context of the United Kingdom, see Roger W. Suddards, *Listed Buildings*, 2nd ed. (London: Sweet and Maxwell, 1988).

7. The text of the Burra Charter is reproduced in a number of ICOMOS documents; see, for example, Peter Marquis-Kyle and Meredith Walker, *The Illustrated Burra Charter: Making Good Decisions About the Care of Important Places* (Sydney: Australia ICOMOS, 1992).

8. "Cultural significance" is the set of attributes that gives rise to the value of cultural capital.

9. For a discussion of costs of regulation, see Anthony I. Ogus, *Regulation: Legal Form and Economic Theory* (Oxford: Clarendon Press, 1994), 155. For a discussion that focuses specifically on compliance costs, see Alan Peacock, et al., eds., *The Regulation Game: How British and West German Companies Bargain with Government* (Oxford: Basil Blackwell, 1984), chap. 3.

10. George J. Stigler, "The Theory of Economic Regulation," *Bell Journal of Economics and Mangement Science* 2, no. 1 (Spring 1971): 3–21.

11. See, for example, James M. Buchanan and Gordon Tullock, "Polluters' Profits and Political Response: Direct Controls versus Taxes," *American Economic Review* 65, no. 1 (March 1975): 139–47, and Robert D. Tollison, "Rent-Seeking: a Survey," *Kyklos* 35, no. 4 (1982): 575–602; rent seeking in the cultural field is examined in William D. Grampp, *Pricing the Priceless: Art, Artists and Economics* (New York: Basic Books, 1989).

12. For an account of regulation as a bargaining process between the regulators and the regulated, see Martin Ricketts and Alan Peacock, "Bargaining and the Regulatory System," *International Review of Law and Economics* 6 (1986): 3–16.

13. Alan Peacock, *A Future for the Past: the Political Economy of Heritage* (Edinburgh: The David Hume Institute, 1994), 23.

14. These issues are discussed in specific contexts in, for example, Peacock, *The Regulation Game,* and Cento Veljanovski, ed., *Regulators and the Market: an Assessment of the Growth of Regulation in the UK* (London: Institute of Economic Affairs, 1991).

15. Such a view has been advanced by Baumol and Oates in their discussion of policy instruments in the environmental field. They note that their support for the use in some circumstances of direct controls "represents a sharp departure from the economist's usual policy recommendations." William J. Baumol and Wallace E. Oates, *The Theory of Environmental Policy*, 2nd ed. (Cambridge: Cambridge University Press, 1988), 156.

16. An overview and critical assessment of contingent valuation methods is provided in J. A. Hausman, ed., *Contingent Valuation: a Critical Assessment* (Amsterdam: North Holland, 1993).

17. Bruno S. Frey, "The Evaluation of Cultural Heritage: Some Critical Issues," paper presented at the Conference of the Association for Cultural Economics International, Catania, Italy, November 1995.

18. As discussed, for instance, in Chris Johnston, *What Is Social Value? A Discussion Paper,* Technical Publications Series no. 3 (Canberra: Australian Heritage Commission, 1992).

19. See David Throsby, "Culture, Economics and Sustainability," *Journal of Cultural Economics* 19, no. 3 (September 1995): 199–206.

20. Nevertheless, a gloomy picture of the dominance of mass tastes in heritage matters is painted in Robert Hewison, *The Heritage Industry: Britain in a Climate of Decline* (London: Methuen, 1987).

21. In practice, of course, the definition of "levels" in this context must have regard to the institutional and administrative structures that determine law-making and revenue-raising capacities in particular countries.

22. A useful summary view of which is contained in Keith D. Suter, "The UNESCO World Heritage Convention," *Environmental Planning Law Journal* 8, no. 1 (March 1991): 4–15.
23. Netzer, Dick, "Local, Central and Supra-National Governments in Heritage Protection and Artistic Production," paper presented at the Workshop on the Economics of Art and Culture, Technical University of Lisbon, November 1994.
24. Françoise Benhamou, "Is Increased Public Spending for the Preservation of Historic Monuments Inevitable? The French Case," paper presented at the 8th International Congress on Cultural Economics, University of Witten/Herdecke, Germany, August 1994.
25. Ismail Serageldin, "Revitalizing Historic Cities: Towards a Public-Private Partnership," in *Culture and Development in Africa*, ed. Ismail Serageldin and June Taboroff (Washington, D.C.: World Bank, 1994): 337–63.
26. See, for example, Organization for Economic Cooperation and Development, *Guidelines for the Application of Economic Instruments in Environmental Policy*, Background Paper no. 1 (Paris: OECD Environment Committee, 1991).

References

Bardach, Eugene. "Social Regulation as a Generic Policy Instrument." In *Beyond Privatization: the Tools of Government Action*, edited by Lester M. Salamon, 197–229. Washington, D.C.: Urban Institute Press, 1989.

Baumol, William J., and Wallace E. Oates. *The Theory of Environmental Policy*, 2nd ed. Cambridge: Cambridge University Press, 1988.

Benhamou, Françoise. "Is Increased Public Spending for the Preservation of Historic Monuments Inevitable? The French Case." Paper presented at the 8th International Congress on Cultural Economics, University of Witten/Herdecke, Germany, August 1994.

Berkes, Fikret, and Carl Folke. "A Systems Perspective on the Interrelations Between Natural, Human-Made and Cultural Capital." *Ecological Economics* 5 (1992): 1–8.

Buchanan, James M., and Gordon Tullock. "Polluters' Profits and Political Response: Direct Controls versus Taxes." *American Economic Review* 65, no. 1 (March 1975): 139–47.

Frey, Bruno S. "The Evaluation of Cultural Heritage: Some Critical Issues." Paper presented at the Conference of Association for Cultural Economics International, Catania, Italy, November 1995.

Giardina, Emilio, and Ilde Rizzo. "Regulation in the Cultural Sector." In *Cultural Economics and Cultural Policies*, edited by Alan Peacock and Ilde Rizzo, 125–142. Dordrecht: Kluwer, 1994.

Grampp, William D. *Pricing the Priceless: Art, Artists and Economics*. New York: Basic Books, 1989.

Hausman, J. A., ed. *Contingent Valuation: A Critical Assessment.* Amsterdam: North Holland, 1993.

Hewison, Robert. *The Heritage Industry: Britain in a Climate of Decline.* London: Methuen, 1987.

Hutter, Michael, and Ilde Rizzo, eds. *Economic Perspectives of Cultural Heritage.* London: Macmillan, 1996.

Johnston, Chris. *What Is Social Value? A Discussion Paper.* Technical Publications Series no. 3. Canberra: Australian Heritage Commission, 1992.

Marquis-Kyle, Peter, and Meredith Walker. *The Illustrated Burra Charter: Making Good Decisions About the Care of Important Places.* Sydney: Australia ICOMOS, 1992.

Netzer, Dick. "Local, Central and Supra-National Governments in Heritage Protection and Artistic Production." Paper presented at Workshop on the Economics of Art and Culture, Technical University of Lisbon, Portugal, November 1994.

Ogus, Anthony I. *Regulation: Legal Form and Economic Theory.* Oxford: Clarendon Press, 1994.

Organization for Economic Cooperation and Development. *Guidelines for the Application of Economic Instruments in Environmental Policy.* Background Paper no. 1. Paris: OECD Environment Committee, 1991.

Peacock, Alan. *A Future for the Past: the Political Economy of Heritage.* Edinburgh: the David Hume Institute, 1994.

Peacock, Alan, et al., eds. *The Regulation Game: How British and West German Companies Bargain with Government.* Oxford: Basil Blackwell, 1984.

Ricketts, Martin, and Alan Peacock. "Bargaining and the Regulatory System," *International Review of Law and Economics* 6 (1986): 3–16.

Selznick, Philip. "Focusing Organizational Research on Regulation." In *Regulatory Policy and the Social Sciences*, edited by Roger G. Noll, 363–67. Berkeley: University of California Press, 1985.

Serageldin, Ismail. "Revitalizing Historic Cities: Towards a Public-Private Partnership." In *Culture and Development in Africa*, edited by Ismail Serageldin and June Taboroff, 337–63. Washington, D.C.: World Bank, 1994.

Stigler, George J. "The Theory of Economic Regulation." *Bell Journal of Economics and Management Science* 2, no. 1 (Spring 1971): 3–21.

Suddards, Roger W. *Listed Buildings.* 2nd ed. London: Sweet and Maxwell, 1988.

Suter, Keith D. "The UNESCO World Heritage Convention." *Environmental Planning Law Journal* 8, no. 1 (March 1991): 4–15.

Throsby, David. *Linking Culture and Development Models: Towards a Workable Concept of Culturally Sustainable Development.* Paris: World Commission on Culture and Development, 1994.

Throsby, David. "Culture, Economics and Sustainability." *Journal of Cultural Economics* 19, no. 3 (September 1995): 199–206.

Tollison, Robert D. "Rent-Seeking: a Survey." *Kyklos* 35, no. 4 (1982): 575–602.

Veljanovski, Cento, ed. *Regulators and the Market: an Assessment of the Growth of Regulation in the U.K.* London: Institute of Economic Affairs, 1991.

4

J. Mark Schuster

Inciting Preservation

When one thinks of state action in historic preservation, one normally thinks first of ownership and operation of historic properties, then, perhaps, of the listing of other properties on historic registers, and, finally, of the promulgation of regulations concerning those properties. But if one wants to have the fullest possible influence on the preservation of the built environment, one needs to consider other forms of government action that shape and affect the context within which preservation might be encouraged or discouraged. Indeed, this is the fundamental premise of this volume.

Increasingly, these considerations must include a careful accounting for the financial context within which decisions about the built environment are made. When society's view of the important elements of the historic built environment was relatively narrow, the number of properties so identified was relatively limited. At that point it was conceivable, both financially and logistically, that the most important government tool to promote preservation would be direct ownership and operation of historic properties. But, as a broader view of preservation that included a wider variety of elements of the built environment developed, the definition had to be extended to more and more properties that were in private hands. It became clear that the full burden of preserving such properties could not be borne by the state and would have to be shared either with the private owners of these properties or with other private groups that had been or could be formed in support of the heritage. This broadening process led to a wider use of strategically designed incentives better adapted to the financial environment within which those incentives had to work.

Undoubtedly, other factors contributed to this shift as well. It may be that because of their labor-intensive nature, the cost of preservation activities has increased faster than others of society's expenses. State action may be necessary to close that gap. Also, the fundamental nature of preservation activity has changed so that full-scale period restoration is no longer the sole

49

form of preservation that society wishes to undertake. And, finally, in an era in which private initiative is supplementing if not replacing state initiative, there is a strong argument for considering new forms of state intervention. All of these forces led to an increase in the use of incentives as tools of state action.

Reasons for Using Incentives

If one were to catalog specific reasons for the state to use incentives, that list would certainly include the following:

- The state wishes to leverage other sources of support for preservation.
- The state wishes to counteract forces that threaten historic resources, including forces that the government may have unleashed itself (such as land use policies), but does not wish to acknowledge this through the use of more direct tools.
- The state wishes to provide a level playing field in the private marketplace between rehabilitation, on the one hand, and new construction or abandonment, on the other.
- The state wishes to compensate owners who may be burdened by other forms of historic preservation intervention.

Richard Roddewig, one of the few commentators who has written explicitly about the use of incentives in historic preservation, is very clear about the role of incentives in historic preservation.[1] In his view, incentives have two specific roles in the preservation process: (1) to generate more rehabilitation of historic structures than would be possible, presumably, through other forms of government action, and (2) to provide a reasonable economic return to owners of buildings protected and restricted by strong landmark laws. In part, he argues, incentives provide compensation while they counter economic forces or government policies that create high land values and threaten even well-maintained historic buildings. Accordingly, his typology of incentives is focused on the question of economic return: incentives that help cover operating costs, incentives that assist with the financing of a project including acquisition costs and construction costs, and incentives designed to help find equity investors. We will see, however, that the incentives actually used around the world today to further preservation goals go well beyond this list.

Donald Haider points out that incentives are undoubtedly important in another way.[2] He suggests that they are particularly well suited to a noncentralized pooling of resources that promotes collaborations and partnerships. In an era in which there is an increasing perception that public resources are limited and that private initiative should be taken more seriously, even as a guide for public sector intervention itself, forms of intervention that draw out and promote multiple partners are generally seen as a good thing.

The Fundamental Message of Incentives

The idea of pooling resources through collaborations and partnerships underlies the fundamental message that the government is sending out when it chooses to take its actions through incentives—"If you do X, the government will do Y." Marya Morris, putting a slightly different spin on preservation incentives, has characterized them as providing a contract of sorts: "If you take care of your property, the public will give you some public money."[3] The basic logical structure is still the same. Whichever way one prefers to cast this message, the key to understanding incentives is the conditional nature of the offer being made. The individual or organization in line to receive the incentive chooses whether or not to accept the offer. Most often the targeted recipient is the individual owner of an historic property, but it might also be a nonprofit organization or even another level of government.

Moreover, incentives have another not inconsiderable attribute: because there is a choice that is followed by a deal if the condition is accepted, the whole takings issue embedded in historic preservation is avoided. Whether or not government intervention with respect to preservation should be considered a taking away of some of the property owner's value in a historic property (therefore necessitating some form of compensation) is at the heart of many of the controversies about government involvement in preservation issues. But for a deal to be struck through an incentive, both parties have to consider it fair and be willing to accept it. An action cannot be considered a taking if the owner has agreed willingly to the deal. This is why in many countries preservation legislation requires the consent of an owner before a property is even listed, because that action might lead to the constraints of regulation as well as to the availability of incentives.

Studying Preservation Incentives

If one wants to find out about incentives from the historic preservation literature, one confronts a rather surprising problem. Many forms of incentives, particularly grants of cash and in-kind contributions, are underexplored in the preservation policy literature. Many examples of incentives are presented in that literature, but the literature is anecdotal rather than analytical. It is almost as if these kinds of incentives have become so much a part of accepted practice that it occurs to no one that they ought to be subjected to analytic scrutiny.[4] (I do not believe that it would be unfair to suggest that there seems to be little tradition of policy analysis in the preservation field more generally.)

The one exception to this lack of analysis is the area of tax-based incentives, in which there is a very rich analytic tradition (though not necessarily emanating from within the field of historic preservation itself). Tax incentives have attracted the attention of economists who find the analytic questions particularly interesting in this area, and this partially explains why any bibliography on incentives (including the one at the end of this chapter) is skewed toward tax incentive questions.

Writing on incentives, particularly tax-based incentives, is often vaguer than it should be to give a completely accurate picture of the actual form of an incentive. For example, in my research for this chapter, I have come across a number of descriptions of tax incentives allowing expenditures to be deducted, that do not explain exactly how the incentive is structured (for instance, the quantity from which the expenditure can be deducted is often not spelled out). This problem is exacerbated when relying on translations from other languages. Often, the best one can do is to get a general sense of the structure of a particular incentive in a particular place. (A notable exception to this observation is comparative work, now nearly twenty years old, undertaken by Ignace Claeys Bouuaert for the Commission of the European Communities.[5]) Until a common analytical vocabulary has been developed and adopted by authors in the field, there will always be the possibility of misrepresenting or overlooking some critical detail of a particular incentive program.[6] Indeed, one of our goals in addressing historic preservation from a government tools perspective is to begin developing such a common perspective and vocabulary.

In exploring the use of incentives for preservation of the built environment I do not intend to offer a complete catalog of the incentives used today. Rather, I have tried to choose a wide range of examples to illustrate the breadth of possibilities and to highlight the issues that come with the use of various forms of incentives. Because not all of the sources on which I have relied for my examples are current, it may be that not all of the examples I cite are either. Also, proposals that are mentioned in one source or another may or may not actually have been implemented. So be forewarned that this is neither a complete nor a completely accurate survey of the use of incentives.

Perhaps, the most important way in which incentives vary is in the prospective recipient. Incentives might be offered to individual citizens, whether or not they own heritage property, to nonprofit citizen groups and organizations, or to one level of government by another—typically by a higher level to a lower level. But in preservation activities, the most important incentives are those offered to individuals of a particular type: private owners of heritage property. If a decision has been made to limit the extent to which a particular government is willing to use an own-and-operate strategy, either because of limited resources or because of an ideological position, then state intervention will target the extent to which individual citizens support and are engaged in historic preservation activities, and there is no better place to begin than with the private owners of properties with particular historic significance.

Direct Incentives to Private Owners

For government incentives actually to provide an incentive for improved and increased historic preservation activity, they have to offer something that private owners want. The first place to turn, probably, is to the provision of direct financial assistance.[7] Many incentives are structured as direct incentives, through which government writes a check and transfers money to another actor in the preservation system.

Grants and Matching Grants

The most common direct incentive comes in the form of grants. Government makes use of a number of different forms of grants; Haider identifies four major types: project grants, formula grants, block grants, and general revenue sharing.[8] Of all of these forms, the one that seems to have been the most important to historic preservation is the project grant. Project grants are normally provided directly to the owners of historic properties for particular purposes (such as maintenance, restoration, or interpretation) or to nonprofit institutions working to further preservation in one way or another. In many places, some of the revenues from the other types of grants may have been used for preservation projects (or for projects with preservation components), but more than likely these projects would be undertaken by lower levels of government with grants from higher levels of government rather than by private owners of heritage properties.

Grants can be designed in a wide variety of ways. In determining eligibility for a grant, one might want to consider, among other things, the nature of the recipient, the purpose/use to which the grant may be put, the geographic distribution of grant recipients and of supported projects, and whether or not previous grants have been made to the recipient and with what success. The variation suggested by these criteria alone is immense, and it would be a gargantuan task indeed to catalog all of the grant programs that have been deployed in the service of historic preservation. But a set of examples can suggest the variety that is possible:[9]

- In the 1970s, Great Britain used an "acknowledgment payments scheme" to provide annual tax-free payments to farmers or timber growers in exchange for respecting ancient monuments on their properties. This particular grant was quite clearly structured in the shape of a deal. But the procedures were so difficult (and, presumably, so costly) to administer that they were replaced with a different scheme. The Ancient Monuments and Archaeological Areas Act of 1979 requires owners of scheduled ancient monuments to obtain permission from the state for the demolition, destruction, removal, alteration, or repair of any monument. If permission is refused, the state is required to pay the owner for any loss incurred. (This flips the logic on its head a bit—"If we do X, you will get Y"—but it still can be understood as a deal, albeit a mandatory deal. Even though it moves the incentive system toward a regulatory stance, it is clearly different from a strict regulatory approach to preservation.)
- Also in Britain, the Historic Buildings and Ancient Monuments Act of 1953 established a program of grants for the maintenance or repair of heritage buildings as long as there is reasonable public access to the building. The amount of the grant may be no larger than 50 percent of the total cost, and applicants for these grants are subject to a means test to establish that they are not able to cover the expected costs themselves. (This grant introduces two characteristics of incentives to which I will return later: the idea of a quid pro quo in exchange for public support and the idea of co-financing, an informal type of matching grant.)
- Again in Britain, "Town Schemes" have also been developed to help maintain and restore ensembles of buildings. In this case, the state pays 25 percent and the local authority 25 percent of the restoration cost; if the county council also participates, the limits are 25 percent state, 12.5 percent county, and 12.5 percent local authority, with the owner contributing at least 50 percent. (Notice again the use of co-financing.)
- Similarly, the Dutch Ministry of Cultural Affairs, Recreation, and Social Work makes grants toward restoration (but not improvements). In the case of grants made to individual owners, the state typically provides 30 percent, the province 10 percent, and the municipality 30 percent, leaving the owner to provide 30 percent; in the case of buildings owned by a public body, the central government percentage might rise as high as 50 percent. In the case of church properties, all public sources provide about 95 percent of the cost, with the church itself having to raise only the remaining 5 percent.
- In France, the Ministry of Culture can contribute up to 50 percent of the cost of upkeep of a heritage property in private hands. But, by the law of 1966, the minister can compel maintenance, in which case the minister

has to contribute more than 50 percent of the cost. (While compulsory maintenance schemes are more appropriately thought of as regulatory, they are often paired with incentives of one sort or another, and therefore deserve mention here.)

- The Austrian Federal Monument Office can provide support to buildings beyond those that are listed monuments through its Facade Action Program. The owners of buildings in designated Facade Action Districts can receive federal grants for a portion of facade work. The remaining costs are shared by the owner, the local government, and the government of the *Land*.

- In Switzerland, where preservation is primarily the responsibility of the cantons, there is, nevertheless, a long tradition of national grant programs and legislation. Since the late nineteenth century, Swiss preservation law has embodied a co-financing principle. A resolution passed in 1886 called for the national government to participate in preservation through financial support that was limited to half of restoration costs. At the outset, the money to provide this financial support was actually administered through a private, nongovernmental organization, the Swiss Society for the Conservation of Historical Art Monuments. In 1917 the ceiling on federal involvement was lowered to 30 percent of costs, but it was raised to 60 percent in 1958. In 1982 the percentage of costs to be covered by the federal government was linked to the relative significance of the historic property—30 to 40 percent of the costs for buildings of national significance, 15 to 25 percent for buildings of regional significance, and 10 to 15 percent for buildings of local significance. Where federal support ends up in each range depends upon the financial strength of the respective canton, which, in any event, is expected to participate by providing some of its own resources.[10]

- Prior to the fall of the communist regime in Poland, the state was authorized to make grants to private owners of listed monuments for up to 30 percent of the total cost of restoration (most such grants actually provided only 15 to 20 percent). The state was also authorized to provide grants for up to 23.5 percent of these costs for nonclassified buildings at the request of the Local Conservator. (To discourage defaults, the owner was required to put up 25 percent of the total cost before receiving the grant.)

With discretionary grants, upon which many grant programs are based, the role of decision making takes on a particular importance. Someone or some group must choose one applicant for a grant over another. This process is fraught with political pitfalls, and the state is well advised to structure the decision-making process carefully. Often these decisions are subject to outside review with a panel of knowledgeable individuals created to make the decisions—a "peer panel review." Yet such a process can also be criticized for creating an in-group with particular interests and biases (as has happened frequently in the field of grant support to the performing and visual arts).

To prevent criticism of discretionary grant-making processes, the state takes great care with who makes the final decisions. Moreover, it often constrains their decisions with explicit definitions of what projects would merit grants, strict limits on the maximum amount that can be granted to any single recipient (and perhaps limits on the minimum amount as well), and clear criteria for geographic distribution.

On this final point, the best interests of preservation and the interests of the political process may well come into conflict. The political process will generate two distinct pressures: one to spread grants across political jurisdictions irrespective of the location of truly valued or truly endangered heritage resources, and the other to satisfy particularly vocal lobbying interests irrespective of the merits of their claims on public resources. Neither of these pressures will necessarily focus grants on the most noteworthy or the most needy historic resources.

Grant programs are often structured as competitive processes. Hopeful recipients present their proposals to the grant program, which compares them before deciding which applicants will receive the grant. When the state wants to target very specific preservation goals and projects, a grant program could, however, be designed so that grants might be offered even if the potential recipient has not formally submitted a proposal.

A second type of direct grant program used in preservation policy includes grants that are structured as a right rather than as the outcome of a discretionary decision-making process. From published descriptions of grant programs, it is not always possible to tell which are as of right and which are discretionary, so I have tried to select some of the clearest examples to make the distinction:[11]

- In the Netherlands, owners of listed windmills have a right to claim an annual maintenance grant from the government (2,000 guilders).
- In both Salzburg and Graz, Austria, local laws establish zones of protection within their historic town centers. Within these zones, regulations are quite strict. In compensation for the additional costs that landlords incur because of the obligation to preserve their buildings, landlords have a legal right to support from a Historic Town Center Preservation Fund.[12] (This makes direct incentives automatic and predictable, qualities more typical of tax-based indirect incentives.)
- From 1960 to 1980, Danish law stipulated that if an owner proposed work on a historic building and the government responded by suggesting

alterations or repairs beyond what had been proposed, the state had to pay the difference. (An interesting element of this incentive is that it actually may function as an incentive to the state to keep its demands reasonable.)

What seems clear from these few examples is that different forms of grants may well reflect fundamental differences in the preservation attitudes of various countries. Anthony Dale, in comparing the grant programs of Great Britain and the Netherlands, for example, points out that, generally speaking, in Great Britain grants are considered discretionary, whereas in the Netherlands they are considered a matter of right.[13] Perhaps this reflects the Dutch view of private owners as trustees of the public interest.

At the extreme of direct grants, I suppose, is compulsory purchase, in which a deal is consummated. But then the tool that is being used by government becomes ownership and operation, unless the state turns around and sells the property to a private owner whom it feels will take better care of the preservation of the property.

As my examples of co-financing grant programs have already suggested, the preservation field is seeing more and more grant programs that are designed to encourage and take advantage of multiple sources of funding. There has been a discernible move from co-financing schemes toward more formally structured matching grants in which the state offers, say, one dollar for every additional dollar that can be raised from other sources toward a preservation project. To design such a matching grant, various ratios might be used, various stipulations might be placed on the grant to target other specific sources of support, and floors and/or ceilings might be placed on the grant.[14]

Indirect Incentives to Private Owners

Direct grants are not the only way that the state can offer incentives to the private owners of heritage properties. An important and growing component of incentive programs in many countries is the indirect incentive. Indirect incentives have rather different attributes. Like direct incentives, they have a financial effect; unlike direct incentives, they involve no direct transfer of money and no state expenditure is recorded.

The best known and most highly touted indirect incentives are tax-based incentives of one form or another, but loans, low interest rate loans, loan guarantees, and guarantees against loss are other examples. Depending on how inclusive one wants to be in identifying government actions that might have some indirect incentive effect on preservation, the list can become quite long indeed.

As a class, indirect incentives have several attributes that may be particularly appealing (though more so in certain political climates than in others). Typically, indirect incentives allow a considerable degree of private sector control over how public sector initiatives are played out. They may be simpler for the government to enact and administer, not requiring any complicated government bureaucracy to oversee them, though the question of how to be sure that the incentive is having the desired effect remains a serious one.

On the other hand, indirect incentives lack one attribute that people often imagine they have. They are often seen as being free to government. When an incentive is provided through foregoing taxes that would otherwise be paid, as happens through tax-based incentives, no direct government check is ever written nor is a direct government expenditure ever recorded. But, of course, the foregone taxes do represent a cost to the state, and the increased difficulty of tracking that cost does not mean that the incentive is without cost. Despite this obvious fact, legislatures are turning to tax-based incentives more and more to limit the size of the public budget and to get programs not considered to be at the heart of the raison d'être of government "off budget." One should not be too surprised to find historic preservation programs on this list. In my account of tax-based indirect incentives below I will endeavor to make explicit the public costs of such programs.[15]

Getting these expenditures off budget through tax-based incentives has an important related consequence. To the extent that indirect incentives become less visible, they become less likely to be subjected to the regular review that one normally expects from state programs, making it even harder to know what the impacts of the programs have been.

Because many of the most well-known indirect incentives are tax-based incentives targeted at the owners of historic properties, I turn first to these.

Tax-Based Indirect Incentives

Tax-based incentives take on one of two broad forms: (1) incentives through which the taxable base is decreased before calculating one's tax liability and (2) incentives through which the taxes owed are decreased directly. To illustrate the difference, consider the example of a program to help owners offset the additional costs of maintaining and rehabilitating historic properties. The government might provide direct grants or it might chose a tax-based incentive approach. If it chooses the latter, there are two basic ways to structure the incentive. In the first, the state might allow the owner to deduct from his or her income the costs of specified maintenance or rehabilitation expenditures for the property, thereby reducing the owner's effective taxable income. This, in turn, results in a tax savings. One might put a variety of limits on this deduction—perhaps a minimum expenditure would be required to receive the benefit, or a maximum—but the basic principle remains: the tax incentive allows specified costs to be deducted from income. (Similarly, one might make a variety of decisions about which of the owner's expenditures are deductible: perhaps they will only be allowed to the extent they exceed "normal" maintenance expenditures, or perhaps all maintenance costs will be allowed.) This form of tax incentive is often referred to as an income tax deduction, but this phrase can be misleading. As we have seen, an incentive of this type does not allow a deduction from one's taxes; rather, it allows a deduction from one's income (or, in the general case, from the taxable base, whatever it happens to be) before calculating the taxes due.

Alternatively, the state might take the total that the owner has spent on specified maintenance or rehabilitation expenditures and allow the owner to subtract a fixed percentage of those expenditures from his or her income tax. This form of tax incentive is typically referred to as a tax credit because the net result of the incentive is a credit against taxes; a 30 percent tax credit, for example, would allow the owner to subtract 30 percent of his or her maintenance or rehabilitation expenditures from the income tax that he or she would otherwise owe to the state.

Either way, the result is a decrease in the net cost of maintenance and rehabilitation, providing an indirect financial incentive for owners of eligible properties to make these expenditures. And, either way, there is a cost sharing between the private owner and the public at large because the public allows the use of foregone taxes to help pay for a portion of the owner's expenditures.

There is, however, an important difference between these two models. In the case of a deduction, the benefit that the individual owner receives via the incentive is a direct function of his or her marginal tax rate. Because most societies have progressive tax systems in which the marginal tax rises with one's income, the effect of a deduction is that the benefit to the owner rises with his or her income. Paradoxically, the result is a regressive incentive.

A tax credit, on the other hand, does not have this property. It treats all owners' expenditures the same and offers the same percentage break on every expenditure—in the example above, 30 cents on the dollar. Some countries, recognizing the equity problem embedded in structuring tax incentives as deductions, have systematically replaced existing deductions in their income tax law with credits. This has happened in Canada in recent years. Interestingly, though the United States tends to choose deductions as its preferred form of tax incentives, the federal tax incentives offered in the field of historic preservation have tended to be structured as tax credits.

Paul McDaniel has pointed out one other attribute of tax-based incentives that is worth noting: programs implemented through tax incentives, because they are as of right rather than discretionary government programs, are effectively given priority over all direct programs.[16] By this he means that direct programs can only be funded out of the tax revenues that result from the collection of taxes that are due after various tax incentives have reduced one's tax liability.

Income Tax Incentives

To the extent that an American style of intervention in historic preservation can be isolated and described independently, that style must be characterized by its reliance on tax-based incentives for preservation activities. A whole variety of tax-based incentives are at work, but, broadly speaking, the most important three are:

- incentives that reduce the cost of maintaining and rehabilitating a historic property in private hands;
- incentives that reduce the opportunity cost of keeping a historic property rather than razing it and replacing it with a more profitable form of property development; and
- incentives that promote the flow of resources—cash, in-kind contributions, easements, development rights, and historic properties themselves—to nonprofit groups dedicated to preserving historic resources.

The first of these is discussed in this section of the chapter, the second in the next section, and the third I return to a bit later.

In the United States there have been four milestones in the use of income tax law to provide incentives for preservation activity.[17] The Tax Reform Act of 1976 launched the American experience with income-tax-based incentives. This act allowed owners of commercial historic properties to speed up the rate at which they could depreciate expenditures made for approved rehabilitation of certified properties. This resulted in more immediate tax savings and brought historic properties more in line with newly constructed properties. On the disincentive side of the ledger, the act disallowed the deduction of expenses of demolition of a historic property as a business expense, effectively making demolition more expensive. Finally, the act allowed charitable deductions for the donation of facade easements on historic properties. (I will return to this last point below.)

The 1978 Amendments to the Tax Reform Act of 1976 introduced, for the first time, a 10 percent tax credit for rehabilitation expenditures. This tax credit induced an immediate and substantial flow of capital into the rehabilitation of certified historic properties.

The major watershed came with the Economic Recovery Tax Act of 1981, which expanded the incentives introduced in 1978. This act put in place a generous three-tiered investment tax credit intended to assist in the rehabilitation not only of historic properties but of older buildings more generally. The tax credit for certified rehabilitation of historic properties was increased to 25 percent; a tax credit of 20 percent was established for the rehabilitation of all commercial properties over forty years old; and a tax credit of 15 percent was established for the rehabilitation of all commercial properties over thirty years old. A tremendous amount of rehabilitation is attributed to the Economic Recovery Tax Act of 1981 as, all of a sudden, the rehabilitation of older properties became much more financially attractive.

Unfortunately, the effect of the 1981 legislation was blunted somewhat with the passage of the Tax Reform Act of 1986. This act, passed at the beginning of a period of relative government austerity, cut back the tax incentives for commercial properties: the tax credit for certified rehabilitation of certified historic structures was reduced to 20 percent, and the tax credit for older, non-historic commercial buildings was set at 10 percent, but only for buildings over fifty years old. In addition, the act intended to limit the value of the tax credit by allowing it only to be applied to taxes on income realized on the building itself (rather than on other sources of income, which had made the earlier tax credit particularly attractive). This was relaxed somewhat in the final bill, but the economics of rehabilitation had, nevertheless, become less attractive than they had been over the previous five years.

Although it is perhaps the best known, the American story is not the only story worth telling with respect to the use of income tax-based incentives. France, Austria, and Germany offer just a few examples:[18]

- France offers owners of heritage properties a 50 percent tax credit for expenditures on maintenance and improvements. A 100 percent tax credit is possible if the building is open to the public according to a set of rules: either it must be open fifty days per year, of which twenty-five are holidays between April and September; or it must be open forty days between July and September. A reduced credit is offered for the portion of the building occupied by the owner, and a portion of the admission fees can be realized tax-free by the owner.
- A 1978 amendment to the Austrian Law for the Protection of Monuments allowed property owners tax benefits for the restoration of buildings classified as monuments. The owner was offered two options: (1) A 50 percent tax credit for restoration costs could be taken in the first year with one fifth of the remaining costs (10 percent of total costs) credited against income taxes in each of the following five years. This amounted to a 100 percent tax credit, though one that was spread over six years; or (2) the costs could be deducted equally over a ten-year period, resulting in a 10 percent tax credit each year, effectively a 100 percent tax credit spread over ten years. The law has since been changed, making only the second option available.

- Similarly, in West Germany, rehabilitation costs necessary for the preservation and use of any listed monument can be deducted over a ten-year period. Deductions must not exceed 10 percent of total income taxes per year. (My source is not precise enough for me to know exactly what is deducted from what in this scheme.) Maintenance expenses can be deducted over a two- to five-year period.

Note that these and other income tax incentives tend to affect only commercial and investment properties, not owner-occupied housing properties. There have been some attempts to offset this. For example, Maryland authorized an income tax incentive for preservation in which expenditures on certified rehabilitation of nondepreciable (that is noncommercial) owner-occupied property could be deducted (presumably from income) before calculating the owner's state income tax liability. As far as I know, however, this law has not been implemented.

Such tax incentives might be adjusted in a wide variety of ways. For example, in the Netherlands the incentive is lowered by any direct grants received by private owners; once they have subtracted the amount of grants they have received from the state from the maintenance costs for a listed building, owners are, apparently, allowed a 100 percent tax credit for the remaining costs.[19]

Property Tax Incentives

Preservation tax incentives are often offered through property tax legislation, as well. Incentives that reduce the local property tax on a property lower one of its main operating expenses, thus reducing the cost of holding and using that property productively. In the United States, property-tax-linked incentives are offered by local government because that is the level of government that uses the property tax as a revenue raising instrument, but these incentives generally have to be authorized through state legislation. Some state governments have considered requiring themselves to reimburse municipalities for revenues lost through such state laws.

Property tax incentives are a government response to two particular problems that accompany the process of rehabilitating historic properties: (1) the high costs of rehabilitation expenditures and (2) the rising property values and the accompanying increases in property tax assessments that result from successful preservation activities.

Property tax incentives take two basic forms, which parallel the two forms of income tax incentives discussed above: lower assessments of the value of the property and lower tax rates. In practice, one sees many variations on these basic forms: frozen assessments, assessments at current use (as opposed to highest and best economic use), assessments at a set percentage of full value, lower property tax rates, and complete exemptions from property taxation, among others. Moreover, any of these forms might be applied permanently or for a limited period of time.

A few examples will indicate the rich variety of property-tax-based incentives used in preservation programs. But let me repeat my caution: because the literature is even weaker when it comes to describing adequately the available property tax incentives, much has to be based on reasonable conjecture rather than on definitive descriptions. [20]

- The state of Oregon has implemented a fifteen-year freeze on property tax assessments for rehabilitated historic properties in exchange for an agreement to maintain the property in the condition it was in at the time of the freeze and to open it to the public at least one day each year.
- Maryland state law authorizes individual counties to give tax credits against local property taxes to offset rehabilitation expenditures as an incentive for private restoration. It allows a credit of (1) up to 10 percent of an owner's expenditures for restoration and preservation of historic property or (2) up to 5 percent of the cost of constructing a new building that is compatible with its surrounding historic district with a five-year carry-forward provision if all of the credit cannot be used in one year. According to one source, however, none of the Maryland counties have seen fit to enact such an ordinance.
- The District of Columbia assesses historic properties at current use value rather than at their highest and best use. In practice, though, this incentive is of little value in the District of Columbia because so many of the historic properties belong to government agencies and various non-profit organizations, which are already exempt from property taxation. (This example illustrates well the broader issue of carefully targeting incentives and raises the question of whether indirect incentives can be sufficiently targeted.)
- In West Germany, monuments whose conservation was deemed to be in the public interest were subject to property tax at 40 percent of their value. Moreover, the owner could receive a total exemption from property taxes if the monument were accessible to the public, the owner submitted to conditions stipulated by the appropriate State Conservation Office, and the monument had been in the owner's family for twenty years or more. This provides a particularly striking incentive not only to retain the property in private ownership but to do so with familial continuity, which, presumably, increases the family's attachment to the property. (Also, in cases where these three conditions were met, inheritance taxes could be reduced to 60 percent.) But the owner could only take advantage of these incentives if the annual costs of the property consistently

exceeded the annual income from the property. The result is that this incentive only functions for truly exceptional properties such as castles or fortresses. Moreover, the incentive is not available unless the owner is legally obliged to preserve the property (typically the result of listing), and thus it may be understood partly as an offer to compensate the owner for the effects of heritage regulations.

- In a similar vein, property taxes on historic properties unlikely to yield a commercial profit can be reduced through lower assessments in Austria.
- In Turkey, cultural properties identified as Class I or Class II are exempt from all property taxes. In addition, repair or construction work on these properties is exempt from all taxation, and imported materials for this work are exempt from customs duties and taxes.

Given all the parameters in the property tax that one can change in order to present an incentive to an owner, it is hard to know exactly how one would set the levels of these various parameters to balance the public benefit of preservation with the increased public cost of foregone taxes, but it is clear that many places have used property tax incentives as a tool in preservation.

Other Tax-Based Incentives

Undoubtedly, there are many other tax-based incentives at work in historic preservation in one place or another. Some places offer an exemption from sales tax on materials purchased as part of rehabilitation projects. In West Germany, taxes on the sale of historic real estate were reduced or waived in some situations. In a number of places, the government authorizes the issuing of tax-exempt bonds to raise capital for the finance of historic preservation projects. Though even less is written about these less frequent forms of incentive, many of the analytical questions I have raised above still apply.

Issues in the Use of Tax-Based Incentives

The use of tax-based incentives is not without controversy. Any tax regime is, first and foremost, implemented to raise revenues for the operation of government programs. Any tax-based incentive, no matter what its purpose, erodes the tax base and results in fewer resources available to the state and/or costs redistributed in the form of higher taxation.

It is probably fair to say that one should use the tax system to achieve public purposes only if (1) the objective is of clear importance to society and (2) the objective can be achieved most easily through the tax system. But notice the trap in the word "easily." It may be easier to put tax incentives in place than pass direct budgetary allocations, as Lester Salamon and Michael Lund have pointed out,[21] but that does not necessarily mean that it will purchase more preservation per dollar of state investment. If the tax-based incentive works in encouraging more private investment to flow in this direction, it may well be preferable to more direct ways of achieving the same goal. But, although tax incentives may be cheap and simple to implement, to the extent that they must be linked to a certification and compliance process to be truly effective, much of this benefit may be lost.

Other Indirect Incentives

Tax-based incentives are not the only indirect incentives offered to owners of historic properties to further historic preservation goals.

A careful analysis of the barriers to preservation activities in a specific place might reveal that the major hindrance is a lack of access to capital. If the government can act in a manner that increases the credit available for a particular purpose, then it will have provided an incentive leading in that direction.

Private lenders might be unwilling to provide loans for preservation projects because it is their perception that such projects are risky investments (particularly if the project in question is one of the first to be undertaken in an area that has not yet undergone restoration). But the public sector might believe that such investments are actually less risky. In such a circumstance, the government could structure ways for capital to be provided to preservation projects through a loan mechanism. The simple willingness of the state to offer such loans might make an important difference in getting preservation projects off the ground. On the other hand, if a major constraint to preservation is the cost of borrowing, then the provision of loans with subsidized (below market) interest rates might be the key.

A loan-based intervention might take one of several forms: the provision of loan guarantees (through which the state guarantees the loan between a private lender and a borrower by cosigning the loan), the provision of loans, or the provision of loans with subsidized (or even no) interest rates. To take just a few quick examples:

- In Poland, the government has offered rehabilitation loans at a 3 percent interest rate.
- In Atlanta, Georgia, the government provides mortgage guarantees at a lower cost than commercial lenders for preservation projects.
- At the national level in the United States, loans for historic preservation were authorized by the 1980 amendments to the Preservation Act of 1966, but they were never actually funded.
- Loans are typically made available for facade improvements in a number of countries.

Another set of indirect incentives can be embedded in legislation affecting real estate development. Examples include the exemption of historic preservation projects from parking requirements, which increase costs and may be incompatible in design with preservation projects, and the offering of development bonuses for projects that save historic properties as part of the development project. The latter approach has been tried in a number of American cities as part of plans to preserve and rehabilitate historic theaters threatened by downtown development pressure. The creation of conservation districts can also be seen as a type of real estate development incentive; it provides an incentive to invest because the context is controlled and predictable (even though the main purpose of the conservation district is to regulate new construction, alterations, additions, demolition, and so on).

The government may also purchase historic properties and resell them to private developers at lower costs to provide an incentive for rehabilitation of those properties. In Cracow, Poland, for example, recognizing that 80 percent of the dwelling units were in private hands and many of them in historic properties, the state purchased dilapidated historic housing, restored the units, and then assigned the buildings to various cooperatives.[22]

Finally, a number of incentives used in the field of historic preservation operate even more indirectly than any of the ones I have mentioned so far. Prizes, awards, and competitions may be thought of, in part, as incentives to better historic preservation. There is a question, of course, as to whether they function more as true incentives than as recognition of quality work. Perhaps prizes and awards fall more into the latter category, while competitions fall more into the former. I do not want to try to split this hair too finely, but it is worth pointing out that there is an element of incentive built into these mechanisms, just as there is a strong element of education in them.

Training programs for specialists in historic preservation also have an element of incentive built into them. The city of Salvador, Brazil, discovered that one of the constraints to increased restoration of historic properties in its case was a lack of trained professionals who could handle the design issues. The result was the creation of a training program, which has now been copied elsewhere. This tool also sits at the intersection between incentive and information.

The state can provide design assistance at a reasonable cost or even free to preservation projects, thus providing another form of indirect incentive to ownership.[23] In Amsterdam, for instance, an owner of a listed building can receive free professional advice from the Restoration Office of the City. If the work is then carried out in the suggested fashion, the owner is eligible for a grant. And in France, the state makes specialist architects available to private property owners for a lower fee than would usually be charged.

Incentives Not Targeted at Individual Owners

Incentives can, as I mentioned earlier, be provided to actors in the historic preservation realm other than individual owners of historic properties. Perhaps the most common examples of preservation incentives that are not targeted at the owners of heritage properties are ones offered to get more resources to flow to nonprofit, citizen-based preservation organizations. Here tax-based indirect incentives have been the most important form of incentive, but grants (particularly matching grants) have also played a role.

Nonprofit groups created to promote preservation and to conserve historic properties are generally tax-exempt on their own income. Thus, for example, any revenues from admission fees to nonprofit historic homes and museums are not subject to taxation and can be used in their entirety if they are turned back to the public purposes for which the nonprofit organization was formed.

A more important incentive of this type has been the incentive to charitable contributions to preservation organizations. In contrast to the treatment of maintenance expenditures through tax credits in the United States, tax incentives for charitable contributions to preservation organizations have taken the form of tax deductions. Historic properties, themselves, may be donated to nonprofit organizations or government agencies and a deduction allowed from one's taxable income. The same applies to the donation of easements or development rights for preservation purposes, thus mixing the property rights tool of government with the incentives tool. Cash contributions to nonprofit charitable organizations can, within generous limits, be deducted from the donor's income before calculating one's income tax, as can gifts of various forms of remainder trusts. All of these reduce the net cost of donations to the donor by sharing the cost with taxpayers more generally in the form of foregone tax revenues.

In the United States, some individual states allow charitable contribution deductions as well.[24] Virginia has a particularly generous income tax incentive. Under the Virginia Neighborhood Assistance Act, it offers a 50 percent tax credit for business contributions to neighborhood revitalization projects that include the rehabilitation of older structures in low income areas.

Such incentives for charitable contributions are available in many countries. Most are designed as deductions from income, but some are designed as tax credits. The extent to which these charitable contribution incentives actually incorporate historic preservation organizations undoubtedly varies from country to country. In Germany, for example, income tax deductions are available to individuals or corporations for donations to support preservation activities through government agencies or nonprofit organizations. I know of no recent source in which comparative information has been gathered on tax incentives for contributions to historic preservation.[25]

When tax provisions include an incentive for the donation of property rather than cash, a number of issues arise concerning the valuation of that property. The donation of preservation easements (including scenic easements, facade easements, and interior features easements) has received particular attention in the literature.[26] (As I have already mentioned in passing, allowing the possibility of donation of easements may require a redefinition of the package of property rights inherent in historic properties, employing another of the five tools.) Three questions are of particular interest here: Under what circumstances can an easement be donated? What is the value of the appropriate deduction or credit? What is the relationship between such an easement and the value of the property with which it is associated for continuing property tax purposes?

Some literature on tax incentives for donations questions the extent to which such a regime should be used to encourage contributions of property rather than cash contributions because of the explicit or implicit constraints that might come with a donation of property. If tax-assisted donations were to be restricted to cash, it is argued, recipient organizations would exert some quality control through their preservation decisions—deciding, for example, which facade easements to buy. (For a similar reason, of course, direct state grants for purchase of selected easements might be preferred over indirect incentives that might have similar effects.)

Other indirect tax-based incentives can affect the disposition of historic properties. Great Britain has a particularly refined set of incentives dealing with capital taxation and the national heritage.[27] While primarily focused on movable heritage items, some of the provisions of this scheme do affect heritage properties. For example, land, historic buildings, and their contents can be accepted by the government in lieu of capital transfer tax. Unlike other tax incentives, however, this one has been designed so that it actually results in a financial transfer within government with the cost of acquisition repaid to the Exchequer out of the National Heritage Fund. The amount of credit budgeted to this fund serves as a limit on the total value of in lieu payments that can be accepted in any given year. In a separate British tax incentive, a transfer of a historic house to the ownership of the National Trust upon death is exempt from capital transfer tax. (Wisely, the trust will not accept such a house without an accompanying endowment for its maintenance and operation.)

Incentives might also be offered from one level of government to another, typically in the form of grants. Such incentives are offered to stimulate the lower level's participation in preservation activities. In the United States, many of the state historic preservation offices were formed in response to such an incentive: federal money was offered, but only if matched by state money. These offices continue to receive grants from the federal government and provide critical services in terms of listing historic properties and ascertaining whether or not the renovation and rehabilitation that is being assisted through the tax credits are being done according to acceptable standards. In Switzerland, the federal government is authorized to compensate cantons for especially important protection measures that they have undertaken. In a way this can be seen as an incentive, or as a federal recognition of the national benefit to preservation efforts.

Governments might also make grants to the creation and ongoing operation of nongovernmental preservation groups (such as grants to national trusts in various countries).

Disincentives

A full consideration of incentives also has to take account of disincentives. Here, though, one has to be careful about the boundary between disincentives and regulation. I am not going to attempt to catalog the possible range of disincentives, but a couple of examples are sufficient to suggest the possibilities.[28] In Great Britain, if work is carried out on a listed building without state consent, a penalty is assessed and the local authority can force reinstatement of the building to its former condition. And in Austria, illegal demolition of a historic property is met with a fine of one year's income, and the owner can be forced to reconstruct the property or pay a fine equal to the cost of reconstruction. Various fines and penalties can provide disincentives. But the biggest effect may be realized if the state is willing to withhold funds in cases where the purposes of the incentive program are not being met. Of course, this is easier to do with direct incentives than with indirect ones.

The Public Interest and Quids Pro Quo

I have chosen to describe the implicit message in a government-offered incentive as "If you do X, the government will do Y." In this formulation, each incentive offered expects something in return. And an important component of the design of any incentive program will be the quid pro quo that is expected. For some, this will seem an odd way to characterize a grant, but only because grant programs have a way of being regarded by their recipients as gift programs. And from that point of view, it is not difficult to begin thinking about the program as an entitlement program.

To keep any government assistance program focused on what is expected in exchange for that assistance is not easy. One of the most radical suggestions in a recent strategy document of the Arts Council of Great Britain was that henceforth a grant from the Arts Council would be considered a sort of contract between the council and its client, rather than simply a payment of funds with no other interest attached. That reformulation, if it had been successful, would have transformed the nature of the relationship between the council and its clients.[29] Presumably, a grant is offered to support something that the recipient is doing well and in the public interest.

In many places, the fact that the incentive is providing assistance in one way or another to a historic property is not considered to be sufficiently in the public interest. The state may insist on further public benefits as part of the implicit deal offered through the incentive. These benefits can take many different forms. Owners may have to agree to inspections to insure that maintenance and rehabilitation are up to established standards; owners may have to agree to maintain the property; and/or owners may have to agree to some form of public access to the property. In many cases, owners who accept an incentive are required to attach a restrictive covenant to their deed to assure that the preservation interest will continue with the property.[30]

- In the state of Washington, when an owner takes advantage of a tax incentive, the property must either be visible from the public right-of-way or the owner(s) must agree to open the building to the public at least one day per year. Thus, the rehabilitation and preservation of the property, while being of public interest, is not deemed to be of sufficient public interest without public access to the property.
- An owner who receives a restoration grant from the Swiss government must enter into a contract with the Department of the Interior establishing subsequent federal protection. The owner must agree to maintain the property, to allow inspections, to allow some degree of public access, and to seek approval for subsequent alterations. Failure to fulfill this contract necessitates repayment of the grant to the government. Once the contract has been entered into and the grant has been used to restore the property, this agreement becomes binding on all future owners. Owners of all federally funded projects are required to submit complete documentation to the Federal Archives for the Care of Monuments, thereby developing a rich archive of material on preservation practice. In this way, the information tool is linked to the incentive tool.
- In Zurich, Switzerland, a specified percentage of living space must be maintained in renovated buildings. Assistance is provided for renovations, but the public interest in maintaining an adequate housing stock is insisted upon.

There is one other aspect of the quid pro quo question that deserves mention. One way to view some incentives is as devices used by the state to offset the negative consequences of government preservation regulations. Thus, owners who are prohibited from demolishing historic property in their possession may be offered a tax incentive for rehabilitation expenses or a decrease in property taxes. The Spanish Historic Heritage Act of 1985, to take but one example, made this trade-off unusually explicit, recognizing that the tax incentives built into the act were intended "to compensate for the costs imposed by th[e] Act on the owners of property belonging to the Spanish historic heritage."[31] It is usually more difficult to tell if an incentive is offered as compensation for an overly restrictive regulation, or if accepting the regulation is the quid pro quo offered by the owner in exchange for taking advantage of the incentive.

Other Elements in the Design of Incentives

There are many other elements that one might want to consider in the design of an incentive. What is the trigger that allows the use of a particular incentive? Is there a floor of commitment below which it cannot be used? Or a ceiling of commitment beyond which it becomes too costly to the state? Eligibility rules are important, as is the timing of the incentive. Other design elements may be important as well.

The financial value offered through the incentive is undoubtedly an important factor. It is harder to know how one might calibrate this with indirect, tax-based incentives, but with a grant, one might design it so that its value is a function of the importance of the building, the severity of any threats to that building, the financial capability of the owner, and/or the extent to which the proposed preservation measures are judged to be within the public interest.

Some incentives are targeted to particular areas. In the Netherlands, there are special rates of subsidy in designated rehabilitation areas and special grants for designated historic town centers. Grant programs may be the easiest of all to aim at particular targets. The former West Germany had grants aimed at historic mills, blacksmith shops, bake ovens, small chapels, surplus parish houses, replacing multipane windows that are a distinctive local architectural element, and so on.

The cleverness of incentives is only limited by one's imagination. Consider a grant designed to support additional expenses over and beyond the normal cost of maintenance and repair. How do you calculate "normal"? How do you assure that expenses will not be excessive? (In other words, it is in the public interest that the expenditures not be too low and not be too high.) In Denmark, the notion of "decay per year" has been developed as a measure of the rate at which buildings of various types are in need of rehabilitation. Owners are allowed a tax exemption on repairs to their houses up the maximum set by the decay per year for that type of building. Such a carefully calibrated incentive may not be desirable, or even possible, everywhere, but it does suggest the range of creativity that can be brought to bear in designing incentives.

Comparing Direct and Indirect Incentives

The examples that I have offered in this chapter by no means exhaust the possibilities for incentives (or disincentives). Rather, I have endeavored to organize this variety of incentives into a set of conceptual categories in order to better identify the ways in which incentives might be designed. I now turn to a broader consideration of some of the policy issues entailed in the use of incentives as a tool of government action. Let me begin with a comparison of direct and indirect incentives in an attempt to highlight some of the more salient issues that need to be considered in weighing various options.

Direct incentives are more clearly affected by limited resources than indirect incentives because explicit expenditure decisions have to be made against a predetermined budget. Moreover, a system based on direct incentives, particularly one that is discretionary, can be an uncertain one for potential beneficiaries of those incentives. The beneficiary does not know whether or not he or she will qualify for a grant, for example, until it is actually received. The Dutch seem to have tried to offset this disadvantage by considering many of their grant programs to be a matter of right. This, of course, has budgetary implications, and can only function as long as the public budget delegated to preservation grants is sufficient to satisfy all of the claims on grant money.

A system built around tax-based indirect incentives, on the other hand, is a more certain one for intended beneficiaries. They can tell relatively easily if they will qualify to use one or another tax-based incentive, and their access to the incentive is often automatic. This does not mean that an indirect incentive is without cost to the state, only that the state is less able to monitor and account for the costs of foregone tax revenues. Other forms of indirect incentives may entail a higher level of government decision making and, therefore, a lower level of automaticity and certainty for the intended beneficiaries of the incentive.

Together these points might mean that beneficiaries would, *ceteris paribus*, prefer indirect incentives to direct incentives. On the other hand, to the extent that the state would like to guide the results of the incentives it offers and limit their costs, it might prefer direct incentives. If it finds deciding between various requests for funds for heritage preservation too difficult to manage, it might, however, also prefer indirect, particularly automatic, incentives.

Though indirect incentives clearly have economic costs to the state (often, though by no means always, in the form of foregone tax revenues), that cost is more difficult to account for and estimate. It may be more difficult to limit the use of indirect incentives than direct incentives and presumably more difficult to limit their aggregate cost.

Anthony Dale has characterized differences in preservation styles among different countries by their relative reliance on direct or indirect incentives.[32] France, for example, emphasizes direct incentives with centralized decisions by a group of experts. In countries that emphasize indirect incentives, such as the United States, one finds more examples of collaborative efforts. This is not to suggest that the form of incentive causes a particular style of preservation activity; it may reinforce or simply reflect that style. Choosing among tools undoubtedly involves leaning toward the tool that most corresponds to a society's way of functioning, that is to say, to that society's view of the appropriate relationship between the public and private sectors.

On the Impact of Incentives

Robert Stipe has pointed out that the incentive value of any preservation law depends heavily on the recipient's—usually the individual owner's—circumstances.[33] It is useful to break this statement into its component parts in order better to understand the issues involved in designing effective incentives (indeed, in designing effective interventions of any sort) and in assessing their impact. Let me conclude this chapter by trying to draw a distinction between what might be called the economic value of an incentive and the incentive value of that incentive.

Consider first the economic value of an incentive to its recipient. This economic value is the economic benefit received by the recipient by virtue of the state's action. In the case of a direct incentive, the economic value is clear: it is the amount of money transferred to the recipient. The economic value of indirect incentives is not as easy to measure, but even in these cases it can be estimated with a little analytic care. As we have already seen, however, there are some issues attached to the economic value realized by recipients of indirect incentives. To the extent that the level of an incentive is linked to an owner's income, as it is in a tax incentive based on a deduction from income, the relative value of that incentive goes up with the owner's income. An incentive constrained by various floors and ceilings may also reflect the owner's personal economic circumstances. In either case, the benefit that the owner receives may be linked more to his or her personal circumstances than to the level of the public interest in whatever action the incentive is designed to promote, and it is important to monitor this lest the incentive become divorced from the public interest in preservation.

But the economic value of an incentive is not the only indicator of how well it is working. One also needs a way to think about the incentive value of any incentive. Here the critical question is not what the level of any financial benefit to the target of the incentive is, but, rather, is the incentive actually strong enough to prompt the target to do something in the public interest that he or she would not otherwise have done?

An owner might take advantage of an incentive that he or she has been offered by pocketing the economic value of the incentive without doing anything different from what he or she would otherwise have done in the absence of the incentive. Or, he or she might be encouraged to levels and standards of preservation, conservation, or maintenance that he or she would otherwise have never considered, in which case the incentive would be providing an incentive value in addition to an economic value. Clearly, one wishes to design incentives with incentive as well as economic value.[34]

A major problem with assessing the impact of incentives is that success is often measured by the number of properties that have taken advantage of a particular incentive (or by the economic value of the incentives used, without any assessment of their incentive value). These numbers are relatively easy to measure; the problem is that they ignore the question of the appropriate counterfactual. The number of buildings restored *under* the historic rehabilitation tax credit is not equal to the number of buildings restored *because of* the historic rehabilitation tax credit.

Even if an incentive is ineffective in the sense that no more preservation is completed than the recipient would have done in the absence of the incentive, however, there may be a good public policy reason to provide a economic value to the target of the incentive. Public policy may dictate that the public should share the cost of that preservation activity from which the public derives value. Thus, the public should pay for that value rather than relying on the individual owner to shoulder all of the economic burden. If the goal of a public policy is to bring those who benefit from and those who pay for a public intervention more in line with one another, there may be an argument for shifting some costs without increased activity.

To realize their full effect, incentives may have to rely on conditions outside their control. Preservation is inevitably going to be linked to the real estate development climate. Incentives that are linked to a strong real estate market are going to be less effective when that market is weak. For example, the plan for a Midtown Cultural District in Boston was premised on the use of property tax incentives to restore historic theaters as well as to create new ones. But the value of the incentive was clearly a function of the health of the local real estate market. When that market declined, the value of the incentives eroded to the point where they became ineffectual.

From this review of incentives as they have been used and might be used in historic preservation, it should be clear that there is a rich menu of possibilities that have already been or might one day be explored. It should also be clear that there is a good deal more to learn about the relative effectiveness of various incentives, as well as about their effectiveness compared to other tools of government action. In an era in which the state is turning more and more to nongovernmental actors in the preservation system to ensure that its public policy with respect to the national heritage will be implemented, the role of incentives will become ever greater, and it will be even more important to understand and assess their effects.

Notes

1. Richard J. Roddewig, *Economic Incentives for Historic Preservation* (Washington, D.C.: National Trust for Historic Preservation, Center for Preservation Policy Studies, 1987).
2. Donald Haider, "Grants as a Tool of Public Policy," in *Beyond Privatization: The Tools of Government Action,* ed. by Lester M. Salamon (Washington, D.C.: The Urban Institute Press, 1989), 93–124.
3. Marya Morris, *Innovative Tools for Historic Preservation*, Planning Advisory Service Report no. 438 (Chicago: American Planning Association, 1992), 3.
4. One notable exception in the literature is *Safeguarding Historic Urban Ensembles in a Time of Change: A Management Guide,* the workbook developed for the International Symposium on World Heritage Towns.
5. Ignace Claeys Bouuaert, *Tax Problems of Historic Houses in the States of the European Economic Community*, Report XII/728/79-EN (Ghent, Belgium: Commission of the European Communities, 1979).
6. Even the otherwise commendable set of comparative studies commissioned by the United States Committee of the International Council on Monuments and Sites (US/ICOMOS) to document comparative preservation policies in a series of countries has found it very difficult to get a comparable level of detail and coverage across countries. Often the authors of these reports stop just short of the detail of description that would be necessary to understand the form of a particular incentive in a particular place.
7. It becomes a bit more difficult to categorize a tool in which the government has taken away something first through regulation, and then offers to return some or all of it through an incentive. Consider incentives linked to zoning. Allowing a developer to develop outside of the existing zoning envelope in exchange for something that is perceived to be in the public interest, such as the preservation of an historic building that occupies part of the site, is an incentive only if the restriction placed by the zoning law is there in the first place. This, of course, suggests that regulation could be used to create the scarce resource that could then be distributed through an incentive of one sort or another, though with this rationale, the original regulation might well not hold up in court.

8. Haider, "Grants as a Tool of Public Policy."
9. The examples listed here as well as those included later in this chapter are taken from the excellent series of reports edited by Robert Stipe for the United States Committee of the International Council on Monuments and Sites, Historic Preservation in Foreign Countries, later retitled Historic Preservation in Other Countries. See the list of references at the end of this chapter for the actual report title for particular countries.
10. Another Swiss government agency, the Federal Commission on Nature and Heritage Protection, also makes grants using a similar formula, but its maxima are higher for each type of property: 50 percent, 35 percent, and 25 percent respectively.
11. See note #9 above.
12. Revenues in these funds come from appropriations from the *Land* and the city, repayment of loans made from the funds, investment of the funds' assets, and donations from foundations.
13. Anthony Dale, *Volume I: France, Great Britain, Ireland, The Netherlands, and Denmark*, Historic Preservation in Foreign Countries, ed. by Robert E. Stipe (Washington, D.C.: United States Committee of the International Council on Monuments and Sites, 1982).
14. As far as I know, nothing has been written on the use of matching grants in preservation programs. For a discussion of the use of matching grants in arts funding and of the issues that that form of funding has presented, see J. Mark Schuster, "Government Leverage of Private Support: Matching Grants and the Problem with 'New' Money," in *The Cost of Culture,* ed. Margaret Wyszomirski and Pat Clubb (New York: American Council for the Arts, 1989), 63–97.
15. For a fuller discussion of the issue involved in using tax-based indirect incentives, albeit in a slightly different field, see J. Mark Schuster, "Issues in Supporting the Arts Through Tax Incentives," *Journal of Arts Management and Law* 16, no. 2 (Winter 1987): 31–50.
16. Paul R. McDaniel, "Tax Expenditures as Tools of Government Action," in *Beyond Privatization: The Tools of Government Action,* 167–96.
17. For a more detailed discussion, see John M. Fowler, "The Federal Government as Standard Bearer," *The American Mosaic: Preserving a Nation's Heritage,* ed. Robert E. Stipe and Antoinette J. Lee (Washington, D.C.: US/ICOMOS, 1987). The idea for tax-based incentives for preservation that became embedded in the Tax Reform Act of 1976 had actually been proposed earlier as part of the Historic Structure Tax Act of 1972, which was never passed.
18. See note #9 above.
19. This is one place where my source is particularly vague, but it seems to imply a 100 percent tax credit, though it might also indicate a deduction of the additional costs from income before calculating tax owed.
20. The American examples are taken from Lonnie A. Powers, "State Historic Preservation Tax Statutes: Three Case Studies," in *Tax Incentives for Historic Preservation,* ed. Gregory E. Andrews (Washington, D.C.: The Preservation Press, 1980), 108–24. For the other examples, see #9 above.
21. Lester M. Salamon and Michael S. Lund, "The Tools Approach: Basic Analytics," in *Beyond Privatization: The Tools of Government Action,* 46.

22. See note #9 above.
23. For the source of the examples, see note #9 above.
24. The interaction of such a state incentive with the federal charitable contribution deduction is subtle. Because the state incentive reduces state income taxes, this in turn lowers the deduction the taxpayer can take on the federal income tax form for payment of state taxes. As a result, federal income taxes will rise slightly, offsetting some of the effect of the federal incentive.
25. In my own writing, I once attempted to tabulate these incentives for contributions to the arts and culture, but this tabulation is now well out of date. See J. Mark Schuster, "Tax Incentives as Arts Policy in Western Europe," in *Nonprofit Enterprise in the Arts: Studies in Mission and Constraint,* ed. Paul DiMaggio (New York: Oxford University Press, 1986), 320–60.
26. See, for example, Russell L. Brenneman and Gregory E. Andrews, "Preservation Easements and Their Tax Consequences," in *Tax Incentives for Historic Preservation,* 147–55; and National Center for Preservation Law, "Treasury Department Questions Policy Value of Easement Donation Deductions," *Preservation Law Update* 1988-5 (January 29, 1988).
27. For a fuller discussion of this regime see Schuster, "Tax Incentives as Arts Policy in Western Europe."
28. See note #9 above.
29. Arts Council of Great Britain, *A Creative Future: The Way Forward for the Arts, Crafts and Media in England* (London, England: Her Majesty's Stationer's Office, 1993), 47. Intervening events and a restructuring of the Arts Council have made it difficult to discern whether this intent to reframe grants has been carried out.
30. The Washington example is taken from Marya Morris, *Innovative Tools for Historic Preservation.* The Swiss examples are taken from Margaret Thomas Will, *Volume II: Federal Republic of Germany, Switzerland, and Austria,* in the series Historic Preservation in Foreign Countries.
31. José Luis Alvarez, "Taxation and Heritage Development," *New Ways of Funding the Restoration of the Architectural Heritage,* Architectural Heritage Reports and Studies, no. 13, Report of the Messina Colloquy (Strasbourg, France: Council of Europe, 1988), 98–107.
32. Dale, *Volume I: France, Great Britain, Ireland, The Netherlands, and Denmark.*
33. Robert E. Stipe, "State and Local Tax Incentives for Historic Preservation," *Tax Incentives for Historic Preservation,* 91–101.
34. Much of the economic debate concerning income tax deductions for charitable contributions is on exactly this question. Various attempts have been made to ascertain the extend to which donors pocket the tax savings offered by the deduction, increase their donations but only up to the amount of the tax savings, or actually increase their donations beyond the value of the tax savings. For a particularly complete discussion of the empirical research findings on this issue, see Charles T. Clotfelter, *Federal Tax Policy and Charitable Giving* (Chicago: University of Chicago Press, 1985). Though this book is some ten years old, the methodological approach to tax-based incentives is still most valuable.

References

Andrews, Gregory E., ed. *Tax Incentives for Historic Preservation.* Washington, D.C.: The Preservation Press, 1980. Chapters include: Mortimer Caplin, "Federal Tax Policy as an Incentive for Enhancement of the Built Environment"; Robert E. Stipe, "State and Local Tax Incentives for Historic Preservation"; Joseph H. McGee, "State and Local Taxation: Current Practices, Procedures and Effects"; Lonnie A. Powers, "State Historic Preservation Tax Statutes: Three Case Studies"; Richard R. Almy, "Considerations in Creating Property Tax Relief for Historic Preservation"; R. Lisle Baker, "State Tax Innovations in the Preservation Field"; and Russell L. Brenneman and Gregory E. Andrews, "Preservation Easements and Their Tax Consequences."

Arts Council of Great Britain, *A Creative Future: The Way Forward for the Arts, Crafts and Media in England.* London, England: Her Majesty's Stationery Office, 1993.

Beaumont, Constance E. *State Tax Incentives for Historic Preservation.* Washington, D.C.: National Trust for Historic Preservation, Center for Preservation Policy Studies, May 1992.

Beaumont, Constance E. "What's New in Preservation." *Planning* 47, no. 10 (October 1991): 18–21.

Bouuaert, Ignace Claeys. *Tax Problems of Historic Houses in the States of the European Economic Community.* Report XII/728/79-EN. Ghent, Belgium: Commission of the European Communities, 1979.

Clotfelter, Charles T. *Federal Tax Policy and Charitable Giving.* Chicago: University of Chicago Press, 1985.

Colin, Thomas J. "What Next for a Troubled Industry?" *Historic Preservation* 40, no. 3 (May/June 1988): 32–35.

Council of Europe, *New Ways of Funding the Restoration of the Architectural Heritage.* Architectural Heritage Reports and Studies, no. 13, Report of the Messina Colloquy. Strasbourg, France: Council of Europe, 1988.

Dilley, Steven C., and James C. Young. *The Tax Reform Act of 1986: Taxation of Real Estate Transactions.* Englewood Cliffs, N.J.: Prentice Hall, 1987.

Ellis, T. C. W. "A Decade of Preservation—Quo Vadis, IRS?" Louisiana State Historic Preservation Office 19, no. 3 (April 1992):14.

Gleye, Paul H. "With Heritage So Fragile: A Critique of the Tax Credit Program for Historic Building Rehabilitation." *Journal of the American Planning Association* 54, no. 4 (Autumn 1988): 482–88.

International Symposium on World Heritage Towns, *Safeguarding Historic Urban Ensembles in a Time of Change—A Management Guide.* Quebec: Organization of World Heritage Towns, 1991.

Morley, Elaine. *The Impact of Historic Preservation Tax Incentives in Illinois and Missouri.* Edwardsville, Ill.: Center for Urban and Environmental Research and Services, Southern Illinois University at Edwardsville, October 1985.

Morris, Marya. *Innovative Tools for Historic Preservation.* Planning Advisory Service Report no. 438. Chicago: American Planning Association, 1992.

National Center for Preservation Law. "Treasury Department Questions Policy Value of Easement Donation Deductions." *Preservation Law Update* 1988-5 (January 29, 1988).

Nolan, John R., and James Peters. "Using Tax Credits to Save Historic Buildings: An Update." *Planning* 50, no. 1 (January 1984): 24–27.

Office of Policy Studies, National Trust for Historic Preservation. "Summary of Preservation Tax Incentives in the Economic Recovery Tax Act of 1981," Information Sheet no. 30, Washington, D.C.: National Trust for Historic Preservation, 1981.

Oldham, Sally G., and H. Ward Jandl. "Preservation Tax Incentives: New Investment Opportunities Under the Economic Recovery Tax Act." *Urban Land* 41, no. 3 (March 1982): 4–9.

Robinson, Susan, and John E. Petersen. *Fiscal Incentives for Historic Preservation.* Washington, D.C.: Government Finance Research Center of the Government Finance Officers Association, 1989.

Roddewig, Richard J. *Economic Incentives for Historic Preservation.* Washington, D.C.: National Trust for Historic Preservation, Center for Preservation Policy Studies, 1987.

Rypkema, Donovan, and Ian D. Spatz. "Rehab Takes a Fall." *Historic Preservation* 42, no. 5 (September/October 1990): 51–58.

Salamon, Lester M., ed. *Beyond Privatization: The Tools of Government Action.* Washington, D.C.: The Urban Institute Press, 1989. Chapters particularly relevant to this chapter include: Lester M. Salamon, "The Changing Tools of Government Action: An Overview"; Lester M. Salamon and Michael S. Lund, "The Tools Approach: Basic Analytics"; Donald Haider, "Grants as a Tool of Public Policy"; Michael S. Lund, "Between Welfare and the Market: Loan Guarantees as a Policy Tool"; and Paul R. McDaniel, "Tax Expenditures as Tools of Government Action."

Schuster, J. Mark. "Government Leverage of Private Support: Matching Grants and the Problem with 'New' Money," in *The Cost of Culture,* edited by Margaret Wyszomirski and Pat Clubb, 63–97. New York: American Council for the Arts, 1989.

Schuster, J. Mark. "Issues in Supporting the Arts Through Tax Incentives," *Journal of Arts Management and Law* 16, no. 2 (Winter 1987): 31–50.

Schuster, J. Mark. "Tax Incentives as Arts Policy in Western Europe," in *Nonprofit Enterprise in the Arts: Studies in Mission and Constraint,* edited by Paul DiMaggio, 108–24. New York: Oxford University Press, 1986.

Stipe, Robert E., series ed. Historic Preservation in Foreign Countries, later retitled Historic Preservation in Other Countries. Washington, D.C.: United States Committee of the International Council on Monuments and Sites. Volumes in the series include:

> Dale, Anthony. *Volume I: France, Great Britain, Ireland, The Netherlands, and Denmark.* 1982.
> Will, Margaret Thomas. *Volume II: Federal Republic of Germany, Switzerland, and Austria.* 1984.
> Gleye, Paul H., and Waldemar Szczerba. *Volume III: Poland.* 1989.
> Leimenstoll, Jo Ramsay. *Volume IV: Turkey.* 1989.

Stipe, Robert E., and Antoinette J. Lee. *The American Mosaic: Preserving a Nation's*

Heritage. Washington, D.C.: US/ICOMOS, 1987. Particularly relevant chapters include: Robert E. Stipe, "Historic Preservation: The Process and the Actors"; John M. Fowler, "The Federal Government as Standard Bearer"; Elizabeth A. Lyon, "The States: Preservation in the Middle"; and J. Myrick Howard, "Where the Action Is: Preservation and Local Governments."

Weber, Stephen R. "Historic Preservation Incentives of the 1976 Tax Reform Act: An Economic Analysis" National Bureau of Standards Technical Note 980. Washington, D.C.: U.S. Department of Commerce, National Bureau of Standards, February 1979.

5   John J. Costonis

The Redefinition of Property Rights as a Tool for Historic Preservation

Government can stimulate desired social policies by defining property rights in ways that facilitate behavior in the private sector that is consistent with these policies. One of the best known examples of this strategy is the legislation assigning private rights to resources which otherwise would be used inefficiently or for socially undesirable ends. In his influential essay, "The Tragedy of the Commons," Garrett Hardin decried the incentive for the private sector to overuse such resources, known to economists as "public goods," because access to them is enjoyed by all, rather than limited to holders of private rights in them.[1] Overfishing of public waters, overgrazing of pasturage commons, and the use of air, water, and other environmental media as pollution sinks are problems created by the unlimited access that Hardin deplores. Restricting access to these resources by assigning to private owners property rights in them and the attendant right to exclude offers greater promise that the resources will be prudently managed.

Conversely, public goods essential to the common welfare are underproduced by the private sector because their potential producers, lacking a private right to their sale or distribution, have no incentive to invest in resources that are open to free appropriation by all. Hence, government creates systems of copyright and patent protection, for example, enabling authors and inventors to assert exclusive, but licensable, rights in the products of their work.

Government can induce the efficient use of resources that are "private goods" as well by recognizing novel forms of property rights in them. Anglo-American common and statutory law have done so over the centuries by stacking up the various sticks that today compose the bundle of entitlements associated with land ownership. The same parcel of land, for example, may be owned by A, leased to B, mortgaged to C, and subject to privileged access by D, or, in the alternative, to restrictions on its use by the owner A in favor of D, the holder of an easement in A's property. The title deed, lease, mortgage, and easement are among the principal instruments that government can use to enable the private sector to engage in efficient and socially desirable transactions involving real property. By adding to or redefining the sticks in the ownership bundle, government enables private activities that would either not occur at all or, in the case of historic preservation, require the other more direct forms of government intervention addressed in this volume.

This chapter focuses on one technique—the transfer of development rights—to facilitate the preservation of historic resources. But this focus should not cause us to forget that any number of other techniques are available and, in fact, have been devised for this purpose as well.

One example is the interest in real property called the "facade easement." Let us suppose that the owner of an architecturally distinguished house would be willing to retain or even to restore the building's facade provided that doing so would not prove financially onerous. Let us suppose further that the property rights regime in force permits the owner to divide his ownership in such a way that control over the facade may be granted to government or to a historic preservation association while the owner retains ownership of the building and its land. Under such a regime the owner can convey the facade easement to government or to the association. He may do so either altruistically or to profit from whatever incentives government may offer for such conduct, including the grant of charitable deductions, tax credits, or reductions in the assessed value of his real property. Legal recognition of the facade easement as a valid property interest serves as the predicate for each of these options.

Although the transfer of development rights incorporates elements of the facade easement, it entails a more radical reformulating of property rights than this or other property rights modification devices. But it is at one with them in demonstrating the power of property rights reformulation as a historic preservation tool.

Development Rights Transfer

Setting the Stage

Historic preservation conflicts take various forms, but one recurs so frequently as to be paradigmatic. A good example is the clash ignited by the proposed addition of a fifty-two story tower atop New York City's Grand Central Terminal, a structure officially designated a landmark by the city's Landmarks Preservation Commission. Clearly, the addition of the tower would have substantially enhanced the profitability of the site, assuming a market for rentable office space located in one of the city's prime office/commercial zones. No less clear to the countless admirers of the Grand Central Terminal was that an International Style tower atop this Beaux Arts gem would have been an "aesthetic joke," in the words of the commission's decision objecting to the proposal.

And so the stage was set for conflict among the controversy's various stakeholders, private and public. Preservationists, abetted by the municipal landmarks body, strove to prevent alteration of the landmark, advancing both cultural and economic arguments. The preservation of architecturally distinctive buildings that have become icons in the public's favorable perception of the city, they insisted, enhances basic community and aesthetic values. Just as it would now be unthinkable for Paris to permit alteration of the Eiffel Tower or Rome the adaptation of its Coliseum, New York must not allow modifications that would degrade this secular cathedral. True, banning the tower would prevent the site owner from enhancing the site's profitability, but this loss was outweighed by the benefits of community stability and, perhaps, tourist revenues promised by retention of the landmark in its pristine state. Moreover, permitting degradation of the terminal, one of the city's most beloved buildings would undermine confidence in the city's preservation program as a tool to protect its less distinguished landmarks.

The site owner and others who would have benefited from the proposed tower obviously saw the matter differently. As a matter of basic fairness, the owners wondered why they, alone among contiguous site owners, should have been singled out to provide the claimed public benefits at severe costs to themselves. After all, the city's zoning code allowed their neighbors full use of the development rights that it allocated to their sites. Why should they not be allowed the same or, if not, at least be compensated for their loss, which, again, was directly linked to the public's presumed benefit? Nor was there anything objectionable about the tower from a zoning perspective. It was not, after all, a slaughterhouse or fat rendering plant. On the contrary, it would have provided office space at an optimal location as well as property tax revenue urgently needed to fund essential municipal services.

Lurking behind these policy and utilitarian considerations is a third concern that affords the focus of this chapter: property ownership, as traditionally conceived under Anglo-American law. Key among the rights associated with real property is the entitlement to develop it and, thereby, to realize income from it. So fundamental is this entitlement that its overly severe curtailment by government requires compensation for its owner under the United States Constitution. The Constitution's Fifth Amendment declares that "private property [shall not be] taken for public use" absent payment of "just compensation" to the property owner by the government. The measure of "just compensation"—the price that a willing buyer would pay to a willing seller in the private market—confirms the centrality of the entitlement to the very concept of property itself. Shorn of nearly all of its development rights, real estate is so fallow that, for Fifth Amendment purposes, it can no longer claim constitutional status as property at all.

The tension between conservation of historic resources and the property rights of their owners varies in relation to the severity of the specific prohibition and the degree to which owners are singled out as the target of the prohibition. Sometimes the prohibition actually enriches the owner. Illustrative is the value enhancement often enjoyed by individual parcels within a neighborhood designated by a municipality as a historic district. As owners of residences in New York City's Greenwich Village or Brooklyn Heights know, these designations frequently increase property values by creating or confirming the neighborhood's unique architectural or cultural significance and catalyzing an array of governmental and private investments designed to sustain this significance. Because the resulting development restrictions target all landowners within the district neighborhood, moreover, they do feel singled out for such restrictions as does the owner of the Grand Central Terminal. Occasionally, even the owner of an individual landmark building benefits from landmark designation. The possibility of a building's adaptive use—conversion from its original use to a different use attractive to the contemporary market—can lead to this outcome, as reflected in the conversion of San Francisco's Ghirardelli Square from a chocolate factory to a profitable tourist magnet featuring shops, restaurants, and theaters.

Such happy outcomes are the exception rather than the rule for individual landmark buildings located in downtown commercial districts. Typically, the discrepancy between the high value of the landmark site and the low income-producing capability of the landmark structure prompts the owner's proposal to demolish or otherwise modify the structure in order to use the site's development rights as fully as the municipality's zoning code permits.

Other chapters in this volume identify techniques other than the reformulation of property rights to secure the conservation of historic resources. For example, government could acquire and operate the landmark itself. It could also disseminate information about cultural heritage issues designed to induce landmark owners to secure their buildings' preservation voluntarily. It might choose the regulatory route, clearly the prevalent mode in the United States and Europe for historic resources in private ownership. (In Europe, it merits notice, the regulatory approach aligns more closely than in the United States with cultural attitudes that favor the notion that private property also serves social functions that warrant public restrictions upon its use.) Finally, government might offer the site owner any number of incentives, some of which blur with or build upon the property rights reformulation discussed in this chapter.

The Traditional Conception of Property Rights: An Invitation to Conflict

A closer examination of the Grand Central Terminal controversy discloses that one feature, in particular, of the traditional conception of property rights pre-ordained the conflict. I speak of the premise that the development rights of a site are inextricably wedded to that site and to that site alone. Unchallenged, this premise coupled with preservation regulations virtually guarantees conflict because the site's unused development rights cannot be used on the site, which, by definition, is the only location at which they can be used. Once the New York City Landmarks Commission prohibited the construction of the tower—the proxy for the terminal site's unused development rights—these rights effectively vanished.

The other techniques discussed in this volume accept this outcome as a given, and seek to work with or around it. The government ownership option, for example, simply destroys the landmark's unused development rights, shifting the financial loss of its destruction from the owner to government itself. The information option serves, it is hoped, to induce the owner to incur this loss voluntarily. The regulatory option directly imposes the loss on the owner. While acknowledging that landmark designation destroys the site's unused development rights, it denies that any quid pro quo is required as a matter of public policy. The incentive option is quasi-compensatory: typically government advances some benefit to the owner, such as reduced real estate taxes, which translates into dollars and mitigates, but seldom fully offsets, the owner's loss.

Transferable Development Rights:
Redefining Property Rights to Avoid Conflict

Reformulating property rights to permit the transfer of development rights departs radically from the other options by modifying the core concept of property in three fundamental respects. First, it permits development rights—traditionally conceived to be permanently rooted in their host site—to be severed from their host land or, as referred to here, from their "transferor site." Second, it allows their owner to transfer these newly severed development rights to the owner of a second, non-host site, the "transferee site." The latter may be either another site of the owner or the site of a third party, to whom the owner sells, devises, or otherwise transfers ownership of the transferor site's development rights. (As we shall see, there may also be an intermediate stage between severing and transferring, in which the development rights are banked, or held for eventual, rather than immediate, transfer.) Third, it enables these severed and transferred rights to be attached to the transferee site. Upon attachment, the development rights of the transferee site equal the sum of the rights transferred from the transferor site (all or only a portion of the latter site's development rights may be transferred) plus the development rights originally granted the transferee site by the zoning code.

A useful analogue in Anglo-American legal history to the reconceptualization of property rights discussed here is the reconceptualization of contract rights that allows the contractual rights granted to A by B to be assigned by A to C. Although contract law traditionalists opposed this shift for some three centuries—how, they questioned, could rights created in favor of A be shifted to C?—Anglo-American law finally came to endorse the shift. Among other far-reaching economic and social changes, the shift made possible the introduction of a credit economy, whereby C proves willing to extend credit to A on the strength of A's grant to C of A's contractual rights against B.

Such arrangements are commonplace today. Proprietors of automobile dealerships, for example, typically finance their inventories by assigning to their lenders the rights to future payments owed to the proprietors under the purchase and sale contracts executed by the proprietors with their customers.

Assignment of contract rights is an analogue to, rather than a mirror of, the transfer of a host site's development rights. For centuries, Anglo-American law has treated contract rights as *in personam* rights, that is, rights inhering in the person(s) of the contracting parties. Consistent with the concept that development rights inhere in the land, on the other hand, Anglo-American property law has characterized development rights as *in rem*. In consequence, it has posited that they are inextricably linked to their host sites, and thus cannot be severed from these sites or banked or transferred and attached to some other site.

Introducing a change in the conception of property rights may be likened to changing one's golf swing. It is impossible to modify one dimension of either without changing various other dimensions of the overall activity as well. The following sections address the subsidiary changes that the reformulating has required, first in related property law instruments and, second in the public or regulatory framework governing land use planning in the areas in which the development rights transfers occur.

Private Property Instruments

Transfers of development rights must be manifested in the deeds registries in which these transfers are publicly recorded as changes in the titles both of the transferor and of the transferee sites.[2] Under municipal law, however, administrators of these registries are not permitted to record these changes unless the mechanisms by which they are accomplished are themselves recognized property instruments.

In Anglo-American property law, property rights transfers may pertain to the entire interest in one's land, in which case they are referred to as transfers of the entire fee simple absolute title. Or these transfers may pertain to some lesser quantum of property rights in the land, in which case they are deemed less-than-fee title interests. Development rights transfers come under the latter category because the transferor retains the underlying fee simple absolute title to the transferor site, but has reduced its title in that site by the quantum of the site's development rights that it has transferred in the pertinent transaction. Accordingly, the deeds registry official will seek assurance that some legally recognized less-than-fee instrument has been employed that simultaneously effects both a reduction of the transferor site owner's property rights and a corresponding increase of the transferee site owner's property rights.

Anglo-American property law has recognized three less-than-fee instruments: easements, real covenants, and equitable servitudes. However, because none of these instruments, as traditionally conceived, is suitable to the task, a new less-than-fee instrument, the preservation restriction, has been created. The manner in which the preservation restriction has come to be defined and legally validated itself illustrates the process by which government continually modifies or adds to the bundle of sticks associated with real property ownership.

Preservation restrictions are most often likened to negative easements, which obligate a landowner to refrain from performing acts on his land that would otherwise be permitted as an incident of fee ownership. Landmark owners, such as the proprietors of the Grand Central Terminal, may not build in the airspace over their buildings, for example, nor may they demolish or significantly alter these buildings. But Anglo-American law has normally limited negative easements to a narrow set of purposes: easements for light and air, for support of a building laterally or subjacently, and for the flow of an artificial stream. Although resembling easements for light and air in its restriction against construction above the landmark, a preservation restriction goes beyond the former in its controls over alteration and demolition. In addition, enforcement has traditionally been denied for negative easements that are not appurtenant to the parcel benefited by the restriction, in this case the transferee site, the development rights of which are increased by the transfer. The appurtenancy requirement would not be satisfied when transferable development rights are banked, rather than immediately transferred, because in such cases and for the duration of the banking period, there is no transferee site to which these rights can be deemed appurtenant. Nor would it be satisfied if one of the parties authorized to enforce the preservation restriction against the landmark site were not itself the owner of land benefited by the restriction, as, for example, would be likely if this party were the National Trust for Historic Preservation or the New York City Landmarks Conservancy.

Preservation easements cannot be brought within the rubric of real covenants. Anglo-American courts generally insist that these interests, too, must be appurtenant to a benefited parcel. An additional requirement—privity of estate between the original parties to the transfer—dictates that the benefited (transferee) and burdened (transferor) parcels must initially have been in common ownership and that the burden must have been imposed on the latter parcel at the time the ownership was divided. Otherwise, the burden of the real covenant, that is, the reduction in the landmark parcel's development rights, will not bind subsequent owners of the parcel, a result that, upon conveyance of the parcel to a subsequent owner, would defeat the purpose of the transaction by reinstating the transferor site's previously transferred development rights. Finally, many courts refuse to enforce affirmative duties in real covenants, a qualification that could prove troublesome if, as usually is the case, obligations to maintain the landmark property are featured in the preservation restriction.

Of the three traditional less-than-fee instruments, equitable servitudes come closest to accomplishing the goals of the preservation restriction. Equitable servitudes are not restricted to the limited purposes of negative easements, but may be employed for any legitimate social goal. No privity of estate other than that provided by the agreement between the transferor and transferee site owners is required in order for the agreement to be enforceable against subsequent owners of the landmark (transferor) site. Equitable servitudes are enforceable by injunction and may include affirmative as well as negative obligations. They must reflect the intent to bind subsequent owners, who must have notice of the agreement creating them, requirements easily satisfied by careful drafting and proper recording of the agreement in the deeds registry, respectively. Unfortunately, non-appurtenant servitudes are not enforceable against subsequent owners of the landmark site in many jurisdictions, and they may not be assignable either.

The technicalities attending each of the three traditional less-than-fee interests undermine their usefulness as historic preservation tools. Although courts in some jurisdictions may be willing to assimilate a preservation restriction to one or another of these traditional instruments, the preferable solution is the passage of legislation that recognizes preservation restrictions as a novel but enforceable less-than-fee interest. This route has been pursued by a number of American state legislatures. Directly addressing the difficulties outlined in this section, they have adopted statutes providing that preservation restrictions shall not be unenforceable because of lack of privity of estate or of ownership of benefited land. They also approve the assignability of preservation restrictions, even if the latter are not appurtenant to benefited land. By clarifying an archaic area of property law, these statutes enable government and the private sector to further historic preservation objectives confident that traditional formulations of property rights will not frustrate these objectives.

Although the features that may be included in preservation restrictions vary in individual cases, certain elements tend to recur in these instruments. In addition to specifying the quantum of the development rights subtracted from the landmark site and added to transferee site, typical preservation restrictions detail the legal authority on which they are premised, restrictions on use, maintenance obligations, duration, and remedies for their violation. Use restrictions are as varied as the character and setting of particular landmark structures. Incorporating features of the facade easement, they typically include prohibitions against alteration or demolition of the landmark structure, but go beyond that instrument by imposing additional limitations relating to such matters as signs, subdivision of the landmark parcel, addition of buildings to the site, and specified uses of the landmark. Other provisions may detail procedures for obtaining approval for permitted modifications and for making periodic inspections of the premises to ensure that the restrictions are being honored. Moreover, as noted earlier, preservation restrictions often create enforcement rights not only in the holder of the transferee parcel but in public agencies and in historic preservation associations as well.

Maintenance obligations are variously stated. Landmark owners may agree simply to keep their properties in good repair or they may undertake to comply with standards incorporated into the preservation restriction. Duration of the restriction may be perpetual or limited to a number of years. The instruments reflect the intent of the parties that the benefits and burdens of the restriction will extend to their successors in interest. Remedies clauses specify who may sue for breach of the restriction and the judicial relief that may be obtained. Miscellaneous provisions may comprehend anything from rights of first refusal to express disclaimers of rights of public access to the landmark. Surveys, line drawings, and photographs increasingly appear as appendixes to preservation restrictions, permitting precise identification of prized interior or exterior features such as paneling, fireplaces, and facades.

Public Planning Considerations: The Role of Government

Government performs two essential functions in breathing life into development rights transfer programs. The first, discussed above, is redefining property rights to ensure that development rights are severable, bankable, transferable, and attachable to a non-host site. It may be, as John Locke and the framers of the United States Constitution believed, that property rights are natural rights and hence do not owe their existence to government. It may also be, as Jeremy Bentham insisted, that government's supreme function is the protection of private expectations in these rights. Accepting both propositions, it remains true that government is the sole institution that authoritatively defines and interprets these rights. Hence, the necessity of looking to legislatures and, subsidiarily, to courts to validate not only the reconceptualization of property rights discussed above but also the legal instruments, such as the preservation restriction, that give practical meaning to this reconceptualization.

Government is likewise necessary to create a framework in which development rights transfer programs are both attractive to their intended participants and compatible with a municipality's land use and urban design values. An active market in transferable development rights requires willing buyers and sellers, an appropriate balance between transferor and transferee sites, conditions securing the commercial value of the rights being transferred, and a network of clear, practical, and consistently administered rules.

But government faces difficult trade-offs in establishing such markets. As much as it may wish to facilitate private sector transfers, it cannot permit property owners to deal rights helter-skelter throughout the city, indifferent to the impact of the resulting augmented development on urban design, public service capacities, or neighborhood sentiment. Conventional zoning controls tend to avoid this by taking the individual site or zoning lot as the unit of development control. Following the traditional conception of property rights discussed above, these controls assume that the development rights they allocate for any given site either will be used solely on that site, or will not be used at all. In consequence, they avoid the planning and urban design complications that attend development rights transfers.

Transfer regimes, in contrast, take entire development rights transfer districts as their unit of control, allocating two layers of development rights to each transferee zoning lot within these districts. One layer is the development rights for these lots permitted by the zoning category for the area in which they are located; the second is the quantum of development rights that may be transferred to these lots from landmark sites. This approach—called "density zoning"—posits that appropriate planning considerations will be respected so long as the aggregate density or bulk of the entire transfer district is not increased by the creation of the transfer regime.

Additional planning controls are necessary, nonetheless, to avoid the undue concentration of development rights on any single transferee site within the district. Take the case of the Grand Central Terminal. A building the size of the Empire State Building could have been comfortably contained within the zoning envelope of the terminal's unused development rights. A transfer of this magnitude to only one or a few receiving sites would have created severe urban design and service overloads. While few transfer situations will present such dire risks of abuse, their possibility points up the need for a residual planning/regulatory role for government.

The Chicago Plan: A Hypothetical Development Rights Transfer Program

A transfer program sensitive to the needs both of the market and of public planning values appears in the "Chicago Plan," which I have proposed as a regime for preserving the city of Chicago's downtown commercial landmark buildings.[3] The plan proceeds from four characteristics that are commonplace among America's urban landmarks: their diminutive size; the disproportion between the high value of their sites and the meager revenue-generating capacity of the landmark structure upon them; the concentration of these buildings in a fairly compact central business district; and the availability of ample public facilities and services in these areas, enabling them to sustain individual buildings of substantial bulk and height.

The plan calls upon the municipality to designate one or more development rights transfer districts, which will likely (but not necessarily) coincide with the areas where the downtown landmarks are located. Upon designation of a landmark or at any time thereafter, its owner may transfer its excess development rights to other sites within the transfer district and receive a reduction in the site's real estate taxes proportional to the site's lessened development potential. Transfers of rights deriving from a single landmark site may be made to one or more transferee sites, but increases in bulk on the latter would be limited to defined ceilings as well as to other planning controls designed to preclude unduly large buildings on these sites. Concomitant with these transfers, preservation restrictions, containing the elements listed earlier, must be recorded against the paired sites.

One variant of the Chicago Plan would provide a forceful backup role for the municipality in cases in which landmark owners decline to participate in the transfer program. In such cases, the city may use its eminent domain powers to acquire a preservation restriction and the landmark's associated unused development rights. Acquisition costs would be funded through a municipal development rights bank. The bank would be a depository of such condemned rights as well as those donated by owners of other landmarks or linked to governmentally owned landmarks. The city would meet program costs by selling these pooled rights from time to time, subject to the same planning controls that apply to private owners.

The Chicago Plan would redistribute preservation costs with the goal of making preservation practicable for the landmark owner and the city alike. Transfer cash payments and real estate tax relief would compensate the owner for his losses. The elimination from the owner's title of the now transferred development rights would decrease the site's value and concomitant speculative interest in it. And the landmarks would remain vital commercial structures, not museums.

Variants of the Chicago Plan have been employed in the United States in one form or another over the last thirty years, not only to preserve landmark buildings but also to protect various other types of low density resources, such as wetlands and open space lands, that promise greater profitability if developed at greater intensity.[4] In celebrating the qualified success of these programs, one hesitates to claim too much for them. They have been and are likely to remain less important and less frequently used than traditional regulatory programs.

The experience of the last three decades suggests a number of reasons for this. To begin with, most preservation and related land use limitations on private property stop well short of the point at which they become suspect as unconstitutional "takings" of property under the Fifth Amendment to the United States Constitution. Second, administrators and legislators prefer traditional command and control regulatory techniques to those that, like development rights transfer, give greater sway to the private market. They often eschew the latter techniques altogether or advance lukewarm support for their use. Finally, tension between the unfettered use of development rights desired by the marketplace and the residual regulatory controls needed to preclude urban design damage from such use has often resulted in programs that end by pleasing neither the market nor the regulators, as the Grand Central Terminal case illustrates. New York City did seek to offset the terminal owner's hardship by authorizing it to transfer the site's unused development rights. Yet ten years after this authorization, the owner felt it necessary to go to court to force the city to make good on its action. The city had so hamstrung the transfer authorization with planning controls that it largely undermined the commercial utility of the development rights it authorized the site owner to transfer.

In addition to exemplifying the property rights strategy, the Chicago Plan demonstrates how the various tools addressed in this volume may be combined in a single historic preservation regime. The government ownership tool, for example, appears in the municipality's power to acquire development rights through eminent domain, and to bank them for future sale to developers of transferee sites. The regulation tool underlies the planning controls the municipality imposes to prevent abusive transfers from damaging its underlying land use and zoning values. The municipality uses the information tool in bringing to the attention of landmark owners, developers, and the general public the benefits associated with the transferable development rights option. And it uses the incentive tool by affording landmark owners a subsidiary array of real estate and related tax benefits.

Development Rights Transfer in a New Guise:
Transferable Pollution Emission Credits

Reconceptualizing property rights to aid historic preservation has been joined
recently by a similar effort to reduce the emission of air pollutants, which are
caused by the use of development rights. Instead of transferable development
rights, however, this initiative refers to transferable (or marketable) emission
credits. The pollution programs also envisage the creation of transferor and
transferee lots (or, more accurately, industrial facility sites); the allocation to
each of pollution credits (measurable in tons per year of the emitted pollutant);
the shift to the transferee site of pollution credits initially granted by the pollution control authority to the transferor site; and a cap on the total atmospheric
pollution load prescribed for the area in question.

The purposes of these programs are usually twofold. The first is to permit
economic development to occur in areas whose ambient air is presently in violation of the air quality standards for the pertinent pollutants. The second is
to introduce economic efficiency into the picture by rewarding the manufac-
turers who can reduce their emissions most cheaply, thereby creating an incentive for reduced pollution overall. This reward takes the form of payments
made to the more efficient pollution reducers by the less efficient pollution reducers, who require the transferred emission credits in order to comply with
the pollution limitations established in their operating permits. A sale takes
place because the cost to the purchaser of emission credits (the transferee in
the scheme) of reducing its emissions exceeds the cost incurred by the seller
(the transferor) for similar reductions. The purchaser pays less, therefore, to
acquire the credits from the seller than to make the reductions itself. The
seller, of course, retains for itself as many emission credits as it requires for
its own industrial activities.

The so-called "non-attainment" provisions of the Clean Air Act illustrate
how these schemes are intended to work.[5] They address the problem of permitting new economic development in areas of the country that are in violation
(in "non-attainment") for one or more pollutants for which national ambient
air quality standards have been fixed. The transfer program seeks to resolve
the dilemma of permitting desired additional economic development in the
non-attainment area, on the one hand, while continuing the state's effort to reduce the area's total atmospheric pollution load to levels that comply with national standards, on the other.

An example of an emissions credit transfer may prove useful. Let us assume that Jones wishes to locate a cement plant that will emit 1,000 tons per
year (TPY) of the air pollutant particulate matter (PM) in an area that is already in "non-attainment" for PM. Obviously, if Jones builds the plant without

offsetting reductions, the area will now suffer an additional annual excess of 1,000 TPY of PM. But suppose there are other industrial plants, also emitting PM, whose owners have become so efficient in reducing the emission of PM per unit process that they now collectively control 2,000 unused PM emission credits. Suppose further that the applicable requirements obligate the builder of the new plant to offset the emissions of the pertinent pollutant by a greater than one-to-one ratio, let us say, by a one-to two ratio. Since Jones would be the purchaser of the needed 2,000 TPY of PM allocation, his industrial site would be the transferee site while the sites of the sellers of the PM emission credits would be the transferor sites. Just as a zoning code makes individual lot and aggregate transfer district development rights allocations, so too would the "state implementation plan," required of all states by the Clean Air Act, allocate emission credits to individual sources within the non-attainment area as well as fix the aggregate amount of pollution by specific pollutant for the area as a whole. Jones would pay the sellers of the PM credits an amount that is greater than their costs of reduction but less than the costs he would have incurred had he sought to make these reductions himself. Jones would apply 1,000 TPY of PM to his site's emission credit allocation, thereby meeting the needs of the site. The remaining 1,000 TPY of PM would be permanently retired, thereby enabling the state to make further progress toward bringing its ambient air into compliance with the PM standards by the statutory deadline.

A Concluding Note: Is Development Rights Transfer a Property Rights Strategy, an Incentive Strategy, or a Hybrid of Both?

It is generally assumed throughout this volume that the five historic preservation tools may be used in combination with one another, and that each is distinguishable from the other. The first proposition is illustrated by the earlier discussion of the concurrent use of the five tools within the framework of the Chicago Plan. But the second proposition may be more difficult to sustain, at least in the case of development rights transfer. Is the technique best characterized as a property rights tool, an incentive tool, or some hybrid of the two?

Characterizing development rights transfer as a property rights tool derives from constitutional and real estate law considerations, and implies that the associated zoning adjustments are secondary to both. In the United States, the constitutional underpinnings of the technique derive from the concern that government's curtailment of a landowner's development rights may obligate government to compensate him under the Fifth Amendment's takings clause. Private real estate law comes into the picture as a basis for describing the impact that a development rights transfer will have on the title of the transferor and transferee lots through the medium of the preservation restriction. This impact will occur *whether or not* the authorization to transfer development rights serves to avoid a Fifth Amendment takings claim.

The contrary assertion that development rights transfer is either an incentive or a hybrid incentive/property rights technique merits serious consideration. Central to the argument is its premise that an incentive is a boon that government offers as a matter of largesse, rather than of constitutional necessity. On this view, a strategy cannot properly be labeled a property *rights* tool unless the entitlement being offered by government—here the authorization to transfer development rights—is, in fact, something to which the property owner enjoys a legal entitlement which government is compelled to honor under the Fifth Amendment's property clause.

The incentive-tool argument has two principal sources. The first is the fact that development rights transfer derives from a planning technique commonly labeled the "zoning bonus." Since zoning bonus regimes clearly fall under the incentive tool category, it is argued, their progeny, development rights transfers regimes, must as well.

The second is that the so-called property rights transferred under the latter are not property *rights* at all in most cases, but merely expectancies that government may choose to honor or disregard as it sees fit. If these so-called rights are expectancies only, the reasoning runs, government could, for constitutional purposes, legitimately achieve its historic preservation ends through noncompensatory regulation. Government offers de facto compensation through the development rights transfer scheme not because it is legally compelled to do so, but for other reasons (avoiding the administrative burdens associated with the other tools, for instance, or affording greater equity to landmark owners than that required by constitutional law). So viewed, the option granted landmark owners to transfer their unused expectancies is as much an incentive as the tax credits or other benefits that government chooses to, but need not, make available to them.

There is a great deal to be said for both characterizations. As to the first, it is true that, from a planning perspective, a forerunner of the development rights transfer technique is the zoning bonus, and zoning bonuses do exemplify the incentive tool as the term "incentive" has been defined. Zoning bonuses are simply additional increments of development rights that the municipality grants to developers who agree to include in their projects one or more amenities, such as plazas, arcades, or subway concourses that the city desires but is unwilling to finance itself. In theory, the value to the developer of the quantum of development rights associated with the bonus somewhat exceeds the cost that the developer incurs in providing the amenity.

So long as government does not mandate provision of the amenity, the option of the additional development rights it makes available to the developer reflects an incentive, not a property rights strategy. Because government is under no compulsion to offer the zoning bonus in the first place, a developer could not force its grant through litigation premised on the Fifth Amendment property clause. (The case might be entirely different, if government *compelled* the developer to provide the amenity without providing a compensatory offset for the additional costs he or she incurs in doing so.) Moreover, zoning bonuses are generally calculated to accord the developer a financial return that is somewhat greater than his cost of providing the amenity.

Both zoning bonuses and development rights transfers use additional development rights as a device to induce developers to provide urban design features such as landmarks or plaza-fronted buildings that might not otherwise be provided. From a property rights perspective, however, these rights originate from different sources. The development rights associated with zoning bonuses are created *ex nihilo* by the municipality. One may, if one wishes, regard them as additional increments to the title the developer holds in his parcel, although the matter is seldom viewed this way in actual planning or zoning practice. Typically, the grant of the additional development rights is noted in the zoning permission, rather than recorded against the developer's title in the public deeds registry.

But there are significant differences between the two as well. In the case of development rights transfer, the additional rights derive, quite literally, from the landmark site and, once transferred to the developer's site, they reduce *pro tanto* the development rights formerly attributable to the landmark owner's site. A development rights transfer, therefore, is a private real estate transaction, recorded in a deeds registry, involving the exchange of a less-than-fee interest in real property between two private property owners, albeit an exchange enabled and blessed by the municipality. More important for our purposes, government grants the landmark owner the development rights option for something he previously had, but as a result of the designation of his landmark he has now lost. Theoretically, he is no better off after the transfer than he was before because the quantum of rights lost at the landmark site is equaled by the quantum gained at the transferee site. The developer-recipient of a zoning bonus, in contrast, is being granted rights additional to those he previously had as an inducement for an amenity that the government probably could not have compelled him to provide.

The second consideration is less easily dismissed. The constitutional jurisprudence of the United States Supreme Court confirms that in most, but by no means all, cases, municipalities may substantially reduce the development rights of landmark sites without incurring a Fifth Amendment obligation to compensate landmark owners for the loss of these rights. Despite a spate of recent land use decisions that have found public regulations to be "takings" under the Fifth Amendment,[6] the court has left untouched its basic view that regulations leaving the owner with some residual economic value in his or her property are immune from challenge despite the losses entailed in the reduction of the parcel's development rights by virtue of landmark designation. Indeed, this was the precise holding the court announced when it rejected the takings claim advanced by owners of the Grand Central Terminal site.[7] Although it commented favorably on the development rights transfer option available to the owners, its opinion leaves little doubt that New York City's ban on the proposed tower over the terminal would have been sustained even in the absence of this option.

In light of the court's reasoning, the quantum of development rights authorized for transfer but exceeding those necessary to avoid a takings determination would indeed be a boon for the landmark owner, rather than a constitutional equivalent for his foregone property rights. Insofar as the development rights transfer technique enables him to enjoy these "additional" rights, it may properly be regarded as an incentive or hybrid incentive/property rights tool, as the term "incentive" is defined above. From a strict constitutional perspective, the landmark owner can be said to be better off after the transfer than before because, except for a radical reduction of his development rights, he never had a constitutional claim to the full quantum of the development rights allocated to his parcel by the zoning code. In such cases, the landmarks law trumps the zoning law, though the result may seem unfair to many.

This reasoning supports the conclusion that development rights transfer is not a pure property rights tool—though only if the term "property" means exactly what it does in the Fifth Amendment. But there is no need to demand this identity of usage in the two contexts. The fact is that the private market treats as property all kinds of expectancies that might well lack constitutional status as "property" were they to be subject to the type of draconian public regulation exemplified in the Grand Central Terminal controversy. The market buys, sells, and exchanges these expectancies in countless daily transactions. They are the subject of deeds, leases, and mortgages; they are recorded in governmental deeds registries; and they bear all the accouterments that the marketplace associates with property. To disqualify them as property for the purposes of the five-tool taxonomy in this volume is to confuse one form of discourse with another.

Those who do so, I am convinced, are troubled by a very different issue, which focuses not on the term "property," but on the term "rights." They fear that to accord the status of property rights to development rights would subject municipalities to the constitutional imperative of compensating landmark owners whenever it diminishes the so-called development rights of their sites, no matter how minimally. Indeed, it is for this reason that in the pollution field, pollution entitlements are called "emission credits" rather than "emission rights," since the claim that industry has a right to pollute is problematic at best.

The solution to this problem is not, however, to deny that development rights transfer is a property rights tool, as that phrase is used in this volume. Far more preferable when discussing the Fifth Amendment compensation question would be to parallel the practice in the pollution field and use the more neutral phrase "development credits," which neither affirms nor denies that the credits in question are rights for purposes of this discourse. Whether or not the credits are also rights would then turn on the circumstances of the particular situation. In the great majority of instances, the credits would not merit constitutional status as rights given the Supreme Court takings jurisprudence discussed earlier. But neither does that jurisprudence deny the possibility that the credits might merit that status in some cases. My suggestion would distinguish what essentially is a semantic problem from the fundamentally different constitutional takings problem that historic preservation regulation occasionally poses.

Notes

1. Garrett Hardin, "The Tragedy of the Commons," *Science* 162, no. 3859 (13 December 1968): 1243–48.
2. A more detailed discussion of the real property instruments, including the preservation restriction, addressed in this section, as well as citations to pertinent statutory and case law, may be found in John J. Costonis, "The Chicago Plan: Incentive Zoning and the Preservation of Urban Landmarks," *Harvard Law Review* 85 (January 1972): 611–20.
3. See John J. Costonis, *Space Adrift: Landmark Preservation and the Marketplace* (Urbana, Illinois: University of Illinois Press, 1974).
4. For a recent summary of the use of transferable development rights in various programs throughout the United States, see Edward H. Ziegler, "The Transfer of Development Rights (Part I)," *Zoning and Planning Law Report* 18, no. 8 (September 1995): 61–65 and "The Transfer of Development Rights (Part I)," *Zoning and Planning Law Report* 18, no. 9 (October 1995): 69–74.
5. 42 U.S.C. 7501-7515 (1995).
6. See, for example, *Lucas v. South Carolina Coastal Council*, 112 S. Ct. 2886 (1992); and *Nollan v. California Coastal Commission*, 483 U.S. 825 (1987).
7. *Penn Central Transportation Co. v. City of New York*, 438 U.S. 104 (1978).

References

Costonis, John J. "The Chicago Plan: Incentive Zoning and the Preservation of Urban Landmarks." *Harvard Law Review* 85 (January 1972): 574–634.

Costonis, John J. *Space Adrift: Landmark Preservation and the Marketplace.* Urbana, Ill.: University of Illinois Press, 1974.

Doheny, David A., ed. *Focus on Property Rights.* Special issue of *Historic Preservation Forum* 7, no. 4 (July/August 1993).

Hardin, Garrett. "The Tragedy of the Commons." *Science* 162, no. 3859 (13 December 1968): 1243–48.

Ziegler, Edward H. "The Transfer of Development Rights (Part I)." *Zoning and Planning Law Report* 18, no. 8 (September 1995): 61–65.

Ziegler, Edward H. "The Transfer of Development Rights (Part II)." *Zoning and Planning Law Report* 18, no. 9 (October 1995): 69–74.

Information as a Tool
of Preservation Action

When the General Conference of the United Nations Educational, Scientific, and Cultural Organization (UNESCO) adopted its "Recommendation Concerning the Safeguarding and Contemporary Role of Historic Areas" in 1976, it explicitly noted, apparently for the first time, the need to encourage "research, education, and information" as a way of providing a positive climate for conservation.[1] But while newly recognized by UNESCO, information-based strategies had long figured in the package of tools that the state uses to pursue its heritage preservation policies. These strategies are often underemphasized and underappreciated as components of preservation programs, frequently fading into the background when other, flashier interventions are brought into play. Yet when assembled together and understood as a separate category of government intervention, as they are in this chapter, the rich experience that the state has had using of information in preservation bears witness to the importance of this tool.

It is much too easy to underestimate the value of information as a tool in heritage preservation. Even though we naturally think that strong actions, such as ownership or regulation, are more likely to work than weak actions, such as collecting and providing information, that does not turn out to be the case at all. I hope to demonstrate that there are many situations in which information may be an effective tool for implementing preservation policy and, moreover, that there may well be situations in which information is the only possible tool to use.

At the most basic level, of course, information is necessary to explain how the state is using its other tools to further preservation. Incentives, regulations, and the redefinition of property rights will only work as tools in preservation insofar as they are communicated to and understood by the actors at whom they are targeted. Even with ownership and operation programs, the state is well advised to make its actions clear by providing information about its goals. In this sense, information is an oil that helps for the other tools do their jobs more smoothly. But information as a preservation tool does far more than this.

Nevertheless, information as a form of action has received little analysis in the literature on preservation policy. The explicit recognition of information as a separate tool—albeit one that is most often used in concert with other tools—leads to a wide variety of insights concerning the possibilities for implementing preservation policy.[2] In this chapter I turn an analytic spotlight on the tool of information, highlighting issues that are revealed when one frames a fifth possibility for state action in this way.

The Fundamental Message(s) of Information

Using information, like using any of the primary tools in any field of public policy, carries with it an implied message. In its least directive form, this message might be, "It is possible to do X." In this case the intent would be simply informing others of possibilities that exist. A slightly more directive form of this message might be, "It would be useful for you to know Y in order to do X." Here, of course, the implication is that with the necessary information at their disposal, citizens or citizen groups (or even other government agencies) are more likely to pursue the goals of historic preservation and to pursue them in ways that agree with accepted public policy. Seen in this way, information is a close cousin to incentives.

An even stronger form of the implicit message—one that is also used in the field of preservation—is, simply, "You should do X." When reduced to these few words, this message sounds overly preachy, particularly to ears that have been trained in the American context in which private initiative is generally accorded a higher priority than public initiative. But this may well be how an information-based message is perceived, even if it was not exactly intended in this way. Of course, this stronger message that might be delivered by information is not far from the message offered by regulation—"You must do X." Once again, we see the potential for the (intentional or unintentional) blurring of boundaries between the various tools.

These basic messages also highlight the fact that, like incentives, information is a tool available not only to the state. Information strategies are a mainstay of the many quasi-governmental and nonprofit organizations active in the preservation arena, and much of what I will say concerning the state's use of information can also be said about these nongovernmental actors as well.

Reasons for Using Information as a Tool

Why might one choose to use information as a separate tool of intervention? It seems to me that there are at least three primary reasons for using an information strategy. The first is to inform the public of the various laws and tools that exist to promote preservation and to explain their implications and how to take full advantage of them. We expect no less from our governments; if state actions are to have an effect, they need to be explained. But it is difficult to think of information of this sort as a separate policy instrument; though important, this use of information does not fully exploit the information tool as a way of promoting preservation.

The second reason for the use of information is to make the public more aware of the existence and importance of historic properties and to explain the desirability of preserving them. In a sense, this can be seen as part of the state's responsibility to see that its citizenry is educated and informed. That people be well informed is reason enough for the provision of information as a part of public policy.

An increasingly important motivation for using information comes from the state's realization that public resources are limited and from its resulting desire to involve as many other actors as possible in the preservation of heritage resources. Information is thus a way to spur others to action and to guide them in their actions. The 1985 Convention for the Protection of the Architectural Heritage of Europe puts this point rather nicely when it introduces its Article 14 on the role of citizen participation and nonprofit, nongovernmental associations in preservation. It calls for the establishment of processes to foster the supply of information, consultation, and cooperation, "[w]ith a view to widening the impact of public authority measures."[3] The use of information coincides nicely with the trend toward less interventionist government and the related trend toward furthering the influence of any public action. Just as with incentives, the certainty that a particular property will be preserved either through state ownership and operation or through regulation is traded for the possibility that the overall level of preservation activity will rise when more actors become involved, encouraged by less severe government actions. Another way to say this is that through information the state is contributing to, if not creating, the conditions within which others will act.

The Roles That Information Plays

Many forms of information can be brought to bear in preservation and preservation policy, and there are many ways to map those different forms of information in order to understand and analyze them. Christopher Hood, for example, focuses on the direction of information flow—in his terms, "detectors" and "effectors"—as one way of understanding the options available in an information strategy.[4] In this section I choose to focus on the various roles that information plays in heritage preservation. By focusing on these roles, one highlights both the various moments in the preservation process at which information can and has been used as a point of leverage and one of the dimensions along which the use of information has its most variation.

Identification and Documentation

The Department of National Heritage's booklet, *What Listing Means: A Guide for Owners and Occupiers*, which describes the formal process for listing historic building in the United Kingdom, contains what at first glance seems to be a rather unremarkable sentence: "The purpose of the list is simply to put a mark against certain buildings to ensure that their special interest is taken fully into account in decisions affecting their future."[5] A simple idea, really—to identify publicly certain properties as having particular historic merit so that they will be more widely recognized as having that merit, an important first step in implementing a public policy with respect to those properties.

When one thinks of lists of heritage properties, one normally considers the other implications of being listed rather than focusing on the list as an important intervention in and of itself. Perhaps the act of listing makes a property's owner eligible for grants or other types of financial incentives, or triggers a higher level of regulation that controls what the owner can do with the property. While these other forms of intervention have been considered elsewhere—including elsewhere in this volume—very little thought has been given to the importance of the act of listing itself, an act that entails the provision of information as a distinct tool of government intervention.

Listing is, perhaps, the most familiar form of one role that information plays in heritage preservation programs, the role of documentation. Such information becomes available once a valued heritage resource becomes identified, typically through a formal listing procedure designed to identify and "put a mark against these buildings" in order to signal that they have a recognized importance.

Heritage registers, of course, include more than just buildings. They also include sites, natural landscapes, manmade objects in the physical environment and other highly symbolic elements in the environment. Poland, for example, has conducted an exhaustive search in order to list and protect thousand-year-old oak trees because of their importance in Polish legend and because their location might help establish the historical extent of Polish territory.[6]

Thus the first two steps in an information strategy are a survey of historic resources and a listing of those that have particular merit.[7] The criteria for listing vary somewhat from country to country, but what varies more are the implications of listing, which shift according to the different legislative regimes of a particular place. Taking just one example to establish the context, according to the Georgia Department of Natural Resources, as described in its brochure on the listing of heritage properties, listing accomplishes six tasks:[8]

- it identifies historically significant resources according to the National Register Criteria for Evaluation;
- it encourages their preservation by documenting their significance and by lending support to local preservation activities;
- it enables agencies at all levels of government to consider historic properties in the early stages of planning projects;
- it provides for review of federally supported projects that may affect the listed properties;
- it makes owners of listed properties eligible to apply for federal grants for preservation activities; and
- it encourages the rehabilitation of certain listed properties through tax incentives and discourages their demolition through tax disincentives.[9]

For my purposes, what is important to notice about this list is that four of the six items focus on listing as an information tool. Only two refer to another tool of government action, both examples of incentives. Yet in much of the discussion of lists as an element in preservation policy, their effectiveness has been measured only by the extent to which they trigger incentives or regulations, making it difficult to separate the information role of lists from their other policy roles.

In those circumstances where the list is viewed primarily as a trigger for other government actions, whether or not owners can object to, dispute, or refuse listing becomes an important policy concern because of the added obligations that come with listing.[10] In some places, however, the regulatory or incentive-providing role of the list is separated from its information role. In the German *Länder* of Bavaria, Saarland, and Lower Saxony, for example, lists of historic properties do not have a regulatory effect since regulations can be applied whether or not a building is listed. The addition of a building to the list "is considered a declaratory—or informational—action, and property owners do not have the right to dispute a listing."[11] Examples such as this one are useful in throwing into higher relief than normal the role of the list as an information instrument.

Listing is typically accompanied by documentation. At its simplest level, this documentation includes information on the existence, location, and configuration of the historic resource. Measured drawings might be prepared, careful photographs taken, and written data compiled, as in the Historic American

Buildings Survey or the Historic American Engineering Record, to assure that the most accurate information possible might always be available, even if the resource is damaged or destroyed. Documentation might also contain information on how researchers, visitors, and other interested individuals might gain access to the resource. And because projects in the United States that have benefited from various federal tax incentives are probably subject to the Freedom of Information Act, the documentation might also provide information on the financial aspects of historic preservation.[12]

Some places have given careful thought to how other government actions might encourage better documentation. In Switzerland, for example, property owners who receive federal funds for preservation of their property must deposit complete documentation (including before-and-after restoration plans and photographs) in the Federal Archives for the Care of Monuments, thus building a more generally available body of knowledge on these properties. This archives also houses the records of the Technical Work Service, a program created during the Depression that put unemployed architects to work documenting a variety of historic buildings.[13]

Though our emphasis in this volume has been on the built heritage, it is worth noting that the process of listing is also used for the movable heritage. Here the concern is more illegal export and import, and various international agreements have led to the registration of collections and of transactions involving these heritage objects.

Of course, the documentation useful to preservation policy goes well beyond information on the buildings and sites to be protected. The efficient running of a preservation program requires substantial documentation concerning existing legislation and programs as well as information on the availability of all of the kinds of resources used in the preservation process. Nonprofit preservation organizations have been particularly good at compiling such information.[14]

It is difficult to imagine the state conducting a historic preservation program without a wealth of information on which to base its decisions. Accordingly, documentation has become a sine qua non of government preservation action.[15]

Validation

Listing not only documents heritage sites, it also validates the importance of those sites, perhaps even engendering a bit of societal reverence for them. Selecting historic resources that will become the targets of government policy inevitably involves choices. And those choices, though often beginning with relatively objective rules—"any building over fifty years old is eligible for listing"—quickly turn to value judgments. Why is a particular resource important? To whom is a particular resource important? What element(s) of its form or its history qualify it for particular attention? Information has to be used to validate the choice of a resource for preservation, but validation necessitates a consideration of values, and values introduce controversy into the debate on preservation policy.

When choices are made in preservation policy one should expect controversy, and that controversy is often, though not always, over divergent interpretations of the relevance and importance of the information embodied in a site or building.[16] It is tempting, I suppose, to retreat to cut-and-dried rules for identifying historic resources, but the wide range of societal interests that might be concerned with a particular property are likely to make that difficult. To take just one vexing example, what stance should the newly emerging democracies in Eastern and Central Europe take with respect to the legacy of Soviet modernist-realist monuments that they have been left with? Some would like to tear them down, removing all physical remnants of this period. Others recognize them as important historical artifacts that are a part of the country's story.

These issues are repeated in a slightly different form when decisions are made about how to interpret a historic resource and present it to the public. What material should be provided? What should be the content of any explanatory signs or exhibits? Which aspects of the history of the resource should be emphasized? Whose perspective should be emphasized?[17] Should some form of costumed interpretation be included? These questions occur not only with respect to the experience of visiting the resource, but also with respect to materials that may be distributed away from the resource, such as school curricula and books and other printed materials. All of this is complicated even more when the site has different meanings for different groups and cultures. This issue affects any historic building or site in which some interests would alter the historic fabric in the pursuit of one set of values and other interests would protect and preserve the site.

Though any development controversy involving a heritage resource would provide a case in point, several recent preservation debates in the United States have proven particularly troubling. One occurs between church congregations, who occupy historic structures but can no longer afford to maintain and rehabilitate them except by draining resources from what they see as their primary mission, and preservation activists, whose primary objective is preserving the structure at all costs.[18] Another example comes out of the relatively recent movement to preserve former slave quarters and shotgun shacks in the South, resources that were previously ignored or "erased" both physically and conceptually.

A particularly complex form of this issue of divergent values is the treatment of heritage resources during periods of armed conflict. The history of warfare is filled with examples of heritage resources being destroyed exactly because of their cultural and historical significance to a particular group or nationality. The destruction of much of the fabric of the built heritage as well as of major cultural institutions such as libraries and archives in the former Yugoslavia testifies to this problem. Nevertheless, this is an area in which information-based strategies have continued to be the tool of choice. While some international agreements do have sanctions that can be brought to bear on the perpetrators of these acts—the possibility of being tried for war crimes, for example—most international conventions rely on good will and the willing participation of the signatory states for their success.

Not surprisingly, in such circumstances states see information as a critical mechanism; indeed, perhaps it is the only available mechanism with any chance of having an impact. A 1994 meeting in Sweden to discuss these issues called explicitly for increased information as a tool to protect the cultural heritage during war.[19] This call took two forms: a call for increased information available in advance and widely publicized as to the cultural and historical value of various sites (despite the fact that such information calls attention to the sites and their symbolic importance, which could also make them targets); and a call for the use of "heritage monitors" as members of peacekeeping missions and disaster aid agencies, to monitor critical sites and provide timely information about them. The resolutions of this meeting are a classic example of an information strategy.

Recognition

Going one step beyond identification and validation, it may also be desirable to recognize publicly particularly noteworthy examples of heritage resources and heritage projects; listing, and information more generally, have a role to play here as well. Many countries in their listing procedures make distinctions between various levels of heritage sites, with more stringent criteria applied to higher levels. Often these more important sites are eligible for higher levels of state support through incentives, but they may also be subject to higher levels of regulation.

UNESCO's World Cultural and Natural Heritage List, created in 1972 to recognize heritage resources of international importance, is a case in point.[20] This list was created to recognize that such sites existed and to serve as a gathering point for resources that might be deployed to protect and preserve them. As of December 1994, this elite list included 326 cultural sites, 97 natural sites, and 17 mixed sites in 100 countries. In reading the text of the convention, it is interesting to note how important information is in the actions that it envisions: through the convention UNESCO intends, among other things, to maintain, increase, and diffuse knowledge by assuring the conservation and protection of the world's heritage and by recommending to the nations concerned the necessary international conventions. Article 4 obliges each signatory state to include identification and presentation among the tasks that it agrees to undertake in the service of preservation; in Article 5 each state agrees to adopt policies to do studies and research and to foster training; and in Part VI the states agree to undertake the dissemination of this information.

Indeed, all selective lists of heritage resources are, in part, devices for conveying honorific distinction, and this role should not be underestimated. Owners are typically quite pleased to display the plaque that identifies their property as being listed on the National Register of Historic Places. But there are more explicit devices that can be used by the state to provide this sort of imprimatur. Prizes and awards of various types are used to identify and bring to popular attention particularly noteworthy examples of heritage preservation projects. The Presidential Design Awards at the national level and the Massachusetts Governor's Design Awards at the state level are two examples of American programs that recognize noteworthy preservation projects and programs (as well as other types of design projects).[21] Seen as policy tools, prizes and awards might embody attributes both of an information strategy and of incentives.

Promotion

Increasingly, the state is interested not only in preserving, understanding, and interpreting heritage resources but also in promoting their active use. To the extent that access to public resources is linked to the actual use that the population makes of heritage resources, it becomes important to cultivate the audience for those resources. Often, of course, the motivations of any public intervention are mixed. Is it possible to separate, for example, protection from promotion as a motivation of the World Heritage Convention? Growing out of a concern for safeguarding sites that have an international importance, it also serves to promote those sites as destinations.

Many promotion devices are available to the state. One such device has been the creation of special events and specially designated days, months, or even years. UNESCO's 1962 recommendations on the safeguarding of landscapes and sites included a full section entitled "Education of the Public," in which it urged the designation of national and international days to highlight the heritage and its preservation.[22] The year 1975 was designated the Year of Conservation in West Germany, and the Council of Europe promoted 1975 as European Architectural Heritage Year. The Arts Council of England, as part of its Arts 2000 program, in which a different city, town, or region and a different artistic theme is chosen for each year leading up to the millennium and the concluding Year of the Artist, has designated Glasgow as the U.K. City of

Architecture and Design for 1999 and awarded the city £400,000 for its proposed programs during that year.

These programs are examples of packaging the historic resources of a place in order to promote them; the packaging and the promotion both have high information content. Government agencies have taken this idea in yet another direction by creating heritage parks that bring together a number of heritage elements under a central theme, allowing the resources to be interpreted and marketed together as a single entity. In many cases, the information content of these newly configured parks is at least as important as the actual value of the physical sites included. The Council of Europe has implemented its own version of this idea through its program of Cultural Routes, and it is working with the United Nations in a joint initiative to develop awareness of and activities associated with the Silk Route. These transnational routes organize heritage and education resources at the European scale, identifying them through a mix of signage, maps and publications, exhibitions, events, and other tourism-based activities.[23]

There is, of course, a down side to better promotion of heritage sites. Venice and Prague and various sites in Egypt bear witness to the fact that increased use can erode the resource. In such cases, the goal of preservation itself—an important public interest in preservation policy—might be best served by limiting or discouraging public access—another public interest—a dilemma with which policy for the most popular sites has to contend.

Preservation and Maintenance Technique

Another familiar form of information in historic preservation policy is information concerning appropriate or desirable modes of technical operation in conservation, preservation, and restoration. Numerous government publications, for example, outline the appropriate techniques for a wide variety of preservation projects. Generally, this form of information is targeted at nongovernmental owners of heritage properties with the hope that they will undertake their own preservation projects using what is considered to be good preservation practice.

Information on technique is offered not only in printed form. Often the state provides technical and design assistance to the owners of heritage properties. In the United States, the Secretary of the Interior's Standards and Guidelines for Archaeology and Historic Preservation are very powerful because the technical advice they provide is tied to most government grants and incentives.[24] Seen in this way, assistance based on giving advice is simply another, more active way of providing information to further preservation goals. It can be an important component of a complete information strategy, though it might even be more effective if combined with incentives or regulation.

Coordination

In a preservation system premised on the involvement of a wide variety of both public and private actors (the direction in which many countries' preservation policies are moving), the coordination of their actions becomes an important goal. The simplest form of coordination begins with the state spelling out the goals or intent of public preservation policy, and here information is indispensable. Nothing surprising here. But taking this idea a bit further, historic preservation plans or general urban development plans that take preservation into account can also be seen as a form of information, communicating plans and ideas to others whose actions will affect those resources and their surroundings.

The way in which this planning is implemented, though, varies considerably across countries. It might be implemented quite simply. The regional planning laws of all of the Austrian *Länder* require that Cultural Property Maps be prepared and that these maps be incorporated into land use maps and plans.[25] Requiring that this information be present increases the likelihood that it will be taken into account in land use planning decisions. Moreover, these maps are linked with computerized references to all known archival resources as part of the Regional Planning Register. (This information approach to preservation planning received considerable notice during the 1975 European Architectural Heritage Year.) At the federal level, the Austrian Federal Monument Office has compiled an Atlas of Historical Zones of Protection, which includes photographs and base maps and indicates the various desirable levels of protection applicable to various sites. This atlas is "promoted as a planning instrument, which, although it has no legal force, encourages and guides the integration of ensemble and monument preservation into local development plans."[26] It is an admirable information tool.

Information can also be included directly in government plans. In some contexts, the state's master plan for the development of a particular area is a legally binding document; in this case, the plan is a form of regulation. But in other places, the plan for the area may be more an expression of the state's desires or hopes for an area and have no regulatory ability. In this case, the plan is more an information strategy intended to point to desirable outcomes and to suggest beneficial ways of coordinating development in the area. The plan is an important way to signal what actions the state itself will take, though it must distinguish between a commitment and an intent; the state can accomplish this only by providing clear and consistent information about its actions and its intended actions.

A similar gray area between regulation and coordination appears when the state regulates the process and timing of development so that there will be sufficient time for that development's impact on heritage resources to be assessed, debated, and possibly mitigated. In the public policy literature, this is called a "notifiable incident," which involves gathering as well as disseminating information.[27] One model for using information in this way is Section 106 of the 1966 National Historic Preservation Act in the United States. Section 106 requires any federal agency whose actions may affect a property on or eligible for the National Register to "take into account the effects of its undertaking" and to afford the Advisory Council on Historic Preservation (which was created by the act) reasonable opportunity to comment on the agency's proposed actions.[28]

Note that regulation is at work here, but it is regulation of the process of developing information on a proposed federal action. The objective is to generate a fuller consideration of potential impacts, and it is achieved through the development and presentation of information. In other words, the regulatory element is what makes the information element possible and more effective. The federal agency that is the project proponent must be able to demonstrate that it has taken into account the impact of its actions on historic resources. As with the Environmental Impact Statements required by the National Environmental Policy Act in the United States, which seek information on the impact of proposed developments on historic resources as well as on many other environmental impacts of development, the theory here is that the more fully the potential impacts are understood, the more likely the various actors in any development proposal will take those impacts into account along with all of the other factors in the development decision.

This is not only an American idea, of course. In Germany, for example, it is typical for preservation laws to require federal agencies "to give special consideration to preservation matters within the scope of their activities."[29] At first glance "requiring" and "giving special consideration to" seem to be contradictory attitudes, but they become compatible when one realizes that such a requirement simply creates conditions under which other preservation interests can protest if the state does not take preservation issues into account in decision making; they can assert that the state did not fulfill the requirement imposed upon it.

As I have already suggested, international treaties and conventions constitute another form of state action in preservation that is most appropriately thought of as a use of information for coordination purposes. Although these international agreements are often misunderstood to have a regulatory function, they typically include no legally binding sanctions. They are based, instead, on the willingness of the signatories to cooperate, coordinate their actions with one another, and operate in a parallel manner:

International organizations have drawn up recommendations, conventions, or statements of principle. These are, of course, non-binding; but by offering guidance, setting standards, and providing emphasis, they may unify and stimulate preservationists and give direction to governments.[30]

Seen from this perspective, these agreements are simply a statement of intent to coordinate preservation actions across countries in a particular way. They send a message that states should act in a particular way—recall the fundamental message of information as a tool—and that signatory states have agreed to act in that way. (There is an obvious link between these conventions and what David Throsby elsewhere in this volume has called "soft regulation"—constraints on behavior that operate by agreement. Here the conceptual boundary between regulation and information is indeterminate.) In this sense such documents are a form of information strategy in and of themselves, but, as I have already pointed out, they also suggest informational activities among the actions that they are urging. Thus they make use of informational tools at two different levels.

Education

The state can communicate information concerning heritage preservation more formally through educational networks. It might sponsor seminars and conferences on various preservation issues. It can develop, or help develop, various school curricula and provide the opportunity for school tours and other special events. It might support special training for craftsmen in particular preservation techniques or for interpreters who will be used to make the heritage come alive. And it might create and support university programs in heritage preservation.

Stretching the purview of education just a bit, the state can provide design and technical assistance at low cost or free of charge in order to communicate appropriate, approved forms of preservation activity. An owner of a listed building might be required to seek advice (coupling an information strategy with a regulatory strategy—the requirement that advice must be sought) rather than approval (a more purely regulatory strategy) before making alterations to that property. There is a danger, of course, that "advice" offered by government employees might become a "requirement" stipulated by the state, especially if there is little counter pressure on the state to make its advice reasonable. This is why Danish preservation law at one point stipulated that if government-suggested work exceeded the cost of what the owner had planned and for which he or she was seeking permission, the government would pay the difference.[31] It is not hard to spot the problem with this scheme: it would provide a strong incentive for an owner to minimize his or her own plans, thereby increasing the cost to the state.

Education can also take the form of demonstration projects, models, or prototypes. The state or nongovernmental organizations wishing to demonstrate particular forms or methods of renovation and rehabilitation can support model projects that are then brought to the attention of a broader public. Persuasive examples would then be imitated through private initiative. This is the stated intention, for example, of the Historic Cities Support Programme of the Aga Khan Trust for Culture, a nongovernmental, nonprofit organization active in promoting the quality of the built environment in the Muslim world.[32] This idea might also be embodied in public charities in which citizens can participate in determining how heritage resources are to be treated architecturally and programmatically.

Persuasion/Exhortation

The state's use of information might, at times, become even more proactive than those forms of information already mentioned. Such usage would be strategic and political. For example, once relatively complete registers of historic sites and buildings became commonplace and the world community comprehended the sheer volume of important historic resources, it was clear that particularly threatened resources needed higher levels of protection or intervention. As part of its World Heritage program, UNESCO compiles a list of World Heritage in Danger intended to focus attention on a smaller number of the World Heritage Sites. Seventeen sites were on this list as of the end of 1994. This list has two functions: first, it presents information as to which sites are in danger, and, second, it triggers provisions for emergency financial measures to be taken by UNESCO. This list therefore couples an information strategy with an incentive strategy.

In the United States, the National Trust for Historic Preservation annually compiles a list of America's Most Endangered Historic Places and circulates this list with a sophisticated public relations mix of press releases, articles, and video.[33] Similarly, one can easily imagine one level of government launching such a program with the hope of provoking action at another level. It is more likely that international organizations or nonprofit organizations would use such a strategy than a government agency, I suppose, because issuing such a list might suggest that that agency was admitting that it had not been effective in carrying out its responsibilities with respect to these heritage resources.

• • •

This tour of the various roles that information can play is not intended as a complete catalogue of the use of information as a policy tool. Rather, I have intended the examples to provoke a new way of thinking about information, not simply as a necessity for explaining how any particular preservation program works, but as an important tool in its own right, one with considerable potential.

Because the field of preservation policy has not begun explicitly to consider information as a tool with its own characteristics and its own advantages and disadvantages, it would certainly be premature to draw any firm conclusions about its use, though in the next chapter I will advance some tentative propositions about the use of information as compared to the use of other tools.

In the remainder of this chapter I turn to several other themes in the use of information that ought to be considered in choosing preservation actions and that deserve further analysis.

The Creation of Information

Up to this point my primary emphasis has been on the roles and content of the information that government might distribute as part of a heritage preservation information strategy. This, of course, presupposes the existence of the information that is to be communicated. As I have already pointed out, an important component of using information as a tool in preservation policy is the creation of opportunities for information to be collected by the wide variety of interested parties. But the environment in which heritage preservation policy and heritage programs function is not always an information-rich environment, particularly in countries that are just now organizing their heritage preservation programs for the first time; in these cases the state may need to be more explicitly involved in the creation of that information base.

The state has a key role to play in the support of the research that is necessary to build an information base. At least three types of research can make a contribution to the formulation of public policy. The first is historical research intended to document, validate, and interpret a site. This step, after all, establishes the importance of the site to the heritage. While the physical artifact itself is important and often irreplaceable, it is not too outrageous to suggest that much of the heritage value of a site to the general public may reside more in the information about the site and its significance than in any physical attributes of the site itself. There is an important variation here across countries, however. Some countries, such as the United States, tilt their heritage policies toward protecting sites that have important historical links and connotations, while others tilt their policies more toward protecting sites that embody the particular aesthetic values of various moments in history. In either case, there is important research to be done documenting the site's contribution to the shared heritage, though the type of research would be rather different in each case.

The second form of research is state-supported research into the processes of conservation, preservation, and restoration. This research focuses on materials and techniques. Advances in technique can make an important difference in the quality and the duration of these activities.

The final type of research is more explicitly oriented toward public policy. The state, for example, might commission research into the financial needs of heritage preservation, or evaluations of various heritage projects and programs that it has run, or feasibility studies to test the viability of proposed projects, or research on the demographics of the audience for heritage sites or on the perceptions of the public on various heritage issues,[34] and so on.

A state agency that is attentive to the need for information as a part of its overall heritage policy and accustomed to using information as part of its policy implementation arsenal may also be better at receiving information back from the field; in other words, it may be better at serving its constituency. On the other hand, agencies that have received substantial resources for heritage programs and have been able to conduct most of their business through ownership and operation are unlikely to have thought much about the role that nongovernmental partners can play in preservation. They are, therefore, unlikely to have thought much about developing a rich information base and are unlikely to perceive much of a need to elicit information from their potential constituents.

Research is not the only way that information pertaining to preservation can be created. One approach that has been used successfully to generate proposals for preservation and reuse of heritage resources is idea competitions; a design competition is held to elicit a range of ideas on how such a resource might be saved and revalued. Used in this way, competitions are information vehicles, though their more traditional use to select and build a "best" project for a site arguably falls more under the rubric of incentives. In the final analysis, it is less important to classify competitions exactly in terms of the five tools than it is to recognize that competitions can have both an information and an incentive intent.

Information Media

A few words are in order concerning the media that are used to transmit information on preservation policy and actions. The list of standard media that have been employed as information devices in the service of preservation policy is quite familiar. Consider first the print media; lists, registers, books, brochures, journals, reports, plans, guidebooks, and plaques all play an important role. Increasingly, electronic media are being used in the service of preservation. Film and video play a large role in promotion and interpretation, and computer technology is becoming a more important tool. Software developers have harnessed the hypermedia capabilities of computers to develop detailed presentations of the historic resources of an area including multiple levels of graphics and other information. Many preservation resources can now be accessed online; Appendix B indicates how to access the best preservation information sites on the World Wide Web.

But, as I have already suggested, other media are available and have been used for communicating information within the realm of preservation. To take just a few examples, competitions, prizes, awards, technical assistance, seminars, conferences, model projects, and education can all be thought of as alternative media that can be employed as part of an integrated preservation strategy.

Guidelines, Principles, Recommendations, Norms, Criteria, Standards, Codes, and Rules

As the participants in the Salzburg Seminar for which these chapters were originally prepared debated the various forms of government intervention and discussed how they applied to their own national contexts, we found ourselves having to deal with a wide range of vocabulary issues, and we have already referred to some of these difficulties earlier in this volume. But in discussing information strategies we particularly found ourselves stumbling over the implications of one set of closely connected words and concepts: guidelines, principles, recommendations, norms, criteria, standards, codes, and rules.

It would be very useful to have a clear, consistent vocabulary that would allow one to distinguish among various gradations along the scale of action from information at one end to regulation or ownership and operation at the other, in other words, along the scale of permissible flexibility in response to a government action. It seems clear that "rules" occupy the regulatory end of such a scale, but with respect to the other words on this list, there is considerable leeway in usage. In the United States, buildings codes are rules that must be followed in construction, and zoning codes are rules that must be followed in development, but codes of good conduct may be voluntarily adopted agreements about how to behave. The Countryside Code in the United Kingdom is a case in point; it is a list of suggested behaviors that, if followed, will serve to preserve the environment. The link to what David Throsby has termed "soft regulation" is clear; these constraints on behavior operate by voluntary agreement rather than by legal mandate.

The words "standards" and "guidelines" are also ambiguous; in normal discourse these words have more the sense of a suggestion, but in particular uses they, too, can be regulatory in intent. Standards for inclusion on a national register of historic properties typically function as rules, though there are undoubtedly those who would argue that such standards are most often too imprecise to be considered hard and fast rules. In the United States, renovations of properties that take advantage of government assistance programs must meet appropriateness standards. Even recommendations can have a regulatory force when used in circumstances in which the state clearly expects compliance. International agreements, because they are primarily information devices, make full use of the vocabulary of principles, recommendations, and guidelines, and it is not surprising to find these words in their titles.

The key here, it seems to me, is not so much entering into a thankless battle to develop a coherent vocabulary as it is constantly reminding oneself of the underlying messages of the various policy tools. These touchstones are important in understanding how a particular policy is being constructed. If the underlying message is a "should" message, then one is operating in the context of an information strategy; if, on the other hand, the underlying message is a "must" message, then one is operating in a regulatory context. In any event, one should not make the mistake of thinking that each of these words is linked inextricably to only one form of intervention. Practice in the preservation field is too complex for such a simple rule.

The Power of Information

It is quite easy, I think, to underestimate the power of information as a policy instrument. After all, no one—neither the state nor any other actor in the preservation system—is required to do anything in the presence of information, nor is there any clear, immediate benefit to a response as there is with incentives. Methodologically, it is difficult to imagine how to measure the impact of information strategies, particularly since they are often used in conjunction with other tools, thereby masking their particular contributions.

One has to rely, instead, on anecdotal information, and here there is considerable and growing support for the role of information. One document on the Australian experience reports that a major effect of listing—in this case on the World Heritage List—has been the increased provision of resources for strengthening management and improving interpretation and visitor facilities at historic cites. The fact that a site has been listed, it is felt, cultivates local and national pride, developing a feeling of responsibility.[35] This idea is echoed in the National Park Service's own description of the National Register of Historic Places in which it discusses the import of the list: "Listing properties in the National Register changes the way communities perceive their historic resources and gives credibility to efforts of private citizens and public officials to preserve these resources as living parts of our communities."[36] Of course, believing that this is the effect is different from demonstrating that it is the effect.

The most convincing testimony I have come across concerning the effectiveness of information as a policy tool in preservation comes from Gerard Bolla, former deputy director-general of UNESCO. In the late 1980s he gave a presentation at the Massachusetts Institute of Technology in which he discussed at length his experience with UNESCO's Convention for the Protection of the World Cultural and Natural Heritage. The convention had been modeled "to give an institutional framework to the international solidarity displayed at the time of the rescue of the temple of Abu Simbel" from the rising waters caused by the construction of the Aswan High Dam in the Nile River.[37] Initially, many of the states that had urged the adoption of such a convention had argued for the critical importance of creating a World Heritage Fund that could provide grants to projects for world heritage sites. At the same time, the United States insisted on the creation of a formal World Heritage List. While many felt that the fund would prove to be the most important tool in the convention, Bolla argued that the list had turned out to be much more important. While the funds deposited in the World Heritage Fund would always be limited, World Heritage List designation quickly became an important symbol that could be used by many different interests to bring a wide variety of political pressure and a wide variety of resources to bear on the protection and preservation of these internationally recognized sites. In our terms, the information tool of granting formal designation turned out to be more effective than the incentive tool of making grants available.

It seems clear that a lot more work remains to determine under what circumstances an information-based strategy is the most effective form of action and when and how it ought to be combined with other tools.

How Good a Job Does/Can the State Do at Providing Information?

One final issue deserves mention. Even if one allows that there are circumstances in which the use of an information strategy is a powerful policy tool, it does not necessarily follow that the state does—or even can do—a good job at providing information. Government agencies do not always do the best job at providing information concerning their actions and intentions. Those that are unconcerned about their continued existence because they do not need to justify their existence to their constituency may be less attuned to the use of information as a policy tool. Accordingly, one would expect that nongovernmental, nonprofit organizations would do a better job with information because they have an incentive linked to their own institutional survival. On the other hand, some government agencies, because of their circumstances, have to pay more attention to justifying their existence, and can be expected to rely on information strategies to make that case. Moreover, they may have to pay close attention to the cost effectiveness of their actions, and that, too, may lead more frequently to information-based strategies because of their (relatively) low cost compared to other forms of action.

Moreover, there are some constraints on the state's ability to communicate information well. In countries in which the tradition has been of a state with a relatively heavy hand, the population may not actually trust government-provided information, suspecting that there is a political and ideological subtext at work. And of course there are countries that restrict the public's access to information as a matter of course.

If this is not a complicated enough environment in which to develop information-based policies, consider the view, expressed by some during the Salzburg Seminar, that in some circumstances the provision of information on valuable heritage properties might actually endanger them, subjecting them to possible vandalism, theft, and destruction or at least to the wear and tear of increased visitation and use. In these cases the state may actually turn to disinformation as a matter of policy. Used in this way, I intend the word "disinformation" to have a neutral connotation; in the same way that we have already talked about incentives and disincentives, disinformation might also be used to pursue laudable public goals. All of these issues need to be explicitly considered in the design of an information-based approach to preservation action.

Conclusion

From the examples that I have presented in this chapter I hope it is clear that the modern state uses information-based strategies in a number of different ways to further its preservation policies. I also hope that I have established that information is sufficiently distinct from the other modes of government action to be considered on its own merits. Yet it should also be clear that those who have been involved in the implementation of preservation policy have only rarely thought about information in a systematic way. By introducing an explicit consideration of information into policy implementation, one can broaden the menu of possibilities for action, and that by itself can contribute substantially to a balanced preservation policy.

Because a tools approach such as the one suggested in this volume has not, as far as we know, been applied previously to the analysis of government preservation policy, it would be presumptuous to draw definitive conclusions concerning when information is likely to be the tool of choice and how exactly to structure it. Nevertheless, some attributes of information as a way of conducting the state's business deserve our attention.

An information approach to preservation can be considerably less expensive than approaches that rely on other tools, particularly if one carefully accounts for all of the social costs of an intervention, not just the direct costs to the public sector or the direct costs to the private sector. In a resource-constrained environment, information may in fact be the only tool that can be deployed with any effect. An information approach is also well adapted to the emerging importance of nongovernmental actors in heritage preservation. One has only to recognize the impact that listing has had in and of itself, independent of the extent to which it triggers the entry of other tools into the policy mix, to glimpse the possibilities information offers. Moreover, if the state is going to be working with other partners, whether they are private individuals, private nonprofit organizations, or quasi-governmental organizations, the success of that partnership will rely on a clear flow of information among the partners.

Yet information may work better in situations where there is a generally held social consensus as to what is to be accomplished and how it is to be accomplished than in situations where there is considerable contention. And, finally, a related point: Information that emanates from the state will be most effective in achieving public goals when there is a fundamental trust of the state and its actions.

In the next chapter I return to these points as I discuss important considerations in choosing one's tools. Whatever that choice turns out to be, information will be a valuable element.

Notes

1. International Symposium on World Heritage Towns, *Safeguarding Historic Urban Ensembles in a Time of Change: A Management Guide* (Quebec: Organization of World Heritage Towns, 1991), B-8.
2. The one exception to this generalization concerning the preservation literature is the loose-leaf binder prepared by the International Symposium on World Heritage Towns, *Safeguarding Historic Urban Ensembles in a Time of Change: A Management Guide.* This document takes a tools approach, though uses categories that differ from ours. On what I have called "information strategies," see particularly sections D–2, "Documentation and Evaluation," and D–3, "Principles and Standards."
3. Council of Europe, *Convention for the Protection of the Architectural Heritage of Europe.* Granada, Spain, 1985, Article 14, "Participation and Associations."
4. Christopher C. Hood, *The Tools of Government* (Chatham, N.J.: Chatham House Publishers, 1986). See particularly chap. 2, "Advice, Information, Persuasion," and chap. 6, "Tools for Detection."
5. Department of National Heritage, *What Listing Means: A Guide for Owners and Occupiers* (London: Department of National Heritage, October 1994), 3.
6. Paul H. Gleye and Waldemar Szczerba, *Volume III: Poland,* Historic Preservation in Other Countries, ed. Robert E. Stipe (Washington, D.C.: United States Committee of the International Council on Monuments and Sites, 1989), p. 3.
7. There is a considerable literature on appropriate techniques for surveying and listing

historic properties. I have chosen not to enter that literature here, preferring to maintain a focus on information as a tool choice.

8. Georgia Department of Natural Resources, "The National Register of Historic Places: Historic Preservation Fact Sheet No. 2," no date, reproduced in Russell V. Keune, ed., *The Historic Preservation Yearbook: A Documentary Record of Significant Policy Developments and Issues* (Bethesda, Md.: Adler & Adler, 1984), 70–71. The process of listing on the National Register in the United States is based on nominations from State Historic Preservation Offices, so the role of designated agencies such as the Georgia Department of Natural Resources in the listing process is critical.

9. For further detail on this point see Schuster, "Inciting Preservation," elsewhere in this volume.

10. The right of property owners to dispute the listing of buildings individually or within districts on the National Register of Historic Places in the United States (and in local districts in some states) has been significantly increased in recent years.

11. Margaret Thomas Will, *Volume II: Federal Republic of Germany, Switzerland, and Austria,* Historic Preservation in Foreign Countries, ed. Robert E. Stipe (Washington, D.C.: United States Committee of the International Council on Monuments and Sites, 1984), 21.

12. I am grateful to Robert Stipe for having pointed out this possibility.

13. Will, *Volume II: Federal Republic of Germany, Switzerland, and Austria,* 75.

14. One of many excellent examples of this type of document is Russell V. Keune, ed., *The Historic Preservation Yearbook: A Documentary Record of Significant Policy Developments and Issues* (Bethesda, Md.: Adler & Adler, 1984). This volume was undertaken under the auspices of the National Trust for Historic Preservation, a government-chartered, private, nonprofit organization. Unfortunately, the intent of the trust to issue such a handbook on a regular basis has not been realized.

15. But, for some in the preservation field it does not necessarily follow that a national list is a necessary element of that documentation. For a debate on the necessity of a national list see the materials reproduced in the section entitled "The Future of the National Register" in Keune, ed., *The Historic Preservation Yearbook,* 74–79.

16. In some countries, such as the United States, the controversy is more likely to be over the economic implications of a preservation decision.

17. These issues are beginning to be explored more systematically with respect to museum exhibitions, particularly with respect to living history museums. See, for example, the critiques presented in Robert Lumley, ed., *The Museum Time Machine: Putting Cultures on Display* (London: Routledge, 1988).

18. For a useful overview of these issues, see chap. 13, "The Landmarking of Religious Property," in Keune, ed., *The Historic Preservation Yearbook,* 257–89.

19. Meeting of the Central Board of National Antiquities, Swedish National Commission for UNESCO, and ICOMOS Sweden, *Resolution on Information as an Instrument for Protection Against War Damages to the Cultural Heritage,* Stockholm, Sweden, 10 June 1994.

20. UNESCO, *Convention for the Protection of World Cultural and National Heritage,* Paris, France, 16 November 1972, reproduced in Keune, ed., *The Historic Preservation Yearbook,* 34–40. The first twelve sites were listed in 1978.

21. For a further discussion of the Massachusetts Governor's Design Awards Program, see Adele Fleet Bacow, *Designing the City: A Guide for Advocates and Public Officials* (Washington, D.C.: Island Press, 1995), chap. 7.

22. UNESCO, *Safeguarding Landscapes and Sites: An International Recommendation*, Paris, France, December 1962, reproduced in Keune, ed., *The Historic Preservation Yearbook*, 50–53.

23. The designers of this program, however, are quick to point out that it was created not so much to communicate information about heritage at the regional and transnational scale—which it does admirably—as to provide a programmatic model for European cooperation in transnational programs.

24. Keune, ed., *The Historic Preservation Yearbook*, 100–125.

25. Will, *Volume II: Federal Republic of Germany, Switzerland, and Austria*, 116.

26. Will, *Volume II: Federal Republic of Germany, Switzerland, and Austria*, 104.

27. For a further discussion of the "obligation to notify" as a form of state action, see Hood, *The Tools of Government*, 98–100.

28. For a very useful and complete discussion of Section 106 review and the structure and role of the Advisory Council, see Keune, ed., *The Historic Preservation Yearbook*, chap. 11, "The Role of the Advisory Council on Historic Preservation," 185–249.

29. Will, *Volume II: Federal Republic of Germany, Switzerland, and Austria*, 75.

30. Keune, ed., *The Historic Preservation Yearbook*, 33.

31. Anthony Dale, *Volume I: France, Great Britain, Ireland, The Netherlands, and Denmark*, Historic Preservation in Foreign Countries, ed. Robert E. Stipe (Washington, D.C.: United States Committee on the International Council on Monuments and Sites, 1982), 126.

32. His Highness the Aga Khan, speech to the International Union of Architects/American Institute of Architects Conference, Chicago, Illinois, June 1993.

33. See, for example, Alicia Rodriguez, "Can We Save Them?" *Historic Preservation* (July/August 1995), 14–16.

34. For example, David Throsby elsewhere in this volume refers to the use of economic research to measure citizens' willingness to pay for collective cultural expenditures.

35. Australian Heritage Commission, "Implications of World Heritage Listing" (Online, 1995). Available: http://www.erin.gov.au/portfolio/ahc/register.htm1.

36. National Park Service, "The National Register of Historic Places," reproduced in Keune, ed., *The Historic Preservation Yearbook*, 71.

37. Gerard Bolla, "Protection of Historic Towns and Quarters: National and Institutional Legal Standards," paper dated May 1987, presented at Massachusetts Institute of Technology.

References

Bacow, Adele Fleet. *Designing the City: A Guide for Advocates and Public Officials.* Washington, D.C.: Island Press, 1995.

Bolla, Gerard. "Protection of Historic Towns and Quarters: National and Institutional Legal Standards." Paper dated May 1987, presented at Massachusetts Institute of Technology.

Central Board of National Antiquities, Swedish National Commission for UNESCO, and ICOMOS Sweden. *Resolution on Information as an Instrument for Protection Against War Damages to the Cultural Heritage.* Stockholm, Sweden, 10 June 1994.

Council of Europe. *Convention for the Protection of the Architectural Heritage of Europe.* Granada, Spain, 1985.

Department of National Heritage. *What Listing Means: A Guide for Owners and Occupiers.* London: Department of National Heritage, October 1994.

Hood, Christopher C. *The Tools of Government.* Chatham, N.J.: Chatham House Publishers, 1986.

International Symposium on World Heritage Towns. *Safeguarding Historic Urban Ensembles in a Time of Change: A Management Guide.* Quebec: Organization of World Heritage Towns, 1991.

Keune, Russell V., ed. *The Historic Preservation Yearbook: A Documentary Record of Significant Policy Developments and Issues.* Bethesda, Md.: Adler & Adler, 1984.

Lumley, Robert, ed. *The Museum Time Machine: Putting Cultures on Display.* London: Routledge, 1988.

Stipe, Robert E., series ed. Historic Preservation in Foreign Countries, later retitled Historic Preservation in Other Countries. Washington, D.C.: United States Committee of the International Council on Monuments and Sites, various dates. Volumes in the series include:

> Dale, Anthony. *Volume I: France, Great Britain, Ireland, The Netherlands, and Denmark.* 1982.
> Will, Margaret Thomas. *Volume II: Federal Republic of Germany, Switzerland, and Austria.* 1984.
> Gleye, Paul H., and Waldemar Szczerba. *Volume III: Poland.* 1989.
> Leimenstoll, Jo Ramsay. *Volume IV: Turkey.* 1989.

7

J. Mark Schuster

Choosing the Right Tool(s)
for the Task

The authors of the preceding chapters have explored each of the five tools of government action. John de Monchaux and I set that task because we wanted, as much as possible, to separate each tool analytically and to highlight its attributes. This separation was necessary to underscore the point that there is a menu of possibilities from which governments choose in determining how to implement their policies with respect to the built heritage—or, for that matter, with respect to any of the substantive policy areas in which they are engaged. At this level of abstraction there is nothing exclusive to the field of heritage preservation; many of the same issues would come up in any field. The link to heritage preservation comes through examples of actual heritage programs that use these tools, many of which have been discussed in the preceding chapters.[1]

When the authors of the preceding chapters turned to actual examples of heritage preservation practice to illustrate the various tools, however, they found that it was often difficult to find pure examples of each tool in use, and for good reason. Recognizing the advantages and disadvantages of the various tools, the state in its preservation programs uses tools in various combinations, trying to find particularly effective mixes of those instruments. In discussions at the Salzburg Seminar, Lester Borley characterized this variability as each program and project "having its own footprint."

In this volume, we have chosen to place tools into a relatively small number of categories to try to focus our collective attention on the broad choices that can be made among different modes of state action. To some degree, the authors of the preceding chapters have already begun to explore choices, especially within each of the five categories—such as direct versus indirect incentives, or hard versus soft regulation—but for the most part, we have not yet discussed how the government, as an agent in heritage preservation, should choose among the major types of tools.

124

As Lester Salamon has suggested, a tools approach to government action is based upon the idea that "[g]reater precision in matching the characteristics of different tools with the particular requirements of the task can . . . improve program performance."[2] We, too, believe this to be the case, but we also recognize that when one moves from the abstract to an actual case of applied government action, things get considerably more complicated.

To think about the government as choosing among the various tools in the preservationist's toolbox is not merely theoretical. Governments regularly search for tools, particularly for new combinations of tools, as the context within which the government is acting shifts. Especially stubborn problems may require a periodic change in approach to see whether or not any progress can be made toward solving them. Today it seems that all governments, whatever their location or level, are searching for less expensive solutions to the societal problems that they endeavor to address, solutions which often involve different types of tools than have been used before.

Thus external pressures move government toward a reevaluation of appropriate tools. Growing fiscal pressure on government, high ambitions for and expectations of government (despite something of a recent rollback in these ambitions and expectations), and increasing government and international activity all make more complicated the context within which government seeks to preserve the built heritage.

Even though government officials regularly choose how preservation policies will be implemented as they design various heritage programs, they rarely use a systematic and comprehensive approach to the choice of instruments. One can always interpret past actions as revealing implicit choices, but to make choices in a more explicitly self-conscious way while designing these programs would, we believe, result in qualitatively different decisions.

Complex pressures and constraints mitigate against a consideration of the full menu of tools in any particular situation. In some cases there may simply be a level of inertia that comes from overfamiliarity with certain tools and current and past practice; in other cases there may well be a systemic unfamiliarity with the true range of tools that is available. Most important, there may be any number of political, legal, economic, or structural constraints that make completely free choice impossible. In this chapter I have set aside these constraints for the moment, beginning with a theoretical approach to tools choice that assumes a free and unconstrained choice. It would not be unreasonable from a public policy point of view to hope that designers of government programs would go through an explicit consideration of the full range of tool options each time a new program is designed and implemented. It is important, though, to recognize these constraints, and I will return to them later in the chapter.

Other pressures also work against a tools perspective. Many countries, particularly those accustomed to a highly centralized government bureaucracy, are tempted to reduce policy debate in any area of state action to a search for the right law. In this view, any societal problem can be fixed if the right law can be devised, and policy mistakes can be attributed to the fact that the existing law has been poorly crafted. Indeed, in comparative conferences and seminars, one is often asked what the right law should be. In the analytic framework that we have adopted in this volume, this way of thinking has little place. We see the drafting of a law as occurring rather late in the policy implementation process; one begins instead with the policy preferences of the government and of other interested groups and individuals in society. These preferences are hammered into public policy through a political process. The government moves to the design of programs to pursue this policy using one or another combination of the basic tools. Only then might it be necessary to draft a new law to facilitate program implementation.

The choice of tools is not solely a technical task, though our discussion of the five tools may contribute to such an impression. As Christopher Hood points out, often in public policy the choice of instrument is more controversial than the objective that is being pursued, and that controversy may well be the most virulent in those cases where the question of effectiveness is not the fundamental question at issue.[3] It is easy to summon examples from related areas of government action. While there may be a substantial agreement that a society ought to assure that affordable housing is provided to its citizens, for example, we disagree as to whether that should be done through the construction of public housing, the provision of housing vouchers, the provision of incentives to private developers, or the regulation of the mix of housing types and prices that developers are allowed to develop. It should not be too difficult to think of familiar examples from the field of heritage preservation, as well. Consider, for example, the controversy over whether important heritage sites should remain in private hands or in public ownership to best ensure that their value to the broader society will be preserved. Paying attention to the choice of tools that government has at its disposal should provide useful insights into how well the government's preservation apparatus can function.

The metaphor of a toolbox in which one rummages around to choose the best tools helps underline another property of those tools. Only extremely rarely is a new tool invented and added to the toolbox. In the various domains of government intervention, new problems—or new perceptions of old problems—rarely lead to the invention of new tools of state action. Rather, they lead to new combinations of old tools. The contents of the toolbox of state action are well known. It does not necessarily follow, however, that all of their attributes are well understood.

Because a tools approach to heritage preservation is a relatively new idea, this initial attempt at such an inquiry falls well short of developing a definitive set of rules about which tools should be used in which situations. Indeed, it may even be presumptuous to suggest that such a list of rules might ever exist. Perhaps endless tinkering is necessary to fit tools and combinations of tools to the many different contexts in which preservation has to take place. Nevertheless, it is possible to point the way to a few principles, and that is the main task of this chapter. Along the way I will continue to make reference to the more general work of Hood and Salamon, both of whose work has been cited throughout this volume and has been particularly helpful to John de Monchaux and me as we have tried to sort out our own ideas as to how the tools approach can be brought to bear on government preservation activities.

Rules for Tools

Which tools should be chosen in which circumstances? It would be comforting, indeed, to establish once and for all a set of rules that would take the guesswork out of crafting preservation programs from the five basic tools and their variants. But, I suppose, if such a set of unambiguous rules were possible, it would already have been developed. Instead, current literature on the tools of government suggests either broad criteria by which such a choice should be made or a set of variables that one might take into account in making such a choice. The literature presents general signposts that guide the way. By focusing on a particular domain of government action, we should be able to understand a little better what might be entailed in making informed choices among the five tools.

By focusing on the choice of tools, I do not mean to imply that I believe that one is confronted with an either/or choice. Often two or three tools in combination will prove to be the most effective way of proceeding. The state's involvement in heritage preservation begins with a policy, a statement of goals, objectives, and approaches that it intends to pursue. Then various programs are designed to implement that policy, and it is these programs that make use of the available tools in combination. Many of the examples cited in the preceding chapters have made it abundantly clear that the tools are often used in combination to offset their individual weaknesses. Nevertheless, in this section I will continue to maintain some separation among the tools in order to highlight better their various positive and negative attributes.

Existing Guidelines

In a discussion of choice, it is important to remember that there is a fine line between stipulating how choices ought to be made—a normative approach—and attempting to explain how such choices are actually made—a descriptive approach. I will not attempt to maintain too strict a separation between these two approaches here, but it is something worth thinking about as others refine our approach to framing heritage preservation action by the state.

Let me begin with Hood, on whom we have already relied heavily in this volume. When Hood turns to the question of choosing among the tools of government, he proposes five guidelines:[4]

- The tool must be matched to the job.
- One must have reason to expect that the tool (or combination of tools) will be effective in its proposed application.
- Effectiveness is not enough in the current fiscal climate. The use of the tool must also lead to a minimal drain on public resources.
- The tool must satisfy the criteria of justice and fairness.
- The mix of tools should only be selected after an examination of alternative possibilities.

At first glance these guidelines are unexceptional, but that does not mean their implications are completely clear. Consider the first. What does it mean for a tool to be "matched" to a job? What are the factors that one wants to think about in establishing whether or not such a match exists? The choice among tools has been the object of so little research, particularly in the preservation field, that at the moment little is known about this question.

Because there is so much variety in the tools and their application, it may turn out that it will be nearly impossible to specify what will work when. Nevertheless, it is still useful to think about the factors that might influence the choice of tools in a broad way, and to offer some propositions about when which tools are likely to work best.

Both the literature on the tools of government and the literature on state action in historic preservation offer some information on how to make appropriate choices among the tools, but one has to dig through them with care in order to find their insights. In this volume we have cited several times one such thoughtful document, *Safeguarding Historic Urban Ensembles in a Time of Change: A Management Guide*, prepared for the International Symposium on World Heritage Towns.[5] The authors of this volume explicitly consider the choice of tools for the preservation of the built heritage. They see the choice of tools as function of six interrelated factors:

- the resources and the institutional infrastructure that a community has at its disposal;
- the nature of the existing threats to the heritage;
- the particular qualities of the heritage that it is hoped the tool will protect or enhance;

- the climate of support for heritage conservation that exists in the community;
- the impact of using a particular tool on other legitimate public mandates (that is, whether or not the tool has unanticipated secondary effects on other areas of public interest); and
- the time-frame in which it one desires to achieve results.

But once again, this list is presented more as factors that ought to be taken into account in choosing tools than as a set of rules. Nevertheless, these factors do suggest some ideas about what might be important in making choices among the tools.

Thirteen Propositions

Because there has been very little empirical research on the use of tools in heritage preservation, it would be unwise to advance a set of rules, but in order to facilitate and provide direction for such research it might be useful to suggest a number of propositions concerning the circumstances in which one might choose one tool over another. Accordingly I will now suggest such a set of propositions and speculate about the direction in which each proposition might influence the choice of tools. In developing these propositions, I have relied upon the general literature on tool choice, the individual essays in this volume, and the discussions conducted at the Salzburg Seminar. The list is meant to be suggestive rather than definitive.

I have tried to group these propositions roughly by type. The first three have to do with prevailing attitudes concerning the state and preservation, the next five have to do with the infrastructure within which preservation policies operate, and the final five have to do with more technical considerations of program design.

Proposition 1 (Government Attitude): *The choice of tools should reflect the attitude that the state wishes to adopt with respect to the sector. A more interventionist attitude will lead to the use of more interventionist tools.*

In an influential paper in the field of cultural policy, Harry Hillman-Chartrand and Claire McCaughey have argued that the structure of government support for the arts and culture and the tools that are typically used within each form of support are a function of the state's attitude toward the arts and culture.[6] They characterize four types of arts support models—Facilitator, Patron, Architect, and Engineer—and suggest that as the state becomes increasingly interventionist across this scale, the tools of choice change, as indeed they do in their examples.

While these authors do not characterize the tools of state action as carefully as we have in the current volume, their view is quite clear. The state in its role as facilitator tends to use indirect incentives, information, and a base of clearly spelled out property rights; the patron state tends to use more direct incentives; and the architect and engineer states make increasing use of direct intervention, particularly regulation and ownership and operation. For these authors, the choice of an attitude or posture of the state precedes the choice of tools, and the latter is dictated in large part by the former. The choice of an attitude or posture is, in turn, influenced by the style of governing that the state wishes to, or feels it must adopt, as well as by the style of policy it wishes to promulgate in a particular sector. Taken together, these observations suggest that though there is not a natural tool for a particular problem, there may be a natural tool for a particular context.

Proposition 2 (Respect for the State): *The choice of tools should reflect the degree to which the government is respected by its citizens. When the government is widely respected and accepted, all that may be necessary for the desired action to take place is for the state to set the direction of policy and lend its approval and support to private actions.*

The basic point here is contained in the negative form of this statement more than in the positive form. If consensus with respect to the role of the state is low, the state will have to rely on more interventionist tools to accomplish its objectives, such as regulation and direct ownership rather than, say, information or incentives. If, on the other hand, respect for and acceptance of the state are high, other actors in the preservation system are more likely to bring their own actions in line with government policy and will react appropriately to less interventionist tools.

Proposition 3 (Degree of Consensus): *The choice of tools should reflect the degree of societal consensus concerning preservation of the heritage. If there is a shared societal consensus about the desirability of preserving the heritage and about how to accomplish that preservation, it will be less necessary to use tools that mandate behaviors.*

When there is a high degree of consensus (and a high degree of congruence between that consensus and public policy), the government can be more relaxed in its choice of preservation tools, using information and incentives to shape implementation rather than relying on regulation or ownership and operation to mandate compliance. But it is worth pointing out that most successful regulation is supported by society's consensus as well. It is very difficult to require citizens to do something which they do not basically support; it is always easier if there is a predisposition in a particular policy direction. Information plays a particularly important role here because it can help shape that consensus as well as guide action once such a consensus is clarified.

Proposition 4 (Ownership Pattern): *The choice of tools should respond to the prevailing ownership pattern of heritage resources.*

Elsewhere in this volume Lester Borley points out that in many places much of the heritage is already under private ownership and that one must take this ownership pattern into account in deciding which preservation tools to use. If heritage resources are mainly in private hands, property rights, incentives, and information strategies will be particularly appropriate, and regulation may also have a role to play. Ownership and operation, on the other hand, might prove to be a very expensive option. If heritage resources have, over the course of the years, become the property of the state, then one would begin by assessing how the ownership and operation system is working.

Of course, what may be most important here is not the fact that much of the heritage property is held in private hands but that private ownership may be a strongly held societal value. If there is a strong social value ascribed to keeping property in private hands, ownership and operation becomes even more difficult to justify. On the other hand, if collective ownership of heritage properties is a highly held value, whether generally or in particularly symbolic instances—even in the United States certain historic properties are owned and operated by the Department of the Interior—ownership and operation should probably figure more prominently among the tools selected.

Proposition 5 (Organizational Ecology): *The choice of tools should respond to the organizational ecology within which heritage preservation will happen.*

In a number of countries, the only actor traditionally involved in heritage preservation is the state itself, but in other countries there is a richer network of individuals and organizations, many of which are nongovernmental and nonprofit. The more highly developed this institutional ecology is, the more likely it is that incentives and information, in particular, will prove to be useful tools. When government is working in the context of an organizational network that also operates in the field of interest, it is much less likely to rely solely on direct action and much more likely to rely on the other tools. And efforts that are in some sense voluntary may ultimately be preferable to grudging compliance or resigned acceptance. Another way of saying this is that ownership and operation by the state may work against the creation of environments that are self-sustaining by virtue of all the interests that are brought to bear on them.

A rich institutional infrastructure presupposes the willingness of other actors to engage in heritage activities and, *ceteris paribus*, it will be easier for the state to find willing partners in its heritage policies when such an infrastructure exists. The state itself can help to foster such an infrastructure, of course, through the passage of legislation legalizing the formation of nonprofit associations and foundations and setting out rules for their operation.

Here an important point seems to be the need for the creation and nourishment of a natural constituency for heritage projects and programs. If such a constituency exists it may demand more of the state in the form of preservation programs, but it may also alleviate some of the pressure on the state by participating in those programs. Here, too, the tools have a role to play. While ownership and operation and regulation do not help build this sort of natural constituency, information, incentives, and even property rights strategies can. In this way, these tools may have benefits beyond whatever immediate responses they cause.

Proposition 6 (Target Size): *The choice of tools should respond to the size of the entity that is being targeted.*

Some preservation policy may be targeted at a small number of heritage properties (or a small number of individuals), but other policies may need to be more generally targeted. One might imagine a range from individual objects and properties through ensembles of such properties to entire landscapes, with each scale necessitating a different approach. As a general rule, incentives and ownership and operation are the tools that can be most carefully targeted to individual properties or actors. Information might be used as a policy tool in either case, linked directly to single properties and their heritage value, on the one hand, or targeted at broad classes of heritage properties or at broad groups of actors in the heritage sphere, on the other. Property rights and regulation, however, are best suited to more general targeting. Indeed, so-called spot zoning, a form of regulation that targets individual properties rather than more broadly defined zones of properties, is illegal in many national contexts because it is felt that regulations must be generally applicable to be socially acceptable.

Proposition 7 (Identification and Dispersion): *The choice of tools should reflect the degree to which heritage properties are individually identified and the degree to which they are concentrated or dispersed.*

The degree to which the targets of the state's preservation action are actually known and identified and the degree to which they are concentrated (or dispersed) are two related attributes that influence the choice of tools in similar ways. Both identification and concentration call for the use of very targeted tools. Because of their broader nature, property rights and regulation are less useful in these circumstances than are ownership and operation or specifically targeted incentives. Information can be helpful in either case.

Proposition 8 (Fine Tuning): *The choice of tools should reflect the degree of fine tuning that might be necessary in the application of the tool. Very particular instances might require tools that can be finely tuned, whereas other circumstances might be better served with more generally applied tools.*

Closely related to the successful targeting of interventions is the question of what degree of fine tuning is desirable or possible with different tools. If the target size proposition adjusts the breadth of intervention, this proposition adjusts the intensity of intervention.[7] It seems clear that information and incentives as well as ownership and operation can be extremely finely tuned to apply varying degrees of intensity as necessary, whereas regulation and property rights are more difficult to vary within a legal framework that expects equality of treatment. Indeed, the government might hesitate to vary the intensity of information and incentives if it does not want to appear to be treating some individuals, institutions, or properties better (or worse) than others.

Proposition 9 (Incidence of Costs): *Because government tools vary in the extent to which they localize (or generalize) the costs of public policies, the choice of tools should reflect a conscious decision as to who should bear those costs.*[8]

There can be considerable disagreement as to who should bear the costs of preserving the heritage resources of a society. At one extreme is the view that because it is of public value to preserve the heritage, all of the costs involved in preservation activities should be borne by the state, and, ultimately, by taxpayers. At the other extreme is a view, more practical than ideological perhaps, that because there are so many heritage properties in so many places, it is well beyond the ability of the state to support such costs, so individual property owners should be induced or required to bear the costs. In between is the view that in many cases sharing costs would be most appropriate, with private property owners bearing some of the costs in recognition of the fact that they have use of the heritage property, and the state bearing the rest in recognition of the public's interest in seeing that the resource is protected and preserved. When viewed from a cost perspective, the choice among tools can be construed as a choice of who should pay for the public policy that the tool is intended to implement.

At the two extremes of this dimension are ownership and operation, which spreads the costs across the widest class of taxpayers, and regulation, which localizes the costs with the private owner of the regulated property. The property rights alternative has the economic effect of adjusting the return that an individual can realize from his or her property, and using this tool may incur costs or bring benefits to property owners depending on the exact form of alterations to the package of property rights the owner enjoys and can use. Incentives, on the other hand, are particularly well suited to sharing cost among public and private interests. The costs of using information as a tool are generally borne by taxpayers.

In thinking about costs, it is important not to confuse the cost to the state of using a particular tool with the cost to society. Some tools, particularly information, are unlikely to incur large costs to the state, and therefore may look more desirable from a cost perspective than, say, ownership and operation. But with other tools, such a comparison becomes trickier. Regulation, for example, appears to be free. With the exception of enforcement costs, which may or may not be substantial depending on local policy choices, the cost of regulation to the state can be quite small, while the costs to the individual property owners whose use of property may be severely restricted could be quite large; because they are visited on individuals rather than on society as a whole, these costs may not be taken into account in the choice of tools. It is certainly true that the state's choice of tools may be constrained by the resources that it perceives are available at any given point, a point to which I will return, but to ignore the private costs of the choice among tools can have long-term consequences on the precise resources that one is trying to preserve. Thus the state ought to account carefully for costs of all types in choosing its tools.

Here, of course, there is a rather large gap between theory and practice. In many countries, systems of taxation are essentially opportunistic, and choices regarding who should pay have more to do with administrative expediency and politics than with a rational process of determining the proper balance of costs and benefits.[9] This, of course, does not mean that debates about the choice among tools do not consider the issue of who should pay; there is every indication that this is and will continue to be an important, if not a determining, factor in choosing tools for implementation.

Proposition 10 (Timing): *The choice of tools should vary according to the urgency with which one wishes to act.*

Because of sudden changes in governmental structure, many countries are facing an urgent situation with respect to their built heritage. In many cases decisions have had to be made relatively quickly to save endangered resources. Certain tools, most particularly direct incentives and ownership and operation, are best suited to quick action. Others, such as property rights and information, are better suited to long-term development of the economic and attitudinal climate within which preservation activities might be undertaken. Indirect incentives and regulation occupy the middle ground of this dimension, though time-limited, emergency regulation may be able to be used effectively as part of a quick response.

Proposition 11 (Automaticity): *The choice of tools should reflect the degree to which automaticity of action is a desired property of heritage programs.*

In some situations it may be preferable to employ tools that act automatically with little discretionary input on the part of decision makers. This would particularly be the case in situations in which discretionary judgment is not trusted and therefore not accepted as an element of state action.

Regulation and property rights are the two tools that most clearly share the attribute of automaticity. Both are automatically available, though one may have to assert one's property rights in order to obtain their full value. Incentives can be designed to be automatic; this is particularly the case with indirect tax-based incentives. Direct incentives, on the other hand, are typically (though not always) designed around discretionary decision making.

Proposition 12 (Certainty): *The choice of tools should reflect the degree to which certainty about the implications of using a tool is a desirable attribute.*

Individual property owners, in particular, will be concerned about understanding the exact implications of any government action on their ownership of heritage properties. It is reasonable to expect certainty in the application of any state program as well as in the reaction of the state to any individual actions undertaken in response to that program.

As an attribute, certainty is clearly related to automaticity, but ownership and operation has to join regulation and property rights as the tools that are more likely to promote certainty. Information can always be ambiguous, and depending on the actual design of an incentive, it can either provide a great deal of certainty to the intended beneficiary, or it can also be somewhat ambiguous.

Proposition 13 (Design Goals): *The choice of tools should vary according to the goal that has been specified for a particular state intervention.*

The goals of state interventions might be classified into three broad groups: (1) searching for good results, (2) avoiding bad results, and (3) mitigating bad results that have already occurred. These categories provide a particularly useful guide in the field of heritage preservation. If one will be satisfied with avoiding bad results, one might turn to regulation, property rights, or ownership and operation. If one wants to promote good results, on the other hand, one might be more likely to rely on incentives and information strategies. Depending on the mitigation necessary, mitigating bad results might be best accomplished through incentives or ownership and operation.

Taken together these propositions suggest ways of thinking about the problem of tool choice in heritage preservation. Many other factors undoubtedly deserve to be taken into consideration, and there are undoubtedly other, more effective ways to present the ideas I have included here. What is most important at this point, however, is to model a different way of thinking about state action in heritage preservation so that we can begin to discuss thinking about program design through the choice of tools. It is in this spirit that I have presented these thirteen opening salvos.

A North American/Western European Model?

I am quite conscious of the fact that the propositions I have presented above proceed from a rational policy model of the world. Perhaps one might even characterize it as a North American/Western European model of public policy formulation and implementation. The world does not always operate so neatly, and one must recognize the complexity that will affect the choice of tools.[10]

In particular, there may be some doubt concerning the extent to which these tools can be applied in transitional economies or in developing countries. Such doubts were certainly expressed by many at the Salzburg Seminar. "Can action in the preservation/conservation arena wait for optimum conditions to appear?" they asked. "Might not valuable resources disappear in the meantime?" The tools, when presented in their most purified forms, appear to require a functioning capitalist market economy with a stable legal system that is integrated into a well-established and clearly understood private property system. How high does the level of "sophistication" of a society have to be for a tool to work?

A number of conditions clearly affect the deployment of the various tools, particularly in formerly socialist economies as well as in developing countries. These conditions may complicate the choice of tools and are ignored at the policy maker's peril. To wit:

- In many such countries there is a movement to transfer property in public hands—including land, churches, and historic buildings—to private ownership, making huge demands on the development of appropriate administrative and legal systems.
- At the same time, there is very little understanding of the implications of private property ownership and the conditions that can be attached to

such property. The idea of bargaining with government around incentives, for example, is quite unfamiliar.

- In the absence of a stable legal system, it is not surprising that there are few legal provisions for dealing with preservation or conservation matters.
- The tax system, which would normally provide resources and into which indirect incentives might be integrated, is often corrupt. Even when it does gather taxes, it does not necessarily distribute them according to relative need or even according to the law.
- The process of designing and implementing appropriate regulations is cumbersome, particularly when there is no consensus or understanding among the population that conservation and preservation have a priority in government action.
- Legal work in relation to conservation and preservation has no prestige among lawyers and the courts are not geared to handle such cases.
- The government does not have the credibility that is necessary for compliance, particularly when regulations are rarely enforced.
- The regulatory process is contaminated, particularly in the Third World, when the fear of having property listed as a heritage property, subject to government regulations, causes people to hide special properties or raze buildings. This is further complicated by the fact that transitional and developing economies may attach undue symbolic importance to new things, even if in cultural terms they are inferior, replacing natural materials with concrete, for example. In this case the education and information process needs to be particularly convincing. Yet, there is a down side here as well: information about the special merits of a property can be an invitation to theft or vandalism.
- Communication is often poor in these countries, particularly between the state and the citizenry, so information is hard to disseminate.
- Many of the tools—but incentives in particular—depend on a trust in government and credibility in its claim to be a partner in the preservation process. This trust is only rarely present.
- All of the tools (and any system within which they are used) call for a self-consciousness on the part of the population in relation to the government, which reveals itself in a willingness to act, organize, negotiate, and engage in the process of preservation. The populations of formerly socialist countries may not yet have such a relationship with their governments.

I list these examples not to suggest that choice is impossible in these circumstances or that implementation is likely to fail, but to point out that tool choice cannot, by its nature, advance far beyond other, more fundamental societal changes. Rather, a wider choice of tools will become available as the societal context stabilizes. This is not an excuse, however, for not considering a broader menu of tool possibilities right away. A major premise of this volume is that tool choices get restricted much too quickly and much too often, and we want to reopen choices that may have seemed closed. Nevertheless, it may be useful to explore constraints on tool choice more explicitly, and it is to this question that I now turn.

Constraints on the Availability of Tools

During the sessions of the Salzburg Seminar in which the faculty tried to move the discussion to a broader consideration of which tools would be the appropriate choice in which circumstances, we found ourselves continually bumping up against the argument that imagining a free choice among tools was counterproductive because of a set of strong contextual constraints on the availability of tools. We were unable to explore fully the extent to which these constraints were real as opposed to perceived, but given the force with which they were expressed, it is necessary, it seems to me, to consider a bit more carefully the degree to which such conditions actually limit the choice of tools. Up to this point, my discussion of the choice of tools has assumed a relatively unfettered choice among those tools, but would we be deceiving ourselves if we were to imagine that a relatively free choice among the various tools is possible? Are there powerful factors that affect the availability of various tools before one can even begin to consider the possibility of choice?

The constraint argument became prominent one morning at the Seminar when one of the Fellows from Central Europe took the floor and said, "Look. All this theory is fine, but the reality for us is that because the state now has only extremely limited resources, we have only one tool that we can even imagine using—regulation. We can't even use own and operate any more. None of the others will protect our heritage either." The irony in this statement, of course, is that its conclusion is that the heavy hand of a centralized state has to be replaced—with the heavy hand of a centralized state. Moreover, if no resources were available to consider deploying other tools, where would the resources come from to enforce these regulations? It will be useful for us to explore this possibility before adopting a model premised on relatively unconstrained choice.

By challenging the statement that there are powerful preexisting constraints on the availability of tools, I do not mean to belittle the very real frustration that the statement represents, nor do I mean to suggest that the constraints are imaginary or trivial. But I do want to suggest the possibility that a full consideration of the tool options might allow one to work creatively around real constraints and recognize that others are illusory. In order to understand the various constraints, let me divide them roughly into three categories: economic, political, and structural.

Economic Constraints

It would be hard to deny that in many countries there are fewer resources available to the state than there once were, and this is as true with the portion of the state budget dedicated to preservation activities as it is overall. Moreover, in many countries there is considerable political and ideological pressure to shrink the size of the state, so the question of whether more resources could be made available to the state through increased taxes on the citizenry has become moot. Government action costs money—even a strategy that relies primarily on information has costs associated with it—but we know very little about the marginal benefit to preservation that might come from investing available resources in the use of one tool as compared to another. Would an additional dollar offered through an incentive or spent in an information campaign produce more preservation than, say, an additional dollar used in ownership and operation? This would not be an easy question to answer in any event, but the preservation sector is not yet even trained to ask it.

In an environment with limited resources, regulation becomes attractive because it appears cost-free—we will just require someone to do something—and that, I think, is why many countries view regulation as the only available tool. But there is an opportunity cost to that individual when his or her actions are changed by regulation (that is, when he is forced to choose a path of action that he otherwise would not choose), even though the net social benefit may be positive.

One need not accept, however, the premise that resources available to the state for preservation activities though current tax revenues will be limited or perhaps even shrink. This is one constraint around which there has been considerable inventive activity, and a wide variety of new revenue-raising instruments have been used for heritage preservation, effectively relaxing this constraint. In the next section of this chapter, I review a number of examples as to how these "new" public resources have been garnered.

We should recognize that the resource constraint becomes more severe not just through caps on, and cuts in, public budgets. Increases in the public's perception about what resources ought to be preserved, and public recognition that preservation is a problem requiring the involvement of the state both increase the demand for preservation. Is there any place where the register of historic resources is shrinking? Seen from this perspective, an increasingly tight economic constraint may actually be a sign of success (the demand for preservation has risen) rather than of failure (not all of the increased demand for preservation can be satisfied).

It may also be that the value of incentives will be limited by another type of economic constraint that derives from differences between local economies and the international economy. To take but one example, in the Czech Republic the prices of faithful restorations of heritage buildings are high because of the expertise that is necessary, but because taxes (and the tax base) in the local economy are low, it is virtually impossible to design a tax incentive and costly to design a direct incentive that will have any substantial effect.

Another economic constraint may arise because of the close link between preservation of the built heritage and the real estate development industry. This link has prompted a joining of government action to private action, particularly through the increased use of incentives. But incentives that appear attractive and generous in a booming real estate market may be completely ineffective in a weak real estate market. At the same time, if one's goal is simply to make a profit without unnecessary complications, in a booming real estate market it may not be necessary to take advantage of any preservation incentive. In a way, these points are only a subset of more general considerations. In a strong economy, resources are available in both the public and private sectors to support preservation, and many different initiatives become possible. In a weak economy, historic resources may not be endangered through destruction, but there may be little incentive to invest in them. Somewhere in between is where an economic balance is most likely to be achieved.

These examples notwithstanding, it is clear that in many countries the previous governmental system was highly reliant on a rich resource base. This is no longer true. The tools of choice have to change as government becomes less involved in doing things itself and more involved in creating the conditions within which preservation action will take place.

Political Constraints

One disadvantage of taking a tools approach to the study of government action in any particular realm is that it is all too easy to give the mistaken impression that one imagines the state as being all-powerful, deciding what it wants to do from a full range of possible actions and then doing it. But the state's actions are limited not only by money, but also by a number of other considerations, some of which might be termed political. In this sense, the state may behave in ways that will constrain its own choices among the tools. Again, my goal is not to catalog political constraints, or even to offer a water-tight definition of political constraints, as much as it is to recognize their potency.

In this volume we have been relatively silent on the formulation of goals for preservation and, more generally, on the formulation of the public policies that incorporate those goals. We wanted to focus attention instead on the choice of tools and we believe that one is confronted with the same possibilities and the same choices whatever the actual configuration of that policy. However, there do seem to be some cases in which policy goals constrain the choice of tool. For example, governments can be reticent to change their use of tools because they view preservation policy as a way of promoting national pride and the image of the state itself rather than as a way of protecting the asset. Such a view is much more likely to lead to ownership and operation or regulation than to one of the other tools. In this example, the goal leads to a particular choice of tool.

In our discussions at the Salzburg Seminar an issue that came up time and time again was the issue of trust. Lack of trust was seen as a major limit on the effectiveness of government action. This came up most clearly, perhaps, in the context of information. On what basis should one trust information that is provided by the state? But it came up elsewhere as well. Can we trust the government to deliver the part of the bargain it offers through an incentive? Moreover, the view that government provides a locus of expertise on various issues seems to be waning. If this is happening because of a sense that there are multiple loci of expertise in any society, then it is a good change, but if it is happening because of a lack of trust, there is cause for concern.

The issue of trust goes both ways. Citizens may not trust the government, as in the examples above, or the government might not trust its citizens or citizen groups. The latter issue has taken on renewed importance as governments have begun to rely more on intermediary organizations such as nonprofit organizations, foundations, and various quasi-autonomous nongovernmental organizations to help provide socially desirable goods and services. The birth of such organizations has been fraught with difficulty in many countries, and at the heart of these difficulties is the question of whether or not the government is prepared to trust these entities, given that they present independent centers of power and influence and may, on some issues, actually oppose the government's own views and policies. One of the participants at the Seminar picked up this theme, pointing out that "to develop a culture of preservation one has to believe in the generosity of people." If it doesn't trust its citizens, the state might well find its choice among tools constrained, since it will hesitate to use tools such as incentives and information.

Related to the issue of trust is the issue of certainty. To adjust one's own individual decisions concerning heritage property, one needs to understand the policy framework within which one is operating: What rules apply to me? What can I take advantage of? How do I know what my full set of options is? What will be the implications of the various actions I might take?

Finally, it is not always possible to tell whether a tool has been explicitly chosen. In a particular context, a particular tool may only be used because its use has become familiar or even traditional. This is a constraint of a different type.

Structural Constraints

Some constraints have less to do with the politics of operating in the public sphere than with the structure of that sphere. For example, not all tools are available to all levels of government, though the actual correspondence between tools and level of government varies from country to country. This correspondence may be specified in a nation's constitution, which defines and limits the powers of various levels and branches of government, or it may be more informal, relying on years of sorting out and developing conventions for ways of conducting the state's business. In the United States, for example, basic governmental powers reside with the states. The states have granted a limited number of powers to the federal government and grant a considerable degree of power to local government. One implication of this division of powers is that regulation is firmly seated at the state and local levels but that the federal government has very few regulatory powers. As a result, when it wishes to act in the preservation sphere, it has to turn more to incentives, information, and ownership and operation and away from regulation.[11] In the many countries where there is not yet a strong acceptance of regional, provincial (state), or local autonomy, the central government may still only be doing what it thinks it does well—own, operate, and regulate. The level of government may, in many places, provide a powerful constraint as to what tools can actually be used.

The question of appropriate level of government has taken on new importance as states, among them the member states of the European Union, have embraced the principle of subsidiarity. The idea of subsidiarity is that action is taken by the lowest level of government possible so that the decisions made and the actions taken will be made as close as possible to the citizens who will be affected. This principle has led to a rearrangement of the levels of government responsible for particular programs, but it has not necessarily led to a redistribution of the available tools among levels of government. It is possible that under subsidiarity there may not be a match between the appropriate level of government and the appropriate tool.

Another type of structural constraint comes into play when we turn our attention to transnational governmental organizations. While often appearing to be quite powerful, these organizations typically have limited powers and limited tools at their disposal. In particular, because they are severely limited in their ability to own and operate, regulate, and redefine the property rights concerning heritage resources, information and incentives become the mainstays of their heritage programs. The conclusion that Hood has come to in his broad look at the tools of government is that the full range of tools is neither employed nor available at either of the extremes—transnational governmental entities, on the one hand, and local governments, on the other.[12]

Another structural constraint may result from how preservation responsibilities are arranged within, as opposed to across, levels of government. As
preservation responsibilities are parceled out among various government ministries or agencies a de facto choice may be made as to the availability of various tools. Some government agencies, by their inherent structure, may be unable to own and operate heritage properties, for example, while others may be
able to use only this tool. Of course, this constraint may be easier to overcome
through governmental reorganization than constraints that are stipulated by a
constitution. It also is true that some tools may just work more comfortably in
certain corners of government than in others; at the Seminar, Dino Milinovic,
the secretary general of the Croation Commission for the United Nations Educational, Scientific, and Cultural Organization (UNESCO), summarized this
idea as, "Each tool finds its harbor in a different segment of the government."

A structural constraint of a rather different sort may result from government's being the only actor capable of undertaking action vis-à-vis heritage
preservation. What I have in mind here are particularly those places in which
there is not yet a strong nonprofit, nongovernmental sector involved in heritage
preservation and where there is little tradition of, or few resources for, individual citizen action. A system of interventions based upon the presumption that
other actors in the infrastructure will exist, respond, and participate, may have
difficulty taking root in such constrained circumstances. Here the constraint
that can and ought to be relaxed has little to do with preservation per se; it is
tied up instead with the considerable efforts being made in many countries to
encourage the creation of a "civil society," in which citizens would become
more engaged in civic life through a variety of voluntary, nongovernmental,
and nonprofit groups, associations, and institutions. Legislation defining and
regulating the nonprofit sector, changing attitudes about the relative role of the
public and private sectors, the growth of privately available resources, and
time are the ingredients that together will relax this constraint on the choice of
tools.

A final structural constraint on the free use of tools, one that is particularly
critical in the emerging democracies of Central and Eastern Europe, is the lack
of clearly defined property rights, which are necessary for most of the tools to
operate well. In places where private property has not been a primary societal
value and where rapid changes in the system of ownership have led to considerable confusion, the government must define, parcel out, and enforce property rights to establish a clear foundation for the other tools of preservation.

Taken together, these constraints are daunting. Indeed, in some places they
may seem to rule out all of the tools: ownership and operation because it is

expensive and there are only limited resources available; regulation because there is a fear and distrust of a heavy-handed state; information because the population does not trust the state to provide accurate information; incentives because the state and its citizens do not trust one another to fulfill their respective parts of the bargain, the resources to offer incentives are limited, and there is no infrastructure of private interests toward which incentives are typically targeted; and property rights because such rights are poorly defined and ambiguous. But a vigilant optimist (to appropriate a phrase used by Gordon Metz, special projects director of the Mayibuye Centre for History and Culture in Cape Town, South Africa, and a participant at the Seminar) will view each of these constraints as a creative challenge. If there is no societal consensus about the importance of preservation as a public good, however, it will be very hard to design ways for the state to act in the preservation system, and this lack of consensus itself will become the binding constraint on state action. Consensus is a necessary prior condition.

Finding the Resources to Pay for "New" Tools

As governments make fuller use of the preservation action toolbox, new programs and new uses of tools are often grafted onto preexisting preservation programs rather than replacing them. In a period in which the perception, if not the reality, is that public resources are increasingly limited, an important question becomes how the state is going to come up with the additional resources necessary to fund those programs.

This search for increased resources has also intersected with another trend, a desire to achieve a better match between those who reap the benefits of public programs and those who pay for them. It is increasingly difficult to justify state programs in which the benefits are perceived as accruing to individuals who do not bear an appropriate share of the costs of the program. Admittedly, precise calculations of incidence are difficult to pin down in the preservation sector, particularly since many of the societal benefits accrue to future generations. Nevertheless, the preservation sector should be concerned about the impression that the benefits of preservation activity accrue mainly to a relatively limited population of well-off individuals, and it should heed the fact that this criticism has been clearly voiced in recent debates concerning the state's cultural policies more generally.

Together these two factors have led to a creative search for new revenue sources, sources that can simply provide more money as well as sources that can bring the costs and benefits more into line with one another. The Council of Europe has been particularly instrumental in identifying new approaches to financing restoration and rehabilitation of the architectural heritage and has published a series of reports on this question, but one does not have to look too far to observe considerable innovation in finding new resources that have been channeled into preservation programs:[13]

- The State of Arkansas uses a special tax on real estate transfers to finance its historic preservation programs.
- Florida offers a higher incentive for private donations to its Community Contribution Tax Incentive Program, whose income is used in part for preservation programs.
- In Kansas the revenues from a mortgage registration tax go into the state's Heritage Trust Fund for Historic Preservation.
- The country of Nepal imposes a Heritage Tax upon departure from its airport.
- In the United Kingdom, proceeds from the new national lottery are dedicated, in part, to heritage projects through the Department of National Heritage.
- Similarly, in the German *Land* of Baden-Württemberg, preservation funds are supplied from a specified portion of the income of the state lottery. In Lower Saxony a portion of preservation grant funds is derived from a state gambling tax and a portion from interest on natural oil production.
- In Zurich, Switzerland, money for preservation grants comes from two sources: the Fund for Public Purposes, which is supplied by proceeds from the canton's lottery, and the Fund for the Support of Efforts to Protect the Heritage.
- Vienna (and Salzburg and Graz) has created a Historic Town Center Preservation Fund that is funded through the proceeds of the "Cultural Schilling Law," which places a 10 percent tax on radio and television license fees. This fund is used for loans, interest payments, and grants for preservation work not otherwise eligible for support and beyond the financial means of property owners.
- In Dubrovnik, Yugoslavia, a particularly complicated revenue-raising structure was put in place to restore buildings damaged by the earthquake of 1979. In addition to state funds, a particularly rich number of other sources were created and/or tapped: an increase of 0.15 percent in the rate of the local tax on workers' personal incomes; an increase of 1 percent in the special municipal sales tax; special funds from the sale of mutual aid badges; a special 10 percent municipal tax on sales of souvenirs, handicrafts, and fine jewelry; a special extra rent on business premises; a return of 10 percent on the fees collected from organized tours of architectural heritage; and a return of 10 percent on the fees collected for the Ploce-Srd cableway.

What is particularly interesting about Dubrovnik's revenue-raising structure is how it targets those who are likely to benefit in one way or another from the restoration of the built heritage: visitors and tourists who come, in part, because of Dubrovnik's historic resources; and owners of business in the historic city, particularly those who benefit from sales to visitors; as well as those who live and work in the city on a daily basis. This is an example of an attempt to achieve a better alignment between those who pay and those who benefit.

Another approach to identifying "new" resources for preservation has been to invent financing schemes that work simply to keep resources within a particular sector. For example:

- In France the Service des Monuments Historiques has a degree of financial independence from the government because it has the right to retain income from historic buildings that it owns and operates. These funds form the Caisse Nationale des Monuments Historiques.
- In Mexico City it has been proposed that in certain circumstances developers be allowed to purchase the right to exceed the otherwise allowable intensity of land use in specified areas adjacent to historic properties; the money raised would be used for the restoration of these properties, among other uses.[14]
- In the United States, a popular mechanism is tax increment financing in which borrowing for preservation improvements is structured so that the loan can be paid back out of the increased property taxes that will be realized on the improved properties.

My point here has not been to provide a complete catalog of innovative funding practices. Rather, I have tried to suggest that considerable effort has gone into figuring out ways to relax the primary economic resource constraint on preservation action by the state. This, in turn, suggests that many of the constraints one perceives may not be as binding as they first appear.

A consideration of constraints can be discouraging; action can seem to be tightly circumscribed before one ever has an opportunity to consider choices among tools. In the last pages, I have attempted to demonstrate two things: (1) that the perceived constraints are often not real or, with a bit of creativity, can be lifted and (2) that even if a constraint prevents the use of one tool, it can often be avoided by the choice of another—one simply has to consider the full menu of possibilities. Nevertheless, an analysis of the existing constraints can be important when one is considering the appropriate and available set of tools.

A Sixth Tool?

John de Monchaux and I have had more than enough experience with our students in the Department of Urban Studies and Planning at the Massachusetts Institute of Technology to know that once a professor says something as definitive as, "There are only five tools of government action," students are immediately convinced that we must be wrong. Any pronouncement this precise invites disagreement. Surely there must be six, or seven, or more.

There have been many attempts to categorize the tools of government action, though their authors have not always worried about making sure that the categories proposed in their schema are both mutually exclusive and exhaustive. Hood, in the book to which we have referred so often, delineates eight basic tools of government.[15] Salamon, in another volume particularly helpful to our thinking, without claiming completeness, discusses six different tools of government action, and his list, too, is rather different from ours.[16] Salamon has also collected and summarized ten other authors' attempts to categorize government tools; these lists range from a low of five tools (though different ones from ours) to a high of sixteen. At yet another extreme, there is a point of view from which one might argue that—with the possible exception of information—there is only *one* form of government action, the definition and apportionment of property rights, and that every government action can be understood in terms of how it distributes property rights among the various interested parties including the state itself.[17] While there is much to learn from this point of view, our sense is that one slice of pizza, no matter how big it is, will not provide a balanced analytical meal.

Our aim has not been to convince our readers that our five-fold categorization is the best such scheme; rather, we have offered it as a scheme that has helped us understand the options available in preservation program design. In the end, the best test is whether a categorization scheme adequately captures the variation one sees in the tools of government and whether it helps elucidate the choices that government can actually make among the various tools, however they are identified and defined. Nevertheless, it is useful to ask whether there are any candidates as a sixth tool, a topic that engendered considerable discussion at the Salzburg Seminar.

A number of Seminar participants pointed out that planning plays an important role in heritage preservation and proposed it as a sixth tool of government action. But the desire to characterize planning as a different, sixth tool, I believe, derives mostly from a difference in how planning is viewed across countries. Phil Herr, an M.I.T. colleague, defines "planning" as the development of a set of intended actions to which all of the parties that have contributed to it are committed. This view, it seems to me, sees planning as an information tool resulting in a (three-dimensional) statement of desires and intents. But this may be a uniquely American view of planning. In other countries, the plan, once it is formally adopted, has the force of law behind it; that's to say, it becomes more of a regulatory tool. In other words, the transnational ambiguity of planning makes it a different type of tool in different contexts. If one does not recognize that ambiguity, then planning somehow looks like a different beast, perhaps even like a sixth tool.

We also discussed education as a possible sixth tool. Here, too, while one can argue compellingly that education is a separate tool of government action, we feel that it is preferable to view education as a subset of the information tool. But our categorization is not intended as a statement about the relative importance of education as compared to other possible tools. We suspect that many candidates for the sixth tool would be proposed based on their perceived importance rather than on their conceptual distinctiveness. If this becomes the rule for categorization, of course, one rapidly ends up with a long list of tools, each important in its own way.

The points about planning and education, and, indeed, about the definition and distribution of property rights, already included in our schema as a separate tool, do suggest one analytical path that might be worth exploring. It may well be that the order of government actions is important. Perhaps, planning, education, and property rights might be better thought of as a set of tools that establish the framework within which the other tools then operate. They create the conditions within which others actors in the preservation system as well as the government itself act. We are not partisans of this view, but we do recognize that the question of order of action is an important one.

If the focus of one's categorization system is on the choices that government can make, then there is a sixth possibility: the government can choose to do nothing. It can choose simply not to open its toolbox. In many instances this may be a viable option that deserves consideration, even though it doesn't quite fit the metaphor of a tool. Of course, the state might decide to do nothing for a variety of reasons: it might believe that a particular action is more appropriately or more effectively left to the private or nonprofit sectors with no government intervention; it might believe that none of the tools available will work in a particular instance; or it may believe that there is insufficient citizen support for an intervention and that if it does not act, citizen support will eventually grow to the point where the state will be able to intervene. Cynics and skeptics will also point out that the state might choose to say it is doing something about a problem but do nothing. But others, who have been working in the preservation arena and have been confronting what they perceive as a tremendous need coupled with a tremendous shortage of resources, might put a more positive spin on doing nothing—if doing nothing is a viable option, then the government must have already done something!

The usefulness of a set of tools is, finally, that the set, when taken together, allows you to get the job done. If the set is incomplete, it will be more difficult to get the job done. In the end, it is as simple as that.

Becoming a Better Designer of Policy Interventions

In this chapter I have just begun to scratch the surface of the ideas and issues in making an appropriate choice among the tools of action. Such an inquiry should enable those who are charged with implementing government policy to become better designers of the policy interventions for which they are responsible, and this should be no less true in the field of heritage preservation than in any other field of state involvement.

But thinking about the state's toolbox does not come naturally. Constraints on choice seem to many to loom larger than the advantages that opening up the true range of choice might bring. Hood, in arguing for a tools-based approach to thinking about state action, points out that a tools-based analysis provides three important ways of thinking about state action: (1) sorting state actions into a relatively small number of categories serves as a "variety reducer" and focuses the analyst on a set of generic attributes of state action; similarities become as important as differences in understanding the options that are open to the state; (2) at the same time, thinking about tools both separately and in combination serves as a "variety generator," pointing the way to new combinations and possibilities that haven't been tried before (indeed, thinking carefully about the set of logical possibilities may suggest avenues that have not yet been explored); and (3) characterizing state actions as a limited set of tools offers a basis on which comparative analysis can be conducted, a powerful tool in its own right, enabling cross-contextual learning.[18]

It is not enough, of course, to choose the right tool for the job. One also has to design that tool. When one thinks of factors that affect the use of tools, one needs to think of both those factors that affect the initial choice of a tool, which has been the focus of this chapter, and those factors that affect tool design. Tool design has been considered at some length in previous chapters, providing eloquent testimony to the variety that exists within each category of tool. There are undoubtedly also factors that then affect how one uses the tool once it has been chosen and designed.

Salamon concludes his inquiry into the tools of the state with a call for research of three types: descriptive work to identify the operating characteristics of the tools now in widespread use, analytic work to develop new ways of describing and comparing and contrasting the various tools, and empirical work to explore the relationship between the tools chosen, the program design that was based on that choice, and its outcome.[19] His general plea is no less applicable to the field of heritage preservation. While some progress has been made on the descriptive side, most notably through the work and publications of the International Council on Monuments and Sites (ICOMOS) and the International Symposium on World Heritage Towns,[20] with this volume perhaps making a contribution as well, there is considerable work remaining along the analytic and empirical dimensions.

Hood ends his similar inquiry into the tools of government by concluding, "Success in government, in the future as well as in the past, will depend on its ability to apply a relatively fixed set of basic tools imaginatively to each new situation as it arises."[21] This seems right to us.

Nevertheless, with increasing constraints on, and suspicions of, the state, it has become harder and harder to think of the state as a completely independent, exogenous actor that makes cut-and-dried choices from its toolbox. As we have suggested a number of times in this volume, the state is increasingly forging relationships with other actors in society to pursue public goals, and these partnerships have become the hallmark of state action in a new era. We would be remiss if we did not notice and speculate upon this development, and in the second part of this volume we consider these evolving relationships, to complement our single-minded focus in the first part of this volume on the state as a central actor (if not *the* central actor) in heritage preservation.

Notes

1. A number of these examples have been contributed by the participants in the Salzburg Seminar that occasioned this book, and their ideas have informed every page of this volume. I would be remiss in not recognizing their contributions to the current chapter in particular, which was written after the Salzburg Seminar sessions and was able to take full advantage of the rich and provocative discussions that took place there. To the participants: I hope that I have represented your voices well.
2. Lester Salamon, ed., *Beyond Privatization: The Tools of Government Action* (Washington, D.C.: The Urban Institute Press, 1989), 258.
3. Christopher C. Hood, *The Tools of Government* (Chatham, N.J.: Chatham House Publishers, 1986), 136.
4. Hood, *The Tools of Government*, chap. 8. Hood call these points "canons" and explicitly spells out only four of the five, but the fifth is clearly assumed.
5. International Symposium on World Heritage Towns, *Safeguarding Historic Urban Ensembles in a Time of Change: A Management Guide* (Quebec: Organization of World Heritage Towns, 1991), D1.

6. Harry Hillman-Chartrand and Claire McCaughey, "The Arm's Length Principle and the Arts: An International Perspective—Past, Present, and Future," in *Who's to Pay for the Arts? The International Search for Models of Support*, ed. Milton C. Cummings, Jr. and J. Mark Davidson Schuster (New York: American Council for the Arts, 1989): 43–80.

7. Hood uses the term "scalability" to refer to this characteristic of the various tools. Hood, *The Tools of Government*, 146.

8. This proposition inevitably leads one to two interrelated questions: "To whom does the heritage belong?" and "To whom should the heritage belong?" One would not even consider this an issue if one did not think that there was a different answer to this question than that revealed through the current pattern of legal ownership of property.

9. I am grateful to Robert Stipe for pointing out this issue to me.

10. I am particularly grateful to Suzanne de Monchaux, on whose notes from the Salzburg Seminar workshops much of this section of the chapter is based.

11. For a detailed explanation of how this works in the United States, see particularly the first and last chapters of Robert E. Stipe and Antoinette J. Lee, *The American Mosaic: Preserving a Nation's Heritage* (Washington, D.C.: US/ICOMOS, 1987). But note that the actual form of federalism in the United States is constantly shifting and the balance of power and authority among national, state, and local governments remains in a constant state of transition.

12. Hood, *The Tools of Government*, 122.

13. These examples, as well as others, can be found in Council of Europe, *Funding the Architectural Heritage*, Architectural Heritage Reports and Studies, no. 8, report of the York Colloquy (Strasbourg: Council of Europe, 1987); Council of Europe, *New Ways of Funding the Restoration of the Architectural Heritage*, Architectural Heritage Reports and Studies, no. 13, report of the Messina Colloquy (Strasbourg: Council of Europe, 1988); Council of Europe, *Funding the Architectural Heritage*, report drawn up by a group of specialists of the Council of Europe (Strasbourg: Council of Europe, December 1991); International Symposium on World Heritage Towns, *Safeguarding Historic Urban Ensembles in a Time of Change: A Management Guide*; Susan Robinson and John E. Petersen, *Fiscal Incentives for Historic Preservation* (Washington, D.C.: Government Finance Research Center of the Government Finance Officers Association, January 1989); Gregory E. Andrews, ed., *Tax Incentives for Historic Preservation* (Washington, D.C.: The Preservation Press, 1980); and Constance E. Beaumont, *State Tax Incentives for Historic Preservation* (Washington, D.C.: National Trust for Historic Preservation, Center for Preservation Policy Studies, May 1992).

14. I do not know if this proposal has ever been implemented.

15. Without exploring the full details here, Hood begins by identifying the four basic resources of government—nodality, treasure, authority, and organization—and then explores how each can be drawn upon by detecting tools (moving towards government) and effecting tools (moving away from government). This leads him to a four by two matrix, or eight basic types of tools. Christopher C. Hood, *The Tools of Government* , 1–7.

16. The authors that Salamon assembled to contribute to his volume discuss direct

government, grants, loan guarantees, tax expenditures (tax incentives), regulations, and government corporations as different tools of government action. Salamon, *Beyond Privatization.*

17. The writings of B. J. Pearce provide an excellent example of how taking this point of view might lead one to characterize government's tools in a rather different way. See B. J. Pearce, "Property Rights Versus Development Control: A Preliminary Evaluation of Alternative Planning Policy Instruments," *Town Planning Review* 52, no. 1 (January 1981): 47–60; and B. J. Pearce, "Instruments for Land Policy: A Classification," *Urban Law and Policy* 3, no. 2 (June 1980): 115–55.

18. Hood, *The Tools of Government*, 115.

19. Salamon, *Beyond Privatization*, 260–61.

20. See particularly the series of reports edited by Robert E. Stipe and published by the U.S. Committee of ICOMOS, Historic Preservation in Foreign Countries (later retitled Historic Preservation in Other Countries); and *Safeguarding Historic Urban Ensembles in a Time of Change.*

21. Hood, *The Tools of Government*, 168.

References

Andrews, Gregory E., ed. *Tax Incentives for Historic Preservation.* Washington, D.C.: The Preservation Press, 1980.

Beaumont, Constance E. *State Tax Incentives for Historic Preservation.* Washington, D.C.: National Trust for Historic Preservation, Center for Preservation Policy Studies, May 1992.

Council of Europe. *Funding the Architectural Heritage.* Architectural Heritage Reports and Studies, no. 8, report of the York Colloquy. Strasbourg: Council of Europe, 1987.

Council of Europe. *Funding the Architectural Heritage.* Report drawn up by a group of specialists of the Council of Europe. Strasbourg: Council of Europe, December 1991.

Council of Europe. *New Ways of Funding the Restoration of the Architectural Heritage.* Architectural Heritage Reports and Studies, no. 13, report of the Messina Colloquy. Strasbourg: Council of Europe, 1988.

Hillman-Chartrand, Harry, and Claire McCaughey, "The Arm's Length Principle and the Arts: An International Perspective—Past, Present, and Future," in *Who's to Pay for the Arts? The International Search for Models of Support*, edited by Milton C. Cummings, Jr., and J. Mark Davidson Schuster, 43–80. New York: American Council for the Arts, 1989.

Hood, Christopher C. *The Tools of Government.* Chatham, N.J.: Chatham House Publishers, 1986.

International Symposium on World Heritage Towns. *Safeguarding Historic Urban Ensembles in a Time of Change: A Management Guide.* Quebec: Organization of World Heritage Towns, 1991.

Pearce, B. J. "Instruments for Land Policy: A Classification." *Urban Law and Policy* 3 (1980): 115–55.

Pearce, B. J. "Property Rights Versus Development Control: A Preliminary Evaluation of Alternative Planning Policy Instruments." *Town Planning Review* 52, no. 1 (January 1981): 47–60.

Robinson, Susan, and John E. Petersen. *Fiscal Incentives for Historic Preservation.* Washington, D.C.: Government Finance Research Center of the Government Finance Officers Association, January 1989.

Salamon, Lester M., ed. *Beyond Privatization: The Tools of Government Action.* Washington, D.C.: The Urban Institute Press, 1989. Chapters particularly relevant to this chapter include: Lester M. Salamon, "The Changing Tools of Government Action: An Overview"; Lester M. Salamon and Michael S. Lund, "The Tools Approach: Basic Analytics"; and Lester M. Salamon, "Conclusion: Beyond Privatization."

Stipe, Robert E., series ed. Historic Preservation in Foreign Countries, later retitled Historic Preservation in Other Countries. Washington, D.C.: United States Committee of the International Council on Monuments and Sites, various dates. Volumes in the series include:

> Dale, Anthony. *Volume I: France, Great Britain, Ireland, The Netherlands, and Denmark.* 1982.
> Will, Margaret Thomas. *Volume II: Federal Republic of Germany, Switzerland, and Austria.* 1984.
> Gleye, Paul H., and Waldemar Szczerba. *Volume III: Poland.* 1989.
> Leimenstoll, Jo Ramsay. *Volume IV: Turkey.* 1989.

Stipe, Robert E., and Antoinette J. Lee. *The American Mosaic: Preserving a Nation's Heritage.* Washington, D.C.: US/ICOMOS, 1987. Particularly relevant chapters include: Robert E. Stipe, "Historic Preservation: The Process and the Actors"; John M. Fowler, "The Federal Government as Standard Bearer"; Elizabeth A. Lyon, "The States: Preservation in the Middle"; and J. Myrick Howard, "Where the Action Is: Preservation and Local Governments."

II

Partnerships for Action

When Public Meets Private

At a time when, on a global scale, the need for preservation intervention is so great, and the available resources seemingly so scarce, it is clear that neither the state nor private organizations can afford to act alone. This pushes historic preservation beyond the tools of state action in the direction of more creative partnerships, often of an international character. Since it can no longer be assumed that the state will be the only active—or effective—agent in cultural preservation, the onus is on combinations of other players to take a greater role, including nongovernmental organizations (NGOs), quasi-autonomous nongovernmental organizations (QUANGOs), nonprofit organizations, corporate entities, and private individuals, often acting independently of government participation. By building cross-sector relationships that will permit risks and costs, as well as benefits and profits, to be to be shared, organizations involved in historic preservation will address not only the dire problem of funding, but also the challenge of gaining access to the media for the dissemination of information. As J. Mark Schuster has observed elsewhere in this volume with respect to incentives, "In an era in which there is an increasing perception that public resources are limited and that private initiative should be taken more seriously (even as a guide for public sector intervention itself), forms of intervention that draw out and promote multiple partners are generally seen as a good thing."

Partnerships with the private sector, moreover, can provide access to management and business resources that will be valuable in the day-to-day operation of a cultural site or institution. Both NGOs and QUANGOs offer expertise in organizational design and administration, as do corporate partners. Corporate partners also bring with them sophisticated public relations resources and relationships with the media—factors that would surely aid in deploying information on behalf of preservation projects—as well as clout in political circles where regulations and policy are determined. Industry groups can also play a role. One particularly active organization is the American

Cultural Resources Association, which was started in 1995 to serve the needs of the cultural resources industry. With one thousand member firms, employing ten thousand people working in a variety of fields, including historic preservation, history, archaeology, architectural history, historical architecture, and landscape architecture, the association promotes the professional, ethical, and business practices of the industry through lobbying, education and training, and networking. The appendixes to this volume list a number of such useful organizations with complete information about how to contact them.

Of course, the need for partnerships is driven by economics. Squeezed in a vice of rising costs and diminishing government spending, historic preservation projects need all the help they can find to ensure their survival. By looking for financial support from the private sector, including nonprofit institutions and nongovernmental organizations, historic preservation groups can increase their ability to do the work that must be done, without tapping the same source (the government) over and over. If, as Dasha Havel points out in her essay, it is impossible for government to handle the full range of responsibilities involved in conservation, then other forces must be brought to bear upon the problem. In Stefano Bianca's terms, "a fan of well-differentiated modes of intervention" is desirable, and the diversification offered by the many possible combinations of partnership structures permits that wider range of resources and skills to be brought together. On the one hand, Lester Borley describes a national context in which private initiative is not only accepted, it is expected and highly institutionalized through a wide variety of partnerships; on the other hand, Havel speaks from a national context in which private initiatives and partnerships are rather astonishing ideas, and the potential partners that she identifies will have to be convinced to accept the level of collaboration she would find desirable. According to Borley, the active role of nongovernmental organizations in the care of a nation's cultural capital extends beyond the role of watchdog over preservation concerns. Borley points out that the rise in global tourism especially has created a demand for the kind of information that private and nongovernmental organizations can best provide. The field of public/private partnerships in preservation is a complex and quickly changing one. These chapters help to frame the issues in a way that helps us better understand the institutional context within which government tools will have to operate to be most effective.

Partnerships involve each of the tools described in Part I of this volume, but probably are most directly related to government ownership and operation, financial and legal incentives, and information; certain aspects of partnerships (notably, the means by which associations of NGOs, QUANGOs, individuals, nonprofits and corporations can act as lobbying groups) are also related to issues of public policy and regulation. In general, partnership tends to enter the discussion in relation to the ever-pressing problem of money, and the most common image of partnership in cultural preservation involves a major business with deep pockets and either altruistic or ulterior motives (such as breaking into new markets or improving public image) working alongside a nonprofit organization and the federal or local government. This emphasis on business connections is an important element in Havel's essay, in which she relates partnerships to analogous phenomena in biology and business. The idea is to set up a "win-win" situation for both parties, a symbiosis or joint venture in which risks and rewards are shared. She also stresses the need to break down the fixed notion of a donor/recipient relationship, which must be replaced by relationships in which greater equality characterizes the participants, again more along the lines of business agreements.

International business is ripe for connections of this kind. The interaction of corporations and culture is in an era of redefinition due in large part to the perception among business leaders that, rather than being simply a write-off for charitable contributions, cultural projects can be profitable. One example of this is the competition among software companies in the United States and Europe to buy the digital reproduction rights to the cultural treasures of Europe's museums, prompting Microsoft chairman Bill Gates to attempt (unsuccessfully) to structure a deal for the rights to the images from the Louvre in Paris, and Olivetti to make a similar (successful) arrangement with the Uffizi in Florence. These images would be put on CD-ROM or made available on the Internet. Museums and arts organizations have for decades been aware of the importance of partnerships with corporate sponsors, and in particular major international corporations such as Philip Morris, Coca-Cola, Credit Lyonnaise, Ford Motor Company, and AT&T—to name just a few—have used high-profile agreements with important cultural institutions to increase their market presence or to improve their image in communities that patronize the arts. In the case of a few corporate sponsors for museum exhibitions, including Tiffany, Cartier, Ferragamo, and Mattel Toys (which sponsored a Barbie doll retrospective), the perception of conflict of interest and self-promotion was too great to ignore, and controversy detracted from the impact of the exhibitions. But these examples do not provide a reason for not developing partnerships; they simply point out that one should do so with caution.

One way to look at what historic preservation institutions and their corporate or NGO partners stand to gain through their interaction is the notion of intellectual capital or cultural capital. Recognized as a new measure of knowledge-based competitive advantages, it is not just an attribute of top management at major corporations. Intellectual capital is the kind of asset that a small organization can lay claim to as well. Not easily quantified, the added "market value" of knowledge and culture is attracting the attention of investment and management experts. The concept of intellectual capital became popular in 1994 through a series of books and feature articles in business magazines such as *Fortune*, *Business Week*, and *Forbes*. The phrase was coined by Andre Alkiewicz of Perception International, a Connecticut-based think tank that advises corporate clients as well as the White House. Those who believe strongly in the notion of intellectual and cultural capital know that it has the potential to redress the economic and political imbalance between developing nations and developed nations, or between powerful corporations and their financially less potent allies in historic preservation projects. Even if a small entity possesses financial assets that are a fraction of a major multinational, they can be on the same level in terms of intellectual or cultural capital.

While intellectual capital may be the objective of some corporations that become involved in preservation, others target assets of a more traditional kind in the form of historic sites and buildings that can be developed for commercial purposes. The most prominent example in the United States is unquestionably the Disney Corporation, which is currently playing a tremendous role in the redevelopment of Manhattan's Times Square, in part through the renovation of landmark theaters. Another, less famous American corporation involved in similar activities is the Kimpton Hotel and Restaurant Group, a large (3,135 employees), San Francisco-based operator of mainly West Coast hotels and restaurants that specializes in finding uses for landmark buildings. Despite its mixed reputation among advocates of neighborhood businesses, the American bookstore chain of Barnes & Noble has also become involved in the restoration of landmark buildings in New York, Chicago, and San Francisco.

In the eyes of some, particularly those who are more comfortable in the nonprofit field, the prospect of working closely with major corporations is a Faustian bargain. Arrangements often bring in a number of different players, and in some cases those in the field of historic preservation are less than delighted by the idea of working with certain corporate partners. This view was articulated at the Salzburg Seminar by Gordon Metz, the special projects director of the Mayibuye Centre for History and Culture at the University of the Western Cape in South Africa, who noted, "I fear the multinational because it has become so large and so invisible." The implication is that by "selling out" to a corporate sponsor, the nonprofit partners are compromising their own values, and possibly ceding control to organizations that might not maintain the necessary level of sensitivity, integrity, or authority.

Much depends on the structure of the partnership. In business or historic preservation, the key issue is the distribution of control, as well as the distribution of risks and rewards. While businesses often involve "silent partners," it is unusual in historic preservation for any of the involved parties to insist on anonymity. More often, it is the desire for image-building and publicity that draws participants into projects. This makes the formation of partnerships in the field of historic preservation more complex, in that a balance of power is often very difficult to achieve.

The composition of partnerships need not be restricted to the customary public/private combination. Consider the partnership involving the United States Committee of the International Council on Monuments and Sites (US/ICOMOS), the ministry of tourism and antiquities of the Kingdom of Jordan, and Chemonics, an international consulting firm. Together they are working on a cultural and environmental resources management project in Amman, Madaba, and Petra—one classic example of a major private/public partnership effort at a World Heritage site. With the emergence of NGOs as agents of change in the sphere of cultural heritage and development, the way is clear to a range of combinations involving nonprofit institutions, private sector institutions including corporations and entrepreneurs, and government agencies. This greater variety of partnerships mirrors the diversity of situations and problems that must be addressed. In some cases, the state is desperate to give ownership away.

It often makes a great deal more sense for a major corporation to team up with an NGO rather than with a federal or regional government, and a triumvirate of public, corporate, and NGO forces is also a viable approach. The structure of a partnership of this kind, as Havel points out in her essay, relies on an initiator or mediator—such as a community leader, government officer, professional consultant, or NGO (local or international)—who offers not only the preliminary research but also the independent point of view that allays suspicions regarding conflict of interest. In one high-profile example in the United Kingdom, the composer and theater personality Sir Andrew Lloyd Webber, who earns millions of dollars per month in royalties from his musicals and publishing enterprises around the world, endowed his own nonprofit organization to keep open the doors of historic English churches, that would otherwise have closed for lack of funds to pay for security. Within two years, Lloyd Webber hopes, the organization will be able to operate on its own, but in the interim he acts as a partner, together with the churches and local authorities, and in that way satisfies his lifelong love for the architecture of the Victorian church.

The participants in the Salzburg Seminar offered a wealth of heartening examples of partnerships in action. Claudia Hamill, the head of European and overseas relations for the National Trust, discussed her work in developing relations with heritage conservation organizations internationally, and explained the importance of partnerships to the work of the trust. Terry O'Regan, a landscape horticulturist, designer and joint managing director of the Cork-based Birch Hill Landscapes Group, pointed out that the projects on which he has worked involve ownership not only by the governmental Office of Public Works, but also by "semi-state companies" such as the Electricity Supply Board, the Forestry Board, and the Turf Board, as well as by local authorities.

Projects in Eastern Europe seemed to promise the broadest range of opportunities for new types of partnerships. According to Christopher Campbell, an American Peace Corps volunteer at the Hortobaghy National Park in eastern Hungary, a partnership with the Danish government provided the funds for multilingual signs along a bicycle trail aimed at promoting ecotourism in the park. He also points out that partnerships are being developed in the nearby Hajdusagi Landscape Protection Area, a 70,000-acre mosaic of protected forests, pasture lands, and former wetlands also under the aegis of the National Park. Hoping to inform private landowners in the area of their emerging democratic rights of ownership, including the right to improve the economic potential of the land, restore habitats, and protect the environmental qualities of the area, the partnership involves an NGO, the funding agencies, the U.S. Fish and Wildlife Service, and private landowners. Alexandra Bitušíková of the Slovak Republic reported that in Slovakia the Tree of Life youth movement, which began in 1982, is a superb tradition that allows hundreds of young people to spend their summers working on the restoration of monuments including castles, folk architecture, and even industrial landmarks including railways and water mills. The movement is a nongovernmental, nonprofit initiative that depends on contributions from individuals, entrepreneurs, foundations, and the government-endowed Proslovakia fund.

The highly professional, forward-looking character of these partnerships points the way to the possibilities for partnerships in the future. Whether global or regional, high-budget or a simple exchange of information and expertise, the partnerships of the future will exploit the broadening interest in matters of cultural preservation among the nations of the world, and will, one hopes, take up the slack where governmental intervention cannot meet the needs of vital projects. Nevertheless, the tools of state action will still have an important role to play in providing incentives for, sustaining, and shaping those partnerships.

References

Arts Council of Great Britain. *Arts Networking in Europe: A Directory of Trans-Frontier Cultural Networks Operating in the European Arena.* London: Arts Council of Great Britain, 1992.

Gramp, William. *Pricing the Priceless: Art, Artists, and Economics.* New York: Basic Books, 1992.

Hammer, M., and J. Champy. *Reengineering the Corporation.* New York: Harper-Collins, 1993.

Maynard, Herman Bryant, and Susan E. Mehrtens. *The Fourth Wave: Business in the 21st Century.* San Francisco: Berrett-Koehler, 1993.

Robinson, Olin, et al., eds. *The Arts in the World Economy.* Hanover: University Ptess of New England, 1995.

Scott Morton, Michael S., ed. *The Corporation of the 1990s: Information Technology and Organizational Transformation.* New York: Oxford University Press, 1991.

Presentation, Promotion, Persuasion, and Partnerships: The Creative Uses of Information and the Role of National Trusts

This chapter will consider the creative uses of information and examine the media and techniques available to us in three stages of the preservation process: presentation, promotion, and persuasion. Each of these words implies action. Preservation, the overall objective, is the action of keeping from injury or destruction, and plays an essential part in sustaining resources in order to pass them on to future generations. Presentation is the action of preparing or offering for acceptance; promotion is the action of helping forward, or advancing; and persuasion is the action of inducing someone to do or believe something. Governments are concerned with all three actions, but can only achieve their objectives by stimulating or creating wide-ranging partnerships with other players, particularly given that the vast majority (85 to 90 percent) of what is considered to be the national heritage (in Western societies, at least) is in private hands. But, as I will discuss in this chapter and illustrate with the example of the National Trust for Scotland, the initiative for stimulating these partnerships can lie equally with voluntary and non-governmental organizations.

Before examining each of the three main areas of action in detail, this chapter first seeks to establish what is meant by the cultural heritage of a nation, and to clarify the context within which one has to act. The international conventions and protocol agreements between nations that establish the parameters or standards expected of governments and their statutory agencies are an important part of this context. Codes of conduct or voluntary agreements, which flow from discussion between governments and the many public and private entities involved in preserving a nation's cultural heritage, will be more effective if community benefits are clearly expressed.

Cultural Heritage

One needs to be clear about what is meant by "culture." I would suggest an *Oxford English Dictionary* definition: "Culture is the sum of the inherited ideas, beliefs, values, and knowledge, which constitute the shared bases of social action." A people's cultural heritage clearly reflects the interaction of their human and natural environments. People are affected by and affect all the elements in their environment; indeed, so much of what we call natural has actually been shaped or adapted by man for man. Therefore, it is essential, in considering the importance of landmark buildings or other structures, that we adopt a more holistic approach.

We might, therefore, agree that "the cultural heritage of a people reflects the interaction of their human and natural environments." Any or all of the information systems that we might consider will only be useful if we accept that we are dealing with a concept of cultural heritage that is much broader than buildings alone.

I think we should also be clear about what we mean by "an historic monument," and for this I would refer to one of the definitions in the International Council on Monuments and Sites (ICOMOS) Venice Charter of 1966, which dealt with the conservation and restoration of monuments and sites.[1] Its concept of an historic monument "embraces not only the single architectural work, but also the urban or rural setting in which is found the evidence of a particular civilization, a significant development or an historic event." A monument is, therefore, not an end in itself but a means to an end, a sort of signpost to a better understanding of a profound culture. In some societies the concept of the heritage has a spiritual rather than a monumental value. Australian Aborigines, as do members of other indigenous societies, value the cultural landscape with which they identify and which they inhabit in common with other creatures. Hence the Australians drafted the Burra Charter in 1978 to extend the concept of culture to man's ancestral heritage.

In New Zealand, the Maori people, who brought with them traditions from the Marquesas when they migrated a thousand years ago, think it odd that the European settler, the *pakeha*, who arrived only 150 years ago, should devote so much effort to restoring old buildings. In the Maori tradition, once a building has fulfilled its purpose and is no longer useful, its spirit is considered to have died, and it therefore has no value worth conserving.

There is, in fact, an even earlier document that should guide our thinking: the Athens Charter of 1931, which was submitted to the International Committee on Intellectual Cooperation of the League of Nations, a committee that can be said to have been the genesis of the United Nations Educational, Scientific, and Cultural Organization (UNESCO). That charter makes it clear that "the best guarantee in the matter of the preservation of monuments and works of art derives from the respect and attachment of the people themselves."

Professor Mohammed Arkoun, recently retired as Professor of Islamic Thought at the Sorbonne, in a speech in Indonesia in November 1992, concluded that "the class of people engaged in mass tourism are culturally the less prepared to take an interest in the discovery of religious belief systems when they travel abroad. Tourists might be open and eager to discover the authentic values of a country, a religious tradition, but if the natives themselves ignore their own values, or use them in a distorted way, then one cannot expect the visitors to comprehend." He stressed the need for tourist guides to be trained as high-level professionals, for they must be considered what he called the "mediators of the whole cultural identity of their countries when they present it to others from other cultures." This concern presupposes that education and training are high on any agenda for preserving the national heritage, and that the need for public awareness is recognized.

In 1992, world leaders met in Rio de Janeiro and arrived at what we now call the Rio Agreement, which included "Agenda 21," a document setting out principles for the sustainable use of scarce resources. Sustainability is largely a matter of common sense: it presumes that in using natural resources to sustain our way of life, we will not diminish them and will be able to hand them on to future generations. We might wish elsewhere to debate the applicability of the concept of sustainability, but within the realm of heritage preservation, we must be aware of the finite nature of the resources available to us.

Information Technology and Information

The range of media at our disposal is vast, and it might be as well to consider the potential of information technology. Information is a two-way process, and to use it to influence others requires a clear understanding of the information presented and of the limits and opportunities offered by competing media. The choice of medium is critical. Marshall McLuhan, in *Understanding Media: the Extensions of Man*, explained that the "medium is the message," in that the technology introduced a change of scale or pace or pattern into human affairs.[2] He was at that time skeptical of the value of television, which he characterized by adjusting a quotation from *Romeo and Juliet*: "But soft! What light through yonder window breaks? It speaks, and yet says nothing."

Information technology has undergone a massive transformation. The capacity to reduce all forms of information to a digital form has led to a revolution in communication. We have around us an invisible transport system that carries billions of pounds or dollars or yen in and out of countries and financial centers in seconds. Few, however, appreciate the implications of this revolution.

The sophistication of the technology means that a person can influence events on the far side of the world, even from the attic of a remote croft, as an item in *The Scotsman* newspaper recently revealed. One night the computer that runs Hong Kong harbor, one of the world's busiest ports, crashed. A software designer, John Roscoe, who works for the Manchester-based I.C.L., was called from his bed in a remote Scottish croft in the Orkneys, and, after a couple of hours at his computer, solved the problem; the shipping in Hong Kong harbor began to move once again.

We must be sure that the Pandora's box of information technology is accessible to all those we wish to reach with our messages. Recent research in the United Kingdom by MORI on behalf of Motorola, shows that the regularity of use of information technology in Britain echoes the nation's social divides between rich and poor, young and old, men and women, North and South, and those with and without work. Surprisingly, 45 percent of all respondents claim never to use personal computers, mobile phones, pagers, or modems. Predictably, levels of training in information technology decline with age, with the highest percentage of training (73 percent) reported by sixteen- to twenty-four-year-olds. *The Economist* recently reported that Inteco, an American consulting firm, had assessed the prevalence of the "interactive consumer" in Western Europe and the United States and had concluded that if the prospects for profitable interactive services are poor in America, they are terrible in Europe. Inteco projects that by the end of the century almost two-thirds of Europe's homes will still be without a personal computer. It follows from these patterns of usage that we shall have to consider most carefully the relative merits of different media, including less sophisticated tools, to reach different markets and to address different publics effectively and cost-efficiently.

For the moment, however, let us consider the nature of information itself, and its creative uses in presentation, promotion, and persuasion, as well as in the development of partnerships. While traveling in Europe, I read many English-language newspapers on aircraft or in executive lounges. The facts they report as news tend to come from the same small group of news agencies, and this produces a certain sameness across all publications. Differences occur on the editorial pages where the facts are analyzed and a gloss put on them, which in turn informs their readers. To inform means literally to put into form or shape, to arrange or compose. Therefore, we need to be clear that there is a distinction between facts alone and interpretation. Since the fifteenth century at least, information has meant intelligence, implying instruction or enlightenment. Reaching people at different levels of awareness or involvement in the process of preservation is, in a way, educating them.

Presenting the Cultural Heritage of a Nation

What sources of information are available to enable us to deal professionally and practically with the conservation and the presentation of properties?

Professor Ian McHarg at the University of Pennsylvania correlated different sets of data in order to make sensible and sensitive decisions on competing land use options, showing how information could be applied with intelligence.[3] The techniques he used have been enhanced or overtaken by more sophisticated information technology, but such sophisticated media require even more urgently an intelligent interpreter to communicate official policy comprehensibly to achieve realistic responses from other partners.

Many geographical information systems are available to help us achieve this wider understanding of the manmade and natural environments. Remote sensing by satellite or aerial survey and the use of infrared photography enable us to establish graphically the interrelationship of significant landscape elements. The process of mapping resources, and the distinctions that can be made between soils, vegetation, and habitats, help to inform our work in the preservation of historic monuments, which, in turn, reflect the nature of the landscape and the local building materials in their regional styles.

In most countries some attempt is made to list buildings of relative importance. In England, buildings are listed by English Heritage (a statutory agency funded by government) in five categories: (1) all buildings built before 1700 that survive in anything like their original condition; (2) most buildings of 1700 to 1840 subject to some selection; (3) buildings between 1840 and 1914 of definite quality and character (this selection is designed to include the principal works of the principal architects); (4) selected buildings between 1914 and 1939 of high quality; and (5) a few outstanding buildings erected after 1939. In choosing buildings, the agency pays particular attention to four aspects: (1) the special value within certain types, either for architectural or planning reasons, or as illustrating social or economic history; (2) technological innovation or virtuosity; (3) association with well-known characters or events; and (4) group value, especially as examples of town planning.[4]

In this way, almost 500,000 buildings in England have been listed. The buildings are classified in grades that show their relative importance: Grade I—buildings of exceptional interest (only 2 percent of the total of listed buildings); Grade II*—particularly important buildings of more than special interest (some 4 percent of listed buildings); and Grade II—buildings of special interest that warrant every effort being made to preserve them. A scheme of listing of this kind is essential to determining which landmark buildings are worth more attention than others, particularly when distributing limited resources.

While this is the listing procedure of an official agency of the government, the properties categorized are rarely government-owned. The majority of properties listed are privately owned, in many cases by individuals who do not have the resources needed for the proper maintenance and presentation of their property. Thus, governments at the national, regional, and local levels need to adopt policies and to implement schemes to help pay for maintenance, repair, and presentation of buildings that are important to the cultural heritage.

Sometimes groups of buildings, particularly in an urban setting, gain value from their harmonious relationship. In the United Kingdom such areas are called "conservation areas" and considered not only as single buildings, but as a group in the context of their immediate environment. The regulatory control over such buildings and their environment is therefore important, and legislation provides, under Town and Country Planning Laws and other legislation related to the cultural heritage, for the protection of such ensembles. Equally important is giving advice or guidance, that is, information, which statutory agencies should provide to owners of important private property. Listing such properties is not in itself sufficient, and as government grant aid is necessarily limited, creating advisory publications is an essential part of communicating policy.

While the natural heritage is not a primary concern of this current volume, it is perhaps useful to recognize that the United Kingdom protects its natural heritage by designating National Parks, which are areas of outstanding landscape value, as well as Areas of Outstanding Natural Beauty, and, in the case of geological, botanical, or other interest, Sites of Special Scientific Interest. The many international conventions concerning the sustainability and diversity of species could influence our approach to the preservation of landmark buildings in their setting. Under my definition of the cultural heritage, it is important to be mindful of the synergy between the manmade and natural elements of our cultural heritage.

UNESCO initiated the World Heritage Convention in 1972, and this convention has drawn attention to those outstanding human and natural elements within our cultural heritage that are considered to be of universal value. In the last three years experts have agreed upon a similar concept of the "cultural landscape." The term embraces a diversity of examples of the interaction between mankind and his natural environment. UNESCO has concluded that cultural landscapes fall into three main categories: (1) a clearly defined landscape designed and created by man; (2) the organically evolved landscape, in two subcategories—a relict (or fossil) landscape still visible in material form or a continuing landscape in which evolution is in progress; and (3) an associative cultural landscape, reflecting powerful religious, artistic, or cultural associations, rather than material cultural evidence, which may be insignificant.

Recognizing Community Values

Many aspects of the manmade and natural elements of the cultural heritage will appeal to different people at different times and in different ways. People are most aware of their immediate surroundings, often taking the historic development of cities and towns for granted. Structures such as palaces, churches, and other fine buildings are perceived to be the concern of the state, the religious community, or large commercial enterprises. For the most part these structures are maintained in good repair. However, it is the ensemble of buildings, and their facades in particular, that creates the attractive character of many historic cities and towns. The maintenance of these ensembles places an undue burden on the individual owners, who may not have access to the fiscal benefits available to commercial enterprises.

The countryside has been affected by centuries of ownership and development, and while too often taken for granted by the casual observer, it is the varying nature and character of a country's landscape that gives it a unique identity and appeal to those who live in cities or who visit from other countries. The countryside or cultural landscape is often revealed in research to be one of the key motivations for tourism. Traditional land use and farming practices are often not supported by fiscal regimes helpful to the owners. While many large-scale enterprises in the countryside can offset their maintenance and repair costs against profits on other parts of their operation, by and large sustaining the regional or local character of the landscape can only be an increasing burden to the private landowner.

Organizations such as Europa Nostra, itself a consortium of over two hundred conservation societies, have been formed and devote themselves to improving the setting of the communities in which they operate. They recognize that an attractive environment, with urban and rural buildings in good repair, is an essential part of civic pride. This in turn encourages the interest and involvement of the younger generation, for whom historic buildings within an attractive setting often provide the first awareness of a rich cultural heritage. Owners or operators of the cultural heritage of a nation, whether governments or their agencies, private organizations or partnerships of individuals, have a considerable collective responsibility to maintain a sustainable asset for future generations.

Sociologists know that collective behavior and the desire to associate is intrinsic to humans. They group, as Lewis Mumford and Patrick Geddes before him realized, in ancestral forms and patterns. Therefore our concept of what is national heritage must relate to a people's associations. Those things that are closest, traditional, and ancestral will be most meaningful, and education for awareness must be pitched accordingly.

It is an interesting time to observe the political and social changes taking place in the countries of Central and Eastern Europe, where, incidentally, conservation skills of a very high order were fostered under communist regimes. The skills exported to the West earned valuable hard currency for Poland and other countries with a well-established tradition for craftsmanship. As each new nation emerges and asserts itself, we have to reach constantly for the atlas of Europe. As Felipe Fernandez-Armesto has said,

Nothing like today's sudden appearance of previously unfamiliar people has happened in Europe since the fall of the Roman Empire. In the familiar Europe of modern history—the arena of states and empires—people are kicking up the sand, which is settling in new patterns. The unfamiliar names, which we are now relearning, have been present for generations in the folk memory of people. Between 1820 and 1939, 61 million Europeans emigrated to the U.S.A., and the descendants of that great mass movement will of course be familiar with the names of the nations now emerging and share in a common memory or cultural heritage.[5]

Engaging Voluntary Action: The National Trust

The citizens of the United Kingdom assume a collective responsibility for their cultural heritage and have done so for well over one hundred years. The National Trust for England, Wales, and Northern Ireland was established in 1895. While not the oldest conservation body of its kind—the Trustees of Reservations in Massachusetts was chartered in 1891—the National Trust has become the world leader in the presentation and promotion of the properties in its care. There are National Trusts in other countries of the world, each varying to some degree in emphasis, but each offering citizens an opportunity to work together to preserve important elements of their nation's cultural heritage that might otherwise be neglected or irretrievably damaged.

I should like to describe the approach followed by the National Trust for Scotland, which was created in 1931, and of which I was the director for ten years. Like the National Trust in England, the National Trust for Scotland is strengthened in its work by powers granted through private Acts of Parliament. The most important of these powers consists of the right to own property inalienably, which means that once declared, such property can never be sold or taken from the National Trust by government except by another Act of Parliament. A Declaration of Inalienability of any property is a simple process, but it implies a commitment in perpetuity. Governments come and go, but National Trusts, in theory, go on forever.

The second important legal power is embedded in "Conservation Agreements" (once called "Restrictive Agreements"), which can be concluded with the owners of private property who wish to ensure the continuity of their property regardless of its future ownership. This legal provision has advantages for the National Trusts in that they do not have to own the property thus protected or bear any of the cost of maintenance, repair, or presentation. Nothing can be done to alter such property without the express permission of the National Trusts. This applies not only to the fabric of a building but also to any landscape that is protected by a Conservation Agreement. It is a continuing burden on the title of the property, regardless of inheritance or succession.

The National Trust for Scotland owns 125 properties, including castles and country houses, historic sites and birthplace properties, mountains and river valleys, villages and monuments. It is an impressive portfolio bearing an awesome responsibility. The use of resources to maintain, repair, and present these properties requires skillful management planning. The concept of property management planning is largely based on common sense, but I think it is a useful tool for all those who are concerned with similar problems regardless of size or scale.

A sensible management plan requires a fundamental knowledge of all aspects of a property, a description of available resources, an assessment of the nonrecreational use of all the elements, and a statement of the existing recreational use, all of which support a clear statement of aims and objectives for the conservation and management of the property (Figure 1). Every five years the trust surveys the important buildings and structures within each of its properties and works out a financial feasibility plan for the maintenance, repair, improvement, and development of each one over a rolling five-year program. By tackling the needs of each property methodically, the trust can more easily assess priorities among its 125 properties.

National Trusts are charitable, not-for-profit organizations. Government support for the National Trust for Scotland amounts to no more than 10 percent of its annual expenditure. The 125 properties attract up to four million visitors a year (two million to built properties and two million to countryside properties), but the income from admissions and the profit on catering and shop trade also amount to no more than 10 percent of the income required. This means that 80 percent of income depends on membership, donations, income from investment, and other sources of revenue.

As National Trusts are membership bodies, they invite voluntary support and donated skills that might be expensive to retain on a permanent salaried basis. Member involvement in so many aspects of the management and maintenance of properties not only avoids expense, but also gives members an increased commitment and sense of purpose. Both the National Trust in England and the National Trust for Scotland now have considerable memberships, approximately 5 percent of the populations of their respective countries. This is a commitment larger than the membership of any political party, and indicates the strength of feeling that ordinary people share in the concept of the national heritage.

Figure 1: Checklist for a Property Management Plan

1. Introduction

1.1   Background
1.2   Historical Background
1.3   Acquisition
1.4   Repair and Restoration
1.5   Structure Plan
1.6   Local Plan
1.7   Surrounding Area
1.8   Nearby Visitor Attractions

2. Description

2.1   Resources

Ownership	Archaeology	Other Designations
Boundaries	Scheduled	Transport/
Geology and Soils	Monuments	Communications
Landscape	Listed Buildings	Population/Services
Water Regime	Other Buildings	Finance
Ecology	Gardens/Policies	Staffing

2.2   Non-Recreational Use

Access	Leases	Fishing
Nature Conservation	Farms	Vermin Control
Woodland	Crofts	Quinquennial Survey
Superiorities	Minerals	

2.3   Existing Recreational Use

Visitor Management	Ranger Service	Sport
Education	Volunteers	Events
Interpretation		

3. Analysis

4. Aims and Objectives

Source: National Trust for Scotland.

The Relevance of Cultural Tourism

The maintenance, repair, and presentation of the heritage, whether owned by public or private organizations, is unlikely to be a profitable exercise. However, the cultural heritage maintained in good condition and well-presented provides the basis for cultural tourism, which brings social and economic benefits to many people employed in other industries and businesses. Therefore, government investment in the cultural heritage can bring a considerable return, largely through the taxation levied on the profitable enterprises that form part of the business of cultural tourism.

The World Tourist Organisation and the World Travel & Tourism Council have both produced figures showing that travel and tourism is the world's largest industry and the world's largest generator of jobs. Tourism's impact is far-reaching but traditionally underestimated because its economic contribution is spread throughout the business community. The European Travel Commission, a consortium of European countries grouped together for the development and promotion of tourism, uses the shared cultural heritage as the main plank of its appeal to the market in the United States, which has traditionally provided a significant number of tourists for Italy, France, and the United Kingdom. All the research into the United States market for world tourism underlines the consumer's interest in "history and countryside." Europe cannot be complacent about its position in the face of competition from other world destinations, however, and keeping the heritage in good repair and presenting it well maintains a vital source of jobs in the many industries of tourism.

The promotion of a nation's cultural heritage places enormous responsibility on those concerned with it. Legislation in the United Kingdom makes it clear that where there is any conflict between preservation and public access, then the sound principles of conservation must take priority. Each property will have a carrying capacity, which can be measured by the number of visitors in an hour or by the day that can be tolerated without damage to the physical condition of the property. It has become increasingly difficult to protect small buildings even in remote locations from overuse during a period in which car ownership, mobility, and public interest are all growing. Therefore, any discussion of the principles of promotion must be tempered by the priorities of sustainability, and the use of methods to mitigate damage, either through limiting numbers or developing alternative attractions.

The easiest method of protection is to do no promotion at all. But writers such as Goethe, Wordsworth, or Sir Walter Scott, or as far back as Shakespeare himself, have already stimulated public imagination and the wish to discover and enjoy places that form an essential part of one's cultural heritage.

If cultural tourism is to have any depth of meaning, then it must reflect the values that people themselves respect. Too often strangers gain only a superficial impression of the significance of the cultural heritage of a different people or nation, and the revitalizing of the cultural heritage must commence with a clear statement and comprehension of the values of the society that wishes to host visitors.

Research in Western countries, which still provide the vast majority of leisure travelers, indicates that tourists' two principal interests are a country's history and its scenery. However, unless the people of those countries themselves understand and respect the richness of their culture, it would be difficult for the stranger to achieve a satisfactory experience. Cultural significance, which is based on social or religious beliefs and understanding, is something that cannot be grasped easily by a stranger visiting a community for a short time. It is therefore necessary, perhaps, for the host nation to explain the roots of its culture, not only to prevent a stranger from unwittingly causing offense, but also to help him or her comprehend the relationship between the design of buildings, the patterns of land use, and the customs of people.

The skills required to restore and maintain buildings are considerable, but those required to promote the cultural heritage are no less demanding, and in this regard I have always felt that the social anthropologist has as much to offer as any marketing specialist. Training guides and heightening the awareness of those responsible for heritage sites are part of the process of cultural revitalization.

Modern travelers moving between countries and even between continents, discover common themes of a rich cultural heritage. As the countries of Central and Eastern Europe have opened up since the traumatic social and political changes of 1989, we have become increasingly aware of the common cultural links among the countries of Western and Central and Eastern Europe. For two generations we imagined that Europe was divided culturally between East and West. Europe has a long political history of occupation, movement, and change, but the reality of the cultural divide has, of course, always been between North and South. The significance of a Europe divided for two generations with a disruption to the patterns of historic movement is sometimes hard to explain. An equivalent trauma would have been to have divided the United States from Duluth on Lake Superior to Galveston on the Gulf of Mexico, and to have limited access between the two halves through St. Joseph, Missouri, for two generations. The East-West divide is indeed more historically true of the United States than it has ever been of Europe (though, of course, the North-South divide in the United States is important as well).

Research and Planning for Promotion

Research into the needs of the market can reveal the aspirations of many different publics. In most countries, the greatest number of visitors to any site of cultural importance are native. Whether it is to the Abbey at Melk in Austria, or to the Taj Mahal in India, the foreigner or stranger would be greatly outnumbered by the people of those countries showing reverence for their own cultural heritage.

Sound planning is required for the sustainable use of all such monuments and places of attraction. In an ideal world we would start by undertaking an interpretive plan for each property and setting aims for its use and enhancement. Interpretive planning is largely based on good information sensibly used, but it requires training. For many years the National Parks Service in the United States has set a very high standard of interpretive planning, and many other organizations, both public and private, including the National Trust for Scotland, have benefited enormously from their staff being trained in the National Park Service's principles of interpretive planning.

Presenting the essential features of cultural heritage sites usually requires supporting services including parking, rest rooms, and eating and shopping facilities. However, traffic movement should be analyzed and ancillary services should be carefully designed so as not to damage the particular ambiance of the property.

The National Trust for Scotland has identified three specific periods within its visitor season over which the needs of visitors vary. Promotion to the various submarkets, such as education or senior citizen groups in the spring and autumn months, and the high volume of holiday tourism in the summer, has different requirements, not only in marketing but also in the management of the property itself. Different patterns of purchasing have been observed and also different lengths of stay by visitors during each of the three periods. This careful monitoring and analysis leads, in the end, to sensitive management that enables staff to optimize the benefit from visitors while honoring the overriding need to conserve the property.

The education levels of the specific sub-markets are also important, particularly when targeting young people of school age, unemployed people, or retired people. The demand for continuing education is providing new markets for historic properties. Therefore, preparing a property for visitors requires not only a clear interpretive plan and the provision of ancillary services, but also an awareness of the changing needs of the various markets, and regular surveys of the ways the public uses a property. Each year, for example, the National Trust for Scotland reviews and updates the techniques of interpretation at a number of its properties, which means that all properties are refreshed on a regular cycle to maintain their appeal to the public.

**Figure 2: Strengths, Weaknesses, Opportunities, and Threats—
An Example from the Corporate Planning Process of the National
Trust for Scotland**

Strengths	Weaknesses
• Inalienability	• Property Conservation Awareness
• Conservation Agreements	• Appeal to the Young
• Tax Exempt Status	• Nature Conservation
• Project Management	• "Added Value" of Properties
• Fund-Raising Ability	• Headquarters Fragmentation
• Membership Strength	• Committee System
• Volunteers' Commitment	• Management Style
• External Relations	• Clarity of Objectives

Opportunities	Threats
• Public Awareness of Environment	• High Unemployment
• Higher Disposable Income	• Energy Costs and Inflation
• Social Profile of Members	• Shortage of Skills
• Continuing Education	• Competition from
• Self Improvement	—Other Voluntary Bodies
• Inheritance Tax Provision	—Fund-Raising Charities
	• Media Attention
	• European Law (e.g., Health and Safety)

Source: National Trust for Scotland.

The business of promotion is a professional one. Because historic properties in the care of public or private bodies have to meet the needs of a changing market, marketing skills are as important to the organization as conservation skills. The creative use of print media, visual displays, and interactive computers is part of the process of promotion. While the National Trust for Scotland allocates 80 percent of its resources to conservation, it needs only 4 percent of its budget to sustain its work of marketing and promotion. No organization serving the needs of the public at large can afford to be complacent about its performance or about changing taste or fashion in the leisure business, in which cultural heritage and cultural tourism play such an important part.

The National Trust for Scotland integrates the efforts of staff of many disciplines into an overall Corporate Plan, which requires each staff member to recognize the roles of others. A feature of this planning process is an analysis of Strengths, Weaknesses, Opportunities, and Threats (SWOT), which attempts to assess all the good and bad practices and perceptions that influence the effectiveness of the organization. This process of critical self-examination strengthens the corporate planning process (Figure 2).

Persuasion

The responsibility for sustaining the cultural heritage requires consistent presentation and persistent promotion. Practical experience provides a sound basis from which to persuade others of the needs of the organization in particular, and of the overriding need to conserve the cultural heritage in general. Thus we can begin to consider the creative uses of information to persuade.

While such properties are rarely profitable in their own right and are often seen as "loss leaders" for the tourism industry, heritage properties have inherent values that need protection and management whether or not they are viable as commercial visitor attractions. As I have suggested, they must be operated and managed in a businesslike way. However, to maintain their charitable status, they must maintain their stated objectives, which in the case of the United Kingdom is closely monitored by the Charity Commissioners, or by the Inland Revenue in the case of properties in Scotland.

The charitable not-for-profit status of the National Trust for Scotland is a most important asset in the process of persuasion. To begin with, the tax advantages provided in law for National Trusts make it attractive for people to fund projects and also to leave money in legacies on death, free of tax. There is, however, a continuing need for National Trusts to be persistent in fund-raising. The total support from members, during life or on death, comprises 50 percent of the income required to sustain the essential work of conservation. Other income derives from corporate promotion, through which businesses wish to be associated with their local communities and to identify with the cultural heritage. National Trusts have received considerable support from the business community, especially for education and awareness programs for young people.

The techniques of persuading people to donate their money have been learned the hard way in the marketplace. But the resulting support is not only financial, it also arrives in the form of moral support and commitment to sound conservation policies by government agencies and the business community.

The role of a nongovernmental organization is an important one in society as a whole. NGOs are an important third element along with government and business in the life and structure of any society. The strength of the National Trust movement has been that when seeking to influence or persuade government or business about the needs of conservation and protection of the heritage, it has been seen to be a good practitioner, and is therefore able to speak with authority when advancing new policies or principles for more general acceptance by government or business.

This proved extremely important in Scotland in the early 1970s when the discovery of North Sea oil posed urgent planning problems for government and business to establish the essential land-based infrastructure to support offshore exploration. Much of the coastline of Scotland is protected by existing national and international conservation policies, but it was important that government should move speedily, in concert with environmental agencies, to consider the development options. Because of the social and economic importance of these facilities to the well-being of the nation, it would have been irresponsible of the National Trust for Scotland to have tried to block all landward facilities for marine oil exploration. It was possible to work in collaboration with government and business to identify the 90 percent of the coastline that should not be despoiled by the infrastructure of the oil industry, but, more importantly, the 10 percent of the coastline more suited to development and on which no challenge would be made.

There was one test case of the threat of an oil-rig construction yard to have been built on land that the National Trust for Scotland itself owned inalienably (the legal protection that the government would have had to overturn by an Act of Parliament). The National Trust for Scotland resisted the proposal for development on its land, and the government wisely changed its mind, proving that a private organization with strong membership and influence in the wider community could argue with authority and common sense on its side.

Of course, the role of nongovernmental organizations is not always defensive. While guarding against the irresponsible actions of others, particularly with respect to local government's interpretation of national policy, nongovernmental organizations should be anticipating issues that could be of critical importance to the community at large. The National Trust for Scotland studied carefully the rural development policies of government and argued for a restructuring of relevant government departments to produce more coherent rural policy initiatives. The arguments were not adopted by government at the time, but ten years later they have become part of its reorganization. Views expressed on the impact of forestry and fish farming on the landscape led to necessary safeguards being introduced to protect against the long-term damage likely to be created by inappropriate safety measures.

The Role of Europa Nostra

Together with environmental groups, there has been a growing awareness among preservation groups of a common conservation responsibility within wider Europe. The National Trust for Scotland is one of two hundred heritage organizations in thirty-one European countries that belong to Europa Nostra, which, in turn, has united with the International Castles Institute. With the additional support of one hundred local authorities and official agencies and eight hundred well-informed individual members, Europa Nostra has taken several initiatives within Europe. To take but one example, it has argued that value added taxes on repairs to historic buildings should be low in order to give people the incentive to restore buildings that are important to the cultural heritage. Europa Nostra did not win that battle, but gained more ground than had been imagined possible when it initiated the campaign. When the next tax review takes place within the European Union, there is prospect of a wider acceptance of the principle. Because keeping the cultural heritage in good repair is essential for the social and economic value of cultural tourism, the benefits of low taxes on repairs seem self-evident, but the conventional wisdom of treasury officials often works against innovative thinking.

While Europa Nostra is a Europe-wide heritage organization, it realized that it could have a still stronger voice if it joined up with other organizations active in preserving the manmade and natural heritage. This led to the formation of the European Heritage Group, consisting of fifteen major conservation organizations, which forms a platform for discussion at the highest level within the structures and institutions of the European Union and the Council of Europe. The European Union is currently formulating its cultural policy, and it is important that organizations with practical experience in managing the manmade and natural heritage should influence the nature of any funding program envisaged.

Europa Nostra also operates an award scheme, which for seventeen years has recognized outstanding restoration of historic buildings or their surroundings, the restitution of land, and the design of modern buildings that fit well into the sensitive environment of historic cities. Awards and public recognition are one method of recognizing achievement not only by industry and communities, but also by national governments. In some instances, these award ceremonies have involved presentations by heads of state and have received the support of relevant ministries of culture. For ten years the Europa Nostra Award Scheme was sponsored by the American Express Foundation, recognizing the business sense of a cultural heritage in good repair.

The activity of bodies such as the National Trusts or Europa Nostra or the European Heritage Group is of course only one part of a larger effort of persuasion initiated by many special interest groups in Europe or internationally. Legislators and other people of influence have little time, and therefore any argument has to be well-conceived, justified, and long-term.

The Competition for Resources

While voluntary charitable bodies, because of their practical experience, are in a good position to support collective attempts to achieve desirable change in national or international policies, they have to sustain their own future in a very competitive world.

In setting strategy and meeting its targets, the National Trust for Scotland faces many forms of competition. To begin with, it competes for visitors to its properties. In Scotland alone there are fifteen hundred attractions vying for both foreign and domestic visitors, who make the enormous number of day visits that form part of the overall leisure industry. The National Trust for Scotland has to compete for the use of that leisure time and thus the money of the visiting public, seeking to develop committed members for the future and trying to convey to the community at large the nature of the work it does for the nation.

Furthermore, there is competition for membership support because there are many environmental bodies with similar charitable status making strong appeals for limited public resources. This is particularly true during times of economic recession, and therefore the National Trust for Scotland needs to state its goals clearly and campaign actively to maintain the support and commitment of a loyal membership.

Nonprofit groups must also compete for financial sponsorship from businesses that wish to be involved in the life of their communities. Arts and cultural organizations also need community support, particularly at a time when support from central and local government is declining. Such organizations have a great attraction for company sponsorship because they offer opportunities for high-profile involvement as well as entertainment for their clients. The longer-term investment needs of the cultural heritage therefore sometimes seem less appealing. Increasingly, head offices rather than local management decide whom the corporation sponsors, and this too poses problems for heritage organizations that cannot afford to maintain high-level contact at a national or international level. Time is well spent in the analysis of company reports and newspaper coverage given to business performance. Thus, economic journals are as important a part of daily reading as journals devoted to preservation and presentation.

Conclusion

I have attempted to show that information, carefully assessed and used intelligently, lies at the heart of the success of any not-for-profit charitable organization that acts in a business-like way. Responsible in part for the cultural heritage of a nation, such an organization must be able to assess public needs quickly if it is to sustain public awareness and ask the community at large to share responsibility for the conservation and presentation of its properties. The problems of the private sector are therefore not dissimilar to those of government wishing to find partners for the neverending burden of stewardship.

The primary responsibility is, of course, to secure a nation's cultural heritage for future generations, and to sustain each resource in such a way that it can be handed on in good conscience. If governments cannot sustain the cultural heritage of their countries independently, then they must provide mechanisms by which partnerships can be established with community organizations. It is easier to achieve this at present in countries whose political and economic systems have had a longer and more settled existence. It is much harder to achieve in countries where there has been fundamental social and political change and where the pressures of personal survival in daily life must take priority. However, the cultural heritage of any nation will deteriorate without adequate forethought and planning.

In some countries where the World Heritage Convention has been accepted, there is an understandable need to have international recognition of those aspects of the cultural heritage, whether manmade or natural, that are of universal value. This is only right and proper. But so much of the cultural heritage of a nation exists at a local scale that will never justify such international attention; its protection therefore relies on the efforts of its own community.

This is precisely why the words of E. F. Schumacher in *Small is Beautiful* seem more and more relevant: "What is the meaning of democracy, freedom, human dignity, standard of living, self-realisation, fulfillment?" he wrote. "Is it a matter of goods, or of people? Of course it is a matter of people. But people can be themselves only in small comprehensible groups. Therefore we must learn to think in terms of an articulated structure that can cope with a multiplicity of small-scale units."[6]

Organizations concerned with the protection of the cultural heritage sometimes feel isolated or out of step with government policy. The heads of state of the Council of Europe, which met in Vienna in October 1993, began to see that the cultural heritage was an important part of the mandate to examine universal cultural rights, which could also respond to the particular needs of minorities new and old. In the midst of the cultural diversity of a changing Europe, the Vienna Declaration justifies some urgent thinking about the whole question of cultural identity, of which heritage, construed broadly, is the clearest manifestation. The declaration concluded, "Remembering the past makes the world a healthier place. It is our only defense against the eternal return of hatred and unreason."

Notes

1. International Council on Monuments and Sites, "International Charter for the Conservation and Restoration of Monuments and Sites (Venice Charter)," reproduced in Russell V. Keune, ed., *The Historic Preservation Yearbook: A Documentary Record of Significant Policy Developments and Issues* (Bethesda, Md.: Adler & Adler, 1984), 40–41.
2. Marshall McLuhan, *Understanding Media: The Extensions of Man* (New York: McGraw-Hill, 1965).
3. See, for example, Ian L. McHarg, *Design with Nature* (Garden City, N.Y.: Natural History Press, 1969).
4. Department of National Heritage, *What Listing Means: A Guide for Owners and Occupiers* (London: Department of National Heritage, October 1994).
5. Felipe Fernandez-Armesto, *Times Guide to the Peoples of Europe: The Essential Handbook to Europe's Tribes* (London: Times Books, 1994), 9.
6. E. F. Schumacher, *Small is Beautiful: Economics as if People Mattered* (New York: Harper & Row, 1973), 70.

References

Department of National Heritage. *What Listing Means: A Guide for Owners and Occupiers*. London: Department of National Heritage, October 1994.

Duroselle, Jean Baptiste. *Europe: A History of its Peoples*. London: Penguin Viking, 1990.

Fernandez-Armesto, Felipe. *Times Guide to the Peoples of Europe: The Essential Handbook to Europe's Tribes*. London: Times Books, 1994.

Fladmark, J. M., ed. *Cultural Tourism: Papers Presented at the Robert Gordon University Heritage Convention*. London: Donhead, 1994.

Harrison, Richard, ed. *Manual of Heritage Management*. Oxford: Butterworth-Heinemann, 1994.

Keune, Russell V., ed. *The Historic Preservation Yearbook: A Documentary Record of Significant Policy Developments and Issues*. Bethesda, Md.: Adler & Adler, 1984.

McHarg, Ian L. *Design with Nature*. Garden City, N.Y.: Natural History Press, 1969.

McLuhan, Marshall. *Understanding Media: The Extensions of Man*. New York: McGraw-Hill, 1965.

Sayer, Michael, and Hugh Massingberd. *The Disintegration of a Heritage: Country Houses and their Collections, 1979–1992*. Norwich, UK: Michael Russell Publishing, 1993.

Schumacher, E. F. *Small is Beautiful: Economics as if People Mattered*. New York: Harper & Row, 1973.

Preservation and Partnerships in Emerging Market Economies

The changes in the economic and political spheres in Central and Eastern Europe are a part of the wave of global social change resulting from today's information technology revolution. This has led to a reassessment of the position of the individual in society, along with a reevaluation of priorities and aims in life. This chapter examines the special role historic monuments play in today's world as visible witnesses to the cultural traditions and roots of nations, and discusses why important international business and nonprofit organizations are turning their attention to helping to care for and preserve these monuments.

The Changes of 1989

The phrase "emerging market economies" in the title of this chapter suggests a significant difference between developments in Central and Eastern Europe and other parts of the world, not only with respect to economic, environmental, and managerial skills—which cannot be overlooked—but simply in terms of the speed of change in the region. It is as though time had stopped in our region for several decades, and catching up requires an accelerated pace of change. Lester Borley describes in his chapter today's new time-space topology as it has fundamentally reshaped a global hierarchy of values for an era of massive development in democratic countries. In cyberspace, on the Internet and the World Wide Web, everyone can participate wherever he or she may be. The creative use of information, together with what Lester Borley calls "perception at a distance" is a new tool, essential for the experience of virtual reality.

Two centuries ago, John Adams wrote to his wife, "I must study politics

and war that my sons may have liberty to study mathematics and philosophy
. . . in order to give their children a right to study painting, poetry, [and]
music."[1] What Adams, in 1780, laid out as his overarching plan for three generations, we are living through in the course of a few years. The blinding speed
of these changes makes financial power seem omnipotent. As a result, the initial approach to the revitalization of cultural heritage projects in the emerging
democracies of Central and Eastern Europe was based upon the expectation
that it would be simple enough to find a source of money, but this has proven
to be both difficult and insufficient.

At the end of the 1980s, political changes in the region brought the possibility of deep and complete changes in all aspects of society. Unlike the totalitarian regimes, the new mode of governing brought economic freedom through
the establishment of a market economy, and a plurality of possibilities
throughout all aspects of society, including the freedom to choose among these
possibilities. The opening of borders suddenly created space to establish new
relationships, among them new forms of cooperation. Individual projects became the first areas for cooperation, and the seeds were sown to transform society from a selfish to a cooperative entity. For individuals, life's priorities
changed, and many developed these new relationships for themselves. It is not
insignificant that these changes took place in the era of the information technology revolution.

The first step in the transformation process was the transition from a centrally-
planned economy to a market economy. This transfer of ownership and all its
consequences has begun to have a positive effect on development in the Czech
Republic. A banking system was created, and Czech currency reached full
convertibility. Yet most real power is still in the hands of the central government. One issue that remains unresolved is how to empower regional governments with certain rights and establish a regional system of administration.
The country needs to be divided into administrative regions in which each region is given some economic autonomy and, consequently, more responsibility
through managing its own budget.

Moreover, we are discovering that this single-minded focus on creating a
market economy now has to be modified to take into account the diverse needs
of society. The transformation must include directed and accelerated development in an attempt to catch up to the more economically stable European regions. Changes in the administrative structures of management are necessary
for the successful application of a transformed political and legal system.
However, changes in management and administration will be hindered by a
lack of skills in these areas and a lack of willingness to take responsibility for
individual decisions. During the last forty years, social relationships or the culture of behavior have strongly influenced what has been possible. As Václav
Havel noted in his New Year's address for 1991, "We have not just been the

victim of the totalitarian machinery; we all are at the same time its creators."

In the Czech Republic these changes in the economic system have directly influenced the cultural heritage because of the quick transfer of ownership rights from the state to private individuals and organizations. Historic sites that significantly contribute to the economic prosperity of the country through tourism are now largely in private hands. Sixty percent of historical sites were owned by the state in 1990. Today, this percentage is only 7 percent.

Compiling a list of all of the governmental institutions, businesses, nongovernmental organizations, nonprofit groups, foundations, and individual experts who have assisted Central and Eastern Europe since 1989 would be an impossible task. However, I would like to focus on a few examples of significant help from abroad, in the form of both financial aid and technical expertise, that influenced the development, attitudes, and perspectives of the nonprofit sector in the field of cultural heritage and preservation. This list includes the British National Trust, the European Foundation Center, the Council of Europe, the European Cultural Foundation, the Fondation de France, the Getty Grant Program, Program PHARE, the Prague Heritage Trust, the Rockefeller Brothers Fund, and the World Monuments Fund. Thanks to their advice and cooperation, a number of significant programmatic milestones have been accomplished. We have signed the World Heritage Convention and become a member of the prestigious World Heritage Trust. The cities of Prague, Český Krumlov, Telč and Kutna Hora are now listed by the United Nations Educational, Scientific, and Cultural Organization (UNESCO) as world monuments. The Association of Historical Sites, with a membership of more than one hundred Czech towns, has been established, and there is now an active Czech Committee of the International Council on Monuments and Sites (ICOMOS).

In the spring of 1991, during his first visit to Czechoslovakia, the Prince of Wales opened a traveling exhibition, "Threatened Monuments, Threatened Consciousness." This exhibition showed the progressive devastation of historic monuments documented by preservation specialists from regional institutes during the years in which their battle to establish measures for the protection of historic monuments fell on deaf ears. During this period the national consciousness was threatened and dulled. The message of this exhibition was reinforced when the Prince of Wales commented that if this trend of devastation continued as it had in most of Europe during the last fifty years, not much would be left but a desolate cultural wilderness in which we would only get lost, losing our sense of life and roots.

This touring exhibition was one of the first instances of partnership in the Czech Republic. Prepared by the Civic Forum Foundation, it traveled to different locations throughout the entire republic. Our partners were local representatives or nongovernmental organizations and individuals who added their own local monuments to the basic exhibition. In this way, it inspired wider interest in the value of local monuments and collected contributions for their protection.

Regulation and its Problems in the Czech Republic

The administration of care for our country's cultural heritage began in 1850 under the auspices of the Austro-Hungarian empire. One of the best-known associations formed during this time was The Club for Old Prague, which was established in 1900 in reaction to the thoughtless and callous rebuilding of the Old Town and the Jewish Quarter. During the First Republic, an effective structure based on the cooperation between regional municipalities and preservation specialists cared for national monuments. At the time the responsibility for the care of cultural sites was anchored in our postwar constitution. The totalitarian regime did not completely lack proper laws. The current poor state of our castles resulted not from a dearth of regulation or an inadequate system of care, but from negative political and economic forces, the rhetoric of the past regime, and a lack of public awareness.

In 1987 a new law for the protection of cultural monuments was passed. This law has been recently updated, formally changing its terminology. However, while the term "socialist state" was replaced by the term "state," the current law does not reflect the fundamentally new situation in property relations embodied in the Charter of Basic Rights and Freedoms, according to which the proprietary rights of all owners have the same legal status and protection. The present law allows the state, during the change of ownership of a cultural monument, to enforce its preemptive right to acquire the property at a price set by an official estimate. But the law is unclear concerning the extent of obligation of the owner and the possible controls or consequences of his or her not observing this obligation.

The proposal for a new legal arrangement sparked extensive debate. Different opinions on the role of the state, reflected in concrete proposals, mirrored the opinions of different political interest groups. On the one hand, the state was seen as an executive institution and, on the other hand, as the guarantor of public space. The result, in the view of some preservation specialists, is that the proposals are too liberal and give the owner too much freedom in caring for the monument. Others contend that the laws are too rigid and do not give the owner any hope for sustaining the monument. The former opinion represents those who believe financial support for the protection of monuments should continue to be the responsibility of the state. The latter is held by those who see the restrictions as a hindrance to reaching the full practical and economic potential of the heritage.

Let me illustrate the situation in the Czech Republic by using examples of the current state of historic buildings in Prague. The Czech Republic enjoyed a healthy tourist boom (approximately 70 million visitors per year) during the six years after the revolution, and this flood of visitors has shown no signs of abating. The majority of tourists, approximately 17 million a year who stay for an average of five days, pass through the Historic Reserve of Prague; however, none of the profits from this tourism is channeled to the maintenance of the city's heritage—there is no mechanism to establish this link. Despite the fact that the Historic Reserve attracts millions of tourists, the city itself has no income from the tourist industry and depends on the state for financial assistance.

The Prague historic district is composed of 3,700 buildings. Of these, 1,600 are listed buildings guarded by rigid rules. Czech law states that private owners of historic monuments are obligated to care for their monuments properly and to consult specialists. Czech tax legislation addresses repairs and renovations in the following manner:

- Repairs: There is a 100-percent deduction for repairs. In other words, the cost of repairs can be subtracted from revenue before determining profit. This is a positive incentive for homeowners to make repairs. But when a bank loan is used as a resource to finance repairs, the interest is considered an investment until all renovation is completed. Depreciation for such buildings is calculated over a period of fifty years.
- Renovation: Renovation is defined as any work that does not exist in the building already, such as adding a new door or elevator and installing bathrooms or a heating system. This work is considered an investment, and with income taxed at approximately 40 percent, the total income that must be generated to break even is almost 1.6 times greater than the amount that is put into the project.
- Capital investment: Capital for the revitalization of cultural monuments is limited, particularly by the preemptive right of the state. Although the state does not currently enforce this right, mainly due to insufficient means, it places investors in a risky position. After investing in the revitalization of a monument, the owner may wish to sell; however, the state may enforce its preemptive right at a price that corresponds not to the market, but rather to its own estimate according to public notice.

This last point is possibly the most serious obstacle to investment, and one can only hope that the law will soon be changed. The established preemptive right of the state with regard to cultural monuments directly conflicts with the principle of privatization and its implementation. Approximately 80 percent of the housing stock in Prague has been restored to private owners, with most of these buildings in the protected reserve zone. This means that much of the housing stock is owned by people who, over the last forty years, have not had the opportunity to accumulate any capital. They cannot afford to pay for the necessary maintenance and repairs. Moreover, because residential rent is regulated by the government, owners do not have the option to raise rents in order to pay for the costs of renovations, repairs, and general maintenance.

The attempt to find a useful function for a monument that will also help finance its sustainability requires an economic valuation for the property. Both overestimation as well as underestimation are common practices. The unrealistic expectations of owners when selling the property make this trade practically impossible and threaten the monument. If the original owners do sell, the purchaser typically converts the building from residential to commercial and buys out the tenants. Unfortunately, a plan submitted by a group of well-known architects to prevent this transfer from residential to commercial ownership has been rejected. The site owner and others who benefit from the proposed development see the matter differently. Preeminent among the rights associated with real property is the entitlement to develop it and, thereby, to realize income from it. This fact, together with the aforementioned system of taxation and the risks associated with capital investment, make the protection of historic buildings very difficult.

As a result, the center of Prague is being depopulated, creating a new demographic pattern. Traditionally the composition of European cities has been the opposite of American urban demography. Typically the center of a European city, with its towering cathedrals, is surrounded by middle-class homes and, further outward along the perimeter, by factories and lodging for factory employees. In the past, economic crises in Europe drove job-seeking emigrants to America where they settled in the city centers, and as they gradually grew richer, they moved to the periphery. Thus, the demographics of the American population improve towards the city's periphery, that is, toward the suburbs.[2]

Conflicts in historic preservation take various forms; however, they often come down to a difference in point of view between monument preservationists and site owners. To the preservationist, the protection of architecturally distinctive buildings that have become public icons contributes to a favorable perception of the city, enhancing basic community and aesthetic values.

To accomplish all of this, new approaches to the heritage have to be designed, approaches that will rely much more heavily on partnerships than before. But to establish the foundation for partnerships there also have to be changes in legislation, changes in the education of the population, the development of a nonprofit sector, and the increased involvement of the business sector.

Adjustment of Legislation

Following a general policy of privatization, it is necessary to find a well-balanced system of regulations, compensation, tax incentives, and grant programs. Part I of this volume describes the five means by which the government can positively influence the preservation of cultural heritage. A natural trend in democratic countries is that government limits itself to the creation of an appropriate space and its protection. Government activity has changed from focusing on "input" to concerning itself with "output" and "policy." As Lester Salamon has pointed out in *Beyond Privatization*, the role of the government as an agency has shifted to the development of "programs," where the program is a particular combination of authority, organizations, resources, and personnel assembled to achieve specific public purposes. And all of these programs need to be embodied in new legislation.

Education

A nationwide education and awareness-building program needs to be implemented that will raise the overall understanding of cultural heritage issues, instilling a sense of pride in cultural preservation. And to be most successful, a network of nonprofit, nongovernmental preservation organizations will have to be created to assist in this task.

The Development of Civic Organizations

To date there are no official National Trust-type organizations established in any of the former Eastern bloc countries, although efforts toward their establishment are under way. Such entities that own and manage property, provide expert advice, or develop educational awareness programs could aid historic preservation. But before we consider how best to use the skills and know-how accumulated in society, let us look at the role of the different sectors in society.

In simple terms, society can be broken into three sectors. Aside from the role of the state, discussed in previous chapters, a democratic society typically consists of a strong business sector and also a "third sector" of noncorporate, nonprofit, and nongovernmental organizations (NGOs). Rather than financial reward, these organizations have as their primary motivations love, personal relationships and interests, shared experiences, faith, a hierarchy of values, internal goals, intellectual potential, and personal aspirations. These dimensions offer a place for local nonpolitical leaders, charismatic personalities, those who feel a sense of responsibility and the call of a certain task in life, and those who wish to involve the family or the wider community in improving the quality of life in a particular place.

The NGO sector includes a wide variety of educational institutions; cultural, social, and charitable organizations; agencies that represent the disabled, ethnic minorities and other groups of disenfranchised people; religious groups; organizations concerned with emergency aid, health, human rights, and community development issues; hobby clubs; sports clubs; public charities, foundations, and civic associations. The NGO sector is not necessarily the same as the community or general public, even though NGOs are often confused with "community," as if they represented the public in the wider sense of the word. It is wrong to assume that the NGO sector "speaks for the people." Nevertheless, it is often a useful bridge between different sectors and a key player in the partnership building process, as will be shown later. In Central and Eastern Europe, the nongovernmental, nonprofit sector still has an uncertain position in society, and foundations and civil associations are not yet taken seriously as trusted partners.

Business

The raison d'être for any business is economic success as measured by profit-making. The mission of a business is to invest and to reinvest, and the dynamics of this process are reflected in the various quantitative measures of success. A necessary condition for any business's success is its acceptance by society, which includes gaining the support of both clients and employees.

In Central Europe we have a long entrepreneurial tradition. The most famous example is the successful entrepreneur Bata, whose athletic shoes are marketed internationally. In the first half of this century he implemented a system of care for his employees, including developing housing and providing a school system. The town of Zlín, where he implemented his approach, is still very successful in business terms, mainly through the strong tradition of this wider concept. Locally Bata exemplified the ideals that are sought in a business-community partnership.

Clever companies in Central and Eastern Europe are establishing real relationships with their communities to improve their image. This is more than a tool; it is a style of doing business. Today this approach has been practically adopted by most large companies. Paying attention to the needs and opinions of the public has become fashionable as well as necessary.

Business today works on the basis of a wider, more personal moral norm, more attuned to the needs and expectations of all those "in the game" within the context of the new economic system. This means, as the Prince of Wales Business Leader's Forum has stressed, that a successful business not only needs customers, but also employees, partners, and a broader community that offers its understanding, support, education, and prosperity.

Huge international companies are looking for new ways to support community projects and events. Contrary to the many forms of short-term support given by locally based companies to their own employees, international firms are oriented toward the development of long-term partnerships that will improve their business success. This philosophy is beginning to influence the behavior of business in Central Europe and the development of society in general. Many entrepreneurs are beginning to realize that profit-making business transactions are compatible with maintaining the environment, with providing training and other means of education, with aiding small entrepreneurs to develop, and with helping small businesses solve the difficult problems that result from economic changes.

New Forms of Capital

The arrogance of man towards nature, the informational/technological revolution, and the consumer society have created conflict between the human community and its environment. The first individuals to take a position against this threat on a global scale were ecologists. After the environmental summit in Rio de Janeiro in 1992, where the idea of sustainable development was formulated, the policy of the World Bank towards the environment changed. More financing is now dedicated to education and wilderness preservation and less to pouring concrete and clearing forests.

Robert M. Solow, Nobel Prize-winning economist in 1987, explained that what we normally measure as capital is just a small part of what it takes to sustain human welfare. The study "Monitoring Economic Progress" became a new model that could help to refocus development strategies. Since the returns on investment in other kinds of capital are difficult to measure, they have often been underevaluated by economists. This green approach reformulates the criteria by which the wealth of a nation is measured. The World Bank saw its task as generating more comprehensive estimates of wealth that could be compared across time. Its starting point became the existing estimates of physical or "produced" capital. Then the estimates of "natural" capital, a combination of land (divided into categories of use, including protected natural habitat), fossil-fuel deposits, other mineral wealth, and clean water were added. When the economic evaluation of the country is defined by whether the country's total wealth is growing, standard estimates of savings using traditional accounting methods can be misleading. Financial capital is just as important for a healthy economy as is intellectual and social capital for a healthy community. A healthy community has a sufficient amount of contacts in a specific social layer of the community. It follows, therefore, that research into a community's wealth must include the wealth embodied in human skills as well as in health and social organizations.

The World Bank is focusing its attention on long-term trends in human capital investment, and a new accounting system is under development that computes not only GNP but also the strength and value of natural resources, human resources, and social institutions that provide economic opportunities for people. Such a system seeks to assign value to the store of resources as well as to products and trade (which mostly represent the use of resources), thus creating a more balanced view of wealth, nation by nation and globally. Yet, individual areas of the world still differ greatly in the extent to which they are prepared to accept the thought of sustainable development in the wider sense of the phrase, including preserving natural surroundings as well as preserving and cultivating cultural values along with their material representations.

If by the concept "culture" we mean "the sum of the inherited ideas, beliefs, values, and knowledge, which constitute the shared bases of social action," as put forward in Lester Borley's contribution to this volume, and we include all of their material representations, we see a certain tension between the protectors of culture in individual places on the planet and the propagators of cultural tourism who bring the informational/technological revolution with them. Weighing against the economic revenues from tourism is the problem of protecting the heritage against material and spiritual devastation through mass attendance. Historic monuments embody eternal values which are not reproducible. As Peter Passel has observed, from an environmental point of view, "It is important to accept that if cultural tourism is to have any depth of meaning, then it must reflect the values which people themselves respect."[3] Even though the idea of sustainable development is generally accepted as an important step, translating it into the languages of individual disciplines, together with preserving the continuity of the cultural values of individual cultures, and subsequently implementing it into law, cannot be expected to happen overnight.

Even though the independent business sector in Central and Eastern Europe developed from practically nothing, terms like "shares," "funds," and "capital" are rapidly becoming more and more common in public discourse. This accelerated economic transformation gives the impression that economics per se have become the priority. The language of economics prevails in our society, and the language of capital is often used with the assumption that it is universally understood.

French social anthropologist and philosopher Pierre Bourdieu has identified different types of capital—social capital, cultural capital, political capital, symbolical capital, intellectual capital, and so on—as a way of evaluating qualities offered to society by means other than economic ones. But following a suggestion of the American anthropologist Andrew Lass, one can separate capital into three basic types: (1) financial, or the world of money, (2) intellectual, or the world of the wealth of knowledge, and (3) social, or the world of human contacts and communication. According to this model, the roles of the individual sectors are simply, but clearly, categorized. The wealth of an individual is possible to conceive in these three forms, too. One might be rich financially, rich in creativity, or rich in the ability to act in social situations. Lass has observed: "One can be financially not very well off, but intellectually a millionaire. Someone who has invested in his education can benefit by making money with his knowledge that people need. Not only is this person useful, but he can interact with others that have knowledge. Therefore, such a person has two things. Although he may not have much money, he has intellectual and social capital."

Is it possible to transform one type of capital into another? If someone is rich in know-how, perhaps an inventor or architect, some investor or construction company can hire him, but what is actually being bought? His talent is being bought. The person cannot be bought.

In countries in transition some people have become rich quickly and, consequently, feel as though they belong to a higher social echelon. They surround themselves with art and move into historically significant buildings. They may buy a Picasso, but they buy a painting, not the artist. Then comes the question, how to manufacture Picassos, meaning artists. One possible way is by investing in the institutions that support the education of talented people.

In this way financial capital in the form of philanthropy supports the creation of intellectual capital. Social recognition of philanthropy makes it possible to increase social capital. Consequently, the financial capitalist has two possibilities for transforming his capital. He can immediately purchase a painting, sculpture, or castle, or, more interestingly and importantly, he can invest in a school or in culture—in the system that protects cultural heritage. This makes it possible for society to care for the continuity of its own existence. The not-for-profit sector, in a cultural social atmosphere, offers and makes possible the creation of important social capital.

Partnership in Theory

"Conflicts are too expensive" is a familiar and pragmatic slogan in the world of business in the United States. How can one promote cooperation and partnership? For a partial answer, one can refer to the theoretical results of research in social psychology, science, or mathematics. In *The Evolution of Cooperation*, Robert Axelrod remembers the simple question that came up at the beginning of his research: "When should a person cooperate, and when should a person be selfish, in an ongoing interaction with another person? Should a friend keep providing favors to another friend who never reciprocates? Should a business provide prompt service to another business that is about to go bankrupt? How intensely should the United States try to punish the Soviet Union for a particular hostile act, and what pattern of behavior can the United States use to best elicit cooperative behavior from the Soviet Union?"[4]

Axelrod also published an article, "Arithmetics of Mutual Help," in the June 1995 issue of *Scientific American*. In this article he addressed the issue of cooperation through mathematical game theory, in which it is possible to posit models with which one can experiment to better understand the meaning and advantages of cooperative behavior. In mathematical game theory, a game is defined as a process of interaction between two (or more) individuals where each chooses one of many possible acts or moves in view of how the size of his resulting profit or loss will be influenced by the behavior of the other. Certain features define the rules of the game, and the instructions of how to react in a given situation are called the strategy of the game. Simply said, it is possible to distinguish between two types of behavior: selfish and cooperative. Selfish behavior is seen simply as the maximizing of one's own profit with no concern for the other's loss. Cooperative behavior means that one is ready to work with others to share the profit.

For those of us in Central and Eastern Europe, the famous example of the "prisoner's dilemma" in game theory reminds us of our recent past. This dilemma illustrates the consequences of selfish and cooperative behavior. Imagine two prisoners, both trying to escape. The consequences depend on whether they will cooperate on their effort to escape, share the risk, and if successful, receive certain rewards. Will one prisoner behave selfishly, exploiting the other by informing the guards of the other prisoner's plan to escape? His selfish behavior thus earns him a large reward, and the other receives nothing. But, based on the same calculation, the other might not cooperate either, leading to the third possibility that neither will cooperate (both will try to exploit the other) and both will receive only a very small reward.

When the game is played for a long time with the same partners, the players become familiar with one another's strategy. This means that the players will come to learn what to expect from the other player. If each player sees that his best personal option is to defect in the first round, then in ensuing rounds both players will expect the other to defect. Each player's only remaining option is also to defect. Even though it is true that the reward for mutual cooperation is higher, this is manifested only after a longer period of time. Thus, although short-sighted selfish behavior would be safer, more advantageous, and more natural in the short term, in the long term, selfish behavior is not nearly as beneficial as cooperative behavior, even though it is more difficult and demanding.

Axelrod shows that cooperation based solely on reciprocity seems possible and could be a winning strategy in a world where any strategy is possible. In biology, the basic rule is survival. Cooperative behavior evolved from this basic rule, since cooperation improves the chances of survival. And although social life is more complicated than most theory, inasmuch as people are not simply following certain schemata, there are rules, and similar strategic roles, that inform behavior.

Cooperative behavior is needed biologically and is transferred into the rules of ethics. In society, morals and ethics develop in order to facilitate our survival. According to evolutionary psychology, one's behavior is affected by one's dependence on others. The list of ethical norms is an effective and concise tool with which we can make emphatic (though possibly wrong) decisions with minimal time and thought. Face to face with complicated social interactions, the individual has a built-in guide to behavior. Ethical norms are an effective guide, thanks to the additional dimension of mutual dependence which helps to overcome, in concrete situations, the barrier of egoistic wishes, and results in helping others. "For altruism to succeed in biological terms, our biological nature made us altruistic in the moral sense."[5] The question arises: how can a potentially cooperative strategy get an initial foothold in an environment that is predominantly noncooperative? Practical mechanisms are necessary to address and short-circuit these theoretical dilemmas.

Action Planning Weekends

A prelude to forming partnerships that has worked with some success in Central and Eastern Europe has been the action planning weekend. Action planning is a new method of community involvement resulting in the creation and revitalization of the urban environment. The Tools for Community Design program by Nick Wates, Ros Tennison, and John Thompson is especially potent in situations where an intermediary is needed to help find a common understanding between different negotiating parties and/or when a project is too complex to be understood by nonspecialists. Moreover, it works for the living environment and provides the possibility of a continuity of genius loci, together with the creation of close relationships between the community and business spheres during financing and/or moral support of local governmental institutions.

A consensus is emerging from within the public and private sectors that a more effective way to create sustainable development is to get everybody involved in the process. All participants thus contribute their ideas and experience collectively at the outset, rather than test their ideas against those that have already been determined by others. For investors, this approach means a real revolution in the preparation of development projects and can, to a large degree, replace or complement the planning of experts and market research. We become aware of this qualitative shift when we compare classical methods of forecasting (for example, the return on investment in a simple economic model) with modern self-organizing prognostic models working on the principle of neuron computers. In classical prognostic models, exact calculations of theoretically derived, relatively simple relations of model parameters were applied to inexact data, while the self-organizing systems are based on the interactive verifying of the path of development in the course of the creation of the prognostic model. These methods were especially proven for long-term forecasts of the behavior of complex systems.

Planning weekends are a technique by which a collaborative, interdisciplinary dialogue can be created at the formative stage of a project. All of the relevant parties can be involved in this intensive period of working together, whether they have existing or potential interests in the project. They may include local and statutory authorities, the voluntary sector, professionals, politicians, developers, financiers, employers and employees, tenants, residents, and the wider community. The aim is for the collaborative process to continue after the planning weekend and to establish appropriate mechanisms to move the project forward. Projects prepared in this way are not only economically feasible but are also supported and accepted by the community.

Partnerships for Development

Earlier, I showed how the business sector can transform its language of financial investment and capital into other forms of capital. The final consequences are shared by all, as are the basic ideas of cooperation in general. These examples are connected through the parallel of ethical norms, which human behavior follows. For successful economic and business development, cooperation across the three sectors is crucial. Each sector must recognize the interdependence among all of the sectors at the structural (organizational) level and acknowledge the equal value of their roles in society while understanding and fulfilling its own particular role. Working in partnership across sector boundaries is vital for the long-term sustainability of the planet and the development of society as a whole.

Partnership as a new method of cooperation with businesses has been a part of the program at the Prince of Wales Business Leaders Forum (PWBLF), since the early 1990s. To borrow the words of the forum's publications "What is Partnership?" and "Tools for Partnership-Building": "Partnership is a formal cross-sector relationship between individuals or groups in which expectations and commitments are agreed beforehand and which has a shared profit/risk element. It is a relationship built upon fulfilling an obligation or completing a task." The Partnership Unit within the PWBLF was established in 1993 to develop and promote cross-sector cooperation. It aims to do this by:

- helping to build the capacity of each sector to work in partnership for sustainable development;
- sharing experience and communicating examples of successful cross-sector partnerships worldwide;
- acting as a catalyst for new partnerships or for the reinvigoration of existing ones; and
- building the case for partnerships from the perspective of all partners: business, government, or voluntary organizations.

Partnership is something like marriage. Each partner should have a feeling of equal importance. Each character is, of course, different as each belongs to a different sector. In keeping with their roles, the different sectors have developed different skills. The corporate sector has highly developed management skills, marketing skills, and a planning mechanism (all tools needed for income generation and wealth creation). The government can use the five tools to protect the public interest. The nonprofit sector has been identified with work that arises from a passionate commitment to a cause, often with a deep knowledge and the skills needed to bring people together. But will the partners be able to break down the perception of a donor/recipient relationship?

A clear declaration and understanding of the expectations and interests of each partner is necessary from the very beginning. The decision-making process as well as transparent accounting need to be negotiated in advance. In reality many nonprofit organizations that approach businesses for financial help simply present a list of expected expenditures along with a description of their project. Businesses operate on a cash-flow basis and ask what will happen when the project will be completed. How much are operating costs? Where is the source of future income? Who is the manager of the project? Is success guaranteed? But most important, they ask, how does the proposed project fit the objectives of the corporation?

Partnerships can work only if each party benefits with respect to its original mission. Government seeks to protect the public interest, broadly defined businesses seek to make a profit, and nonprofit organizations seek to promote the common interests of their supporters. There is still a great anxiety from NGOs about the behavior of the business sector just as there is concern from businesses about the capacity of the NGO sector. In a partnership the parties must get to know one another, bringing a strong understanding to the partnership relationship. The political program of the government is probably known. But do NGOs really know what the ideas behind the companies operating around them are? What is the agenda of Coca-Cola? Microsoft? How different is the perspective of American Express from that of Visa? Do we really know which kind of business operates in our region? And vice versa? What kind of market research is done by companies to pinpoint the wishes of their clients? Do companies feel that they have proper access to their customers? Do the sophisticated market research methods, forecasts, and opinion polls really map out the client's wishes and the community's expectations?

In emerging market economies, cross-sector partnerships are an entirely new phenomenon. They could be used to develop a completely new approach to preserving the national heritage. Beginning with collaborative efforts such as action planning weekends and expanding them into true development partnerships could become a truly revolutionary method for the implementation of sustainable development in the context of the cultural heritage in Central and Eastern Europe.

The Western European and American situations with respect to the built heritage are relatively stable because of constitutional limitations, legislative authorizations, and the existence of a network of bureaucratic institutions for preservation. In this sense, the choice of tools in these settings may be quite limited. In the former Soviet states, on the other hand, the divestment of preservation policy and authority from central governments, privatization and restitution, and the rush to substitute market for command economies make these countries fertile ground to test theories on the choice of implementation tools and to develop new forms of partnership.[6]

Notes

1. John Adams, letter to Abigail Adams, 12 May 1780, in *The Book of Abigail and John* (Cambridge, Mass.: Harvard University Press, 1975), 260.
2. Cyril Höschl, "Evakuace Praga" (The Evacuation of Prague), *Lidove noviny* 29 (3 February 1996).
3. Peter Passel, "The Wealth of Nations: A 'Greener' Approach Turns List Upside Down," *The New York Times* (19 September 1995), C1.
4. Robert Axelrod, *The Evolution of Cooperation* (New York: Basic Books, 1984), vii.
5. Vojtech Novotny, "Do Good, Retaliate, and in Time, Forgive," *Vesmír* 74 (September 1995), 492–94.
6. I am indebted to Robert Stipe for calling this point to my attention.

References

Axelrod, Robert. *The Evolution of Cooperation*. New York: Basic Books, 1984.

Höschl, Cyril. "Evakuace Praga" (The Evacuation of Prague), *Lidove noviny* 29 (3 February 1996).

Nadace Pro Rozvoj Architektury a Stavitelstvi Ceska Spolecnost Pro Stavebni Pravo. *Ochrana pamatek a stavebni zakon*. Prague: ABF, 1994.

Novotny, Vojtech, "Do Good, Retaliate, and in Time, Forgive." *Vesmír* 74 (September 1995): 492–94.

Nowak, Martin A., Robert M. May, and Karl Sigmund. "The Arithmetics of Mutual Help." *Scientific American* 272, no. 6 (June 1995): 76–81.

Passel, Peter. "The Wealth of Nations: A 'Greener' Approach Turns List Upside Down." *The New York Times* (19 September 1995), C1.

The Prince of Wales Business Leaders Forum. *Assessing the Impact in Central and Eastern Europe: A Review of Business as Partners in Development 1990 to 1995*. London: K&N Press, 1995.

Salamon, Lester M. *Beyond Privatization: The Tools of Government Action*. Washington, D.C.: The Urban Institute Press, 1989.

Štulc, Josef. "Prague: A City Poised at the Cross-Roads." Peter Burman, Rob Pickard, and Sue Taylor, eds. *The Economics of Architectural Conservation*. York, England: The University of York Institute of Advanced Architectural Studies, February 1995.

Wates, Nick. *Action Planning*. London: The Prince of Wales' Institute of Architecture, 1996.

Appendixes

A. Annotated Bibliography

Katherine Mangle

This bibliography was prepared as background material for the Fellows and Faculty of Salzburg Seminar 332, "Preserving the National Heritage: Policies, Partnerships, and Actions." Some of these materials are specifically referenced in the individual papers included in this volume.

Cantacuzino, Sherban. "Blueprint for Conservation in the Third World." *MIMAR: Architecture in Development* 24 (1987): 19–25.

> Based on research in India, this article is intended for the use of state and local government. An implicit idea is that a different conservation "blueprint" is necessary for developing areas.

Costonis, John. *Space Adrift: Landmark Preservation and the Marketplace.* Urbana, Ill.: University of Illinois Press, 1974. ISBN 0–252–01553–3.

> The seminal work on transfer of development rights, *Space Adrift* frames preservation planning and legislation discussion around an innovative landmarks preservation scheme for the city of Chicago. Though this strategy was the model for programs in other cities such as New York and Denver, it was never implemented in Chicago. After illustrating the plan, Costonis discusses its economic, design, and legal impacts.

Costonis, John J. *Icons and Aliens: Law, Aesthetics, and Environmental Change.* Urbana, Ill.: University of Illinois Press, 1989. ISBN 0–7506–0822–6.

> This book explores the relationship between aesthetics and the law. Preservation of historic and otherwise significant buildings often follows trends and fashion, yet must be backed up and interpreted by the judicial system.

Dale, Antony. *Volume I: France, Great Britain, Ireland, the Netherlands.* Historic Preservation in Foreign Countries, edited by Robert E. Stipe. Washington, D.C.: US/ICOMOS, 1982. ISBN 0–911697–00–4.

> The first in a series intended to provide information and models to American preservationists, this book is an inventory of the historic preservation policies in France, Great Britain, Ireland, and the Netherlands. Each section looks at national acts, regional and local activity, inventories/lists of properties, any financial incentives, and voluntary groups. Though care is taken to avoid direct comparisons between very different systems, the book concludes with a list of the best points from each country's system, which could inform a comprehensive legislation.

Gleye, Paul, and Waldemar Szczerba. *Volume III: Poland.* Historic Preservation in Other Countries, edited by Robert E. Stipe. Washington, D.C.: US/ICOMOS, 1989. ISBN 0–91169–705–5.

    A descriptive account of historic preservation practices and projects in Poland, this text follows the movement's progression from the 19th century as a partitioned state, through the political changes of the twentieth century. While policies and the form of preservation activity are emphasized, one chapter is devoted to "Polish Theory and Philosophy," and another to the training of preservation professionals.

Goodland, Robert, and Maryla Webb. *The Management of Cultural Property in World Bank-Assisted Projects.* World Bank Technical Paper no. 62. Washington, D.C.: World Bank, 1987.

    The first section of this paper is a statement on the treatment of cultural property (movable and nonmovable) within World Bank projects, including how consideration for heritage objects and buildings should be taken within projects not explicitly related to culture. The second part contains an index of World Bank-assisted projects with cultural property components, and the appendixes include "Legislation," "International Conventions," and "Non-Governmental Institutions with Expertise in Cultural Preservation."

International Symposium on World Heritage Towns. *Safeguarding Historic Urban Ensembles in a Time of Change: A Management Guide.* Quebec: Organization of World Heritage Towns, 1991.

    Written for the World Heritage Towns Colloquium, this manual is designed to assist town officials by providing models of management and policy in historic towns and cities. The bulk of the guide, "Managing Conservation Programs Within Historic Towns," uses case studies to illustrate the use of various conservation tools. Adaptation of these tools to a specific town's needs is discussed in the intervening text.

Keune, Russell V. *The Historic Preservation Yearbook: A Documentary Record of Significant Policy Developments and Issues.* Bethesda, Md.: Adler & Adler, 1985. ISBN 0–917561–00–7.

    This material presents local, state, and national legislation and agency documents, addressing issues and methods of preservation in the United States. All five policy tools are addressed: ownership and operation, regulation, incentives, property rights, and information. Clearly organized, this has a good balance between informative text and original sources.

Leimenstoll, Jo Ramsay. *Volume IV: Turkey.* Historic Preservation in Other Countries, edited by Robert E. Stipe. Washington, D.C.: US/ICOMOS, 1990. ISBN 0–911697–06–3.

    This final volume of its series describes the historical development of the heritage preservation movement in Turkey, then discusses current methods and institutions through numerous project descriptions.

Listokin, David. *Living Cities*. Twentieth Century Fund Task Force on Urban Preservation Policies. New York: Preservation Press, 1985. ISBN 0-87078-167-7.
    A critical look at the American preservation movement and processes, including what has been and should be done in historic preservation, who should set policy, and what tools are available. The report includes an overview of the evolution, themes, and meanings of the movement, and government regulations and controls at the local, state, and national levels.

Mc Lean, Margaret, ed. *Cultural Heritage in Asia & the Pacific: Conservation and Policy*. Proceedings of a Symposium Held in Honolulu, Hawaii, September 8–13, 1991. Marina Del Ray, Cal.: Getty Conservation Institute, 1993. ISBN 0-89236-248-0.
    A record of the proceedings of a symposium held in Honolulu, this is one of few books addressing heritage conservation in Asia. Though much of the emphasis is on technical preservation approaches, there are policy recommendations as well. These articles draw attention to the Western cultural leanings of the international conventions and make recommendations on heritage conservation.

Medler-Montgomery, Marilyn. *Preservation Easements: A Legal Mechanism for Protecting Cultural Resources*. Denver: The Colorado Historical Foundation, 1984.
    A guide to the development, concerns, uses, and consequences of the legal rights tool of preservation easements.

Morris, Marya. *Innovative Tools for Historic Preservation*. Planning Advisory Service Report no. 438. Chicago: American Planning Association, 1993.
    In light of the American Federal Preservation tax credit cuts of 1986, this report looks at options for state and local governments to encourage or enforce heritage preservation. It considers a variety of approaches (state and local tax relief, conservation districts, down-zoning, and comprehensive plans) with examples from numerous American cities.

Paseltiner, Ellen Kettler, and Deborah Tyler. *Zoning and Historic Preservation—A Survey of Current Zoning Techniques in U.S. Cities to Encourage Historic Preservation*. Springfield, Ill.: Landmarks Preservation Council of Illinois, 1983.
    A survey of current zoning techniques designed to encourage historic preservation in American cities.

Robinson, Susan, and John E. Peterson. *Fiscal Incentives for Historic Preservation*. Washington, D.C.: Government Finance Research Center, 1989. ISBN 0-89125-138-3.
    Part of a project undertaken by the city of Atlanta, Georgia, to integrate historic preservation into its existing planning program, this report spends a great deal of time examining and explaining the implications tax incentives hold for the city budget and the property owner. It includes an economic explanation of tax incentives, including informative graphs showing the effects different incentive programs (abatement, freeze, and credit) have on the property tax.

Roddewig, Richard. *Economic Incentives for Historic Preservation.* Washington, D.C.: National Trust for Historic Preservation Center for Policy Studies, 1987.

Prepared for the city of Atlanta, Georgia, this paper describes the status and use of economic incentives in the United States after 1986. There is a brief discussion of the types of incentives needed, financing and cost-cutting incentives, and finance assistance.

Salamon, Lester, and Michael Lund. "The Changing Tools of Government Action: An Overview" and "The Tools Approach: Basic Analysis." Chaps. 1 and 2 in *Beyond Privatization: The Tools of Government Action*, edited by Lester M. Salamon. Washington, D.C.: Urban Institute Press, 1989.

The introductory chapters of this book explain a "tools" approach to public policy analysis. After addressing the modes of political inquiry from which this method differs, the authors explore the meaning of "tools," and the important factors to recognize when categorizing various mechanisms (such as administrative feasibility, effectiveness, political support, efficiency, and equity).

Stipe, Robert E., and Antoinette J. Lee, eds. *The American Mosaic: Preserving a Nation's Heritage.* Washington, D.C.: US/ICOMOS, 1987. ISBN 0–89133–140–9.

This book is a thorough account of modern American preservation activity, from the policy framework to the more difficult social and economics issues facing the movement. The progression of the American preservation movement is evaluated as the authors examine its policy tools and organizations.

U.S. Department of the Interior. *The Secretary of the Interior's Standards for Rehabilitation and Guidelines for Rehabilitating Historic Buildings.* Washington, D.C.: Government Printing Office, 1983.

This seemingly simple list of technical rehabilitation guidelines has become one of the most powerful preservation information tools in the United States. The twelve standards are the basis of many tax incentive and grant programs.

Wagner, Richard. *Local Government and Historic Preservation.* Washington, D.C.: National Trust for Historic Preservation, 1991.

This book, published by the National Park Service and the National Trust, is a broad guide for preservation on the city level. Wagner not only explains the tax incentives, Secretary's Standards, and the National Register, but also looks into approaches to educating the community and neighborhood revitalization strategies. Case studies from around the United States are included.

Wigg, David. *Of Mosaics and Mosques: A Look at the Campaign to Preserve Cultural Heritage.* New York: World Bank, 1994. ISBN 0–8213–2732–1.

Within this essay, the author relates the story of two cases of World Bank-assisted projects in Cyprus and Pakistan, in which cultural heritage preservation became a multi-disciplinary struggle. Through this he examines the impact of multilateral organizations such as the World Bank.

Will, Margaret T. *Volume II: Federal Republic of Germany, Switzerland, Austria.* Historic Preservation in Foreign Countries, edited by Robert E. Stipe. Washington, D.C.: US/ICOMOS, 1984. ISBN 0–911697–01–2.

Though the works in this series are not meant to be explicitly comparative, this volume allows for cross-referencing due to its organization. With three European countries covered in the same book, each chapter lays out the development of preservation legislation, approaches to listing, property rights, financing, federal legislation, and private or institutional groups.

B. A Guide to Preservation Resources Online

Katherine Mangle

Doing Research on the World Wide Web

Amidst the often superfluous and overwhelming stream of information available on the Internet, valuable sources for serious research on preservation can be found. One can quickly access full texts of official and informational documents. With a little more patience, one can find visual and audio presentations of architectural projects.

The address listed after each of the following titles is the URL code (Universal Resource Locator) for locating the file. Click on the underlined word for a direct connection, or enter the code into the provided space when opening a file from a search interface. Specifics of searching for Internet sites will differ slightly depending on the software in use. For a basic introduction to using the World Wide Web, see *The World Wide Web for Dummies*, which is accessible from the MIT homepage:
<http://www.mit.edu:8001/people/rei/wwwintro.html>

This appendix lists the locations of resources for the preservation of historic buildings and sites. Within most of these files are connections to further resources. For example, the World Wide Web page of the U.S. National Trust for Historic Preservation contains a section on Internet Resources, which can be directly accessed through that site.

Please keep in mind that the virtual landscape is constantly changing, and some of these connections will surely change location or form in the near future. The information contained here was last checked in August 1996 when this appendix was compiled.

Organizations

The following citations lead to the home pages of particular heritage and architectural preservation offices and organizations.

Australian World Heritage Areas (AERIN)
<http://kaos.erin.gov.au/land/conservation/wha/auswha.html>
This section of the Australian Department of Sport and Territories addresses the country's World Heritage Areas by providing information on the sites, how they are listed, and the implications of World Heritage Listing.

International Council on Monuments and Sites
<http://www.icomos.org>
ICOMOS operates a homepage through ICOMOS Canada, which includes international

agreements and standards set by ICOMOS, other international organizations, specialist committees, and information on the new Blue Shield cultural property protection initiative.

Ministére de la Culture et de la Francophonie
<http://www.culture.fr>
Within the directory of the French Cultural Ministry page, a section entitled Public Information on Cultural Patrimony (*La Fondation du Patrimoine*) proposes to create a Biblioteca Universalis which will offer information on the major works and artifacts of the world, including the cultural and scientific heritage, via multimedia technologies. Offered in English and French.

National Trust for Historic Preservation
<http://www.nthp.org>
This new homepage of the United States preservation organization is divided into 12 categories, including information on Historic Places, Preserving Communities, Courts and Congress, and a Resource Directory.

Organization of World Heritage Cities
<http://www.ovpm.org>
(e-mail: ovpm@qbc.clic.net)
Created for the Second General Assembly of World Heritage Cities in 1995, this is the new World Wide Web page of the organization for the 109 cities on the World Heritage List. It includes the 1991 Management Guide, international charters and recommendations, international development assistance organizations and addresses, organization tactics, and conservation policy tools. These are discussed through case studies of diverse historic town projects. Offered in English, French, and Spanish.

PATA Foundation
<http://www.pata.org/patanet/index.html>
This is the Internet location of the nonprofit foundation of the Pacific Asia Travel Association. Pacific Asia travel and tourism depends on the attractions of the area's natural environment and on the diversity of its cultural heritage. These attractions are threatened in many areas, and through its grants, described here, the PATA Foundation contributes to their protection.

United Kingdom Department of National Heritage
<http://www.city.ac.uk/artspol/dnh.html>
The Management of United Kingdom Culture World Wide Web page of the National Heritage Department includes a section on heritage, which provides links to UK government information, as well as to information on world, Commonwealth, and European cultural heritage sites, and to the British Broadcasting Corporation, British museums, and the British Library.

UNESCO World Heritage Center
<http://www.unesco.org> also available at <gopher://gopher.unesco.org/11/Heritage>
The World Heritage Center is the United Nations Educational, Scientific, and Cultural Organization Secretariat for the Convention Concerning the Protection of the World Cultural and Natural Heritage. Within this page are links to the World Heritage List (including sites, criteria, and Heritage in Danger), World Heritage Committee Annual Reports, the 1972 Convention for the Protection of the World Cultural and Natural Heritage, and the 1976 Recommendations Concerning the Safeguarding and Contemporary Role of Historic Areas.

United States National Park Service
<http://www.cr.nps.gov>
This is the World Wide Web server for the Preservation Division of the National Park Service. This site is well-developed, with information on historic places and programs managed by the NPS, including Historic Places, Structures and Landscapes, Grants and Aid, and Where You Live.

World Bank
<http://www.worldbank.org>
The World Bank central homepage provides information on research projects, publications, current events, and the institution itself.

Collections and Resources

These resources are organized by various entities (individuals, preservation organizations, or universities, for example). Once connected to the respective site, one may search for specific resources, such as a UNESCO convention text, the Web page of a local historic preservation board, or a library database system.

Arch Net Cultural Resource Management and Historic Preservation Resources
<http://www.lib.uconn.edu/ArchNet/Topical/CRM/CRM.html>
A directory of Internet resources related to cultural resources management and historic preservation, organized by International Councils and Treaties, U.S. Government Agencies, U.S. Cultural Protection Legislation, and U.S. State Archaeologists and State Historic Preservation Offices. Still the most extensive treatment of national cultural resource legislation and regulation in the United States. Includes a listing of State Historic Preservation Offices with a known presence on the Internet.

Canadian Heritage Information Network (CHIN)
<http://www.chin.gc.ca>
The Conservation Info Network is a computer-based network that serves museums, libraries, and other heritage institutions internationally. CHIN supplies access to over twenty databases, provides advice on information standards, explores and evaluates multimedia technologies, and offers specialized training in museum practices and Internet use.

Internet Resources for Heritage Conservation, Historic Preservation and Archaeology
<http://www.cr.nps.gov/ncptt/irg>
This is a general, well-organized Internet Resource Guide for researching Heritage Conservation, including links to Web pages, electronic journals, images, library catalogs, and fee-based services.

Multilaterals Project
<http://www.tufts.edu/fletcher/multilaterals.html>
The Fletcher School Multilaterals Project Page is the location of most major international treaties, conventions, and lists. The Cultural Protection category includes the following:

- Treaty on the Protection of Artistic and Scientific Institutions and Historic Monuments, 1935.
- Protection of Artistic and Scientific Institutions and Historic Monuments Treaty Between the USA and the Other American Republics, 1935.
- Convention for the Protection of Cultural Property in the Event of Armed Conflict, 1954.
- Convention for the Protection of the World Cultural and Natural Heritage, 1972.
- World Heritage List and the List of World Heritage in Danger
- Convention on the Protection of the Archaeological, Historical, and Artistic Heritage of the American Nations, 1976.
- Convention for the Protection of the Architectural Heritage of Europe, 1985.
- Recommendation Concerning the Preservation of Cultural Property Endangered by Public or Private Works, 1986.
- Measures Likely to Promote the Funding of the Conservation of the Architectural Heritage, 1991.
- European Convention on the Protection of the Archaeological Heritage, 1992.
- Resolution on Information as an Instrument for Protection against War Damages to the Cultural Heritage, 1994.
- Recommendation Concerning Protection, at the National Level, of the Cultural and Natural Heritage, 1994.

The National Trust for Historic Preservation Library
<http://www.itd.umd.edu/UMS/UMCP/NTL/ntl.html>
The United States National Trust's library is located at the University of Maryland, to which one may submit requests for information from their Index to Historic Preservation Periodicals. Also at the site is a telnet connection to the library's catalog and links to historic preservation sites on the Web.

Preserve Net
<http://www.crp.cornell.edu>
Preserve Net includes an interactive information service and a new law service designed to aid lawyers, activists, and owners in understanding the law as it relates to preservation. Begun in December 1994 by the National Council for Preservation Education, Preserve Net is a comprehensive resource "dedicated to enhancing the dissemination of information regarding historic preservation and related disciplines. This Web resource is housed at Cornell University and is operated through the combined efforts of many undergraduate and graduate students, and faculty members across the United States."

Specific Resources

The following citations lead directly to specific historic preservation discussion groups, projects, and mailing lists.

Conservation DistList
<gopher://palimpsest.stanford.edu>
An online preservation discussion group. To subscribe, send the message, "subscribe Cons DistList <yourname@address>" to: consdist-request@lindy.stanford.edu

Preservation Discussion Group
To subscribe, send the message, "Subscribe preservation-l" to: listserv@netcom.com

Risk Map of Cultural Heritage in Italy
<http://www.uni.net/aec/riskmap/english.html>
When completed, this page will use Geographic Information Systems to develop thematic maps of hazards to cultural heritage sites in Italy.

C. Organizations Involved in the Conservation of the Built Heritage

Katherine Mangle

This appendix contains a list of key heritage organizations that was compiled as we were planning the Salzburg Seminar. Addresses, phone numbers, and the Universal Resource Locator for organizations' Web sites change frequently. The information in this appendix was last checked in August 1996.

Advisory Council on Historic Preservation
1100 Pennsylvania Avenue, NW
Suite 809
Washington, D.C.
USA
Phone: (202) 606-8503
Fax: (202) 606-8647
URL: <http://www.achp.gov>

Aga Khan Trust for Culture
Case Postale 2049
1211 Geneva 2
Switzerland
Phone: 41-22-909-7200
Fax: 41-22-909-7292

Civic Forum Foundation
Karolíny Svetlé 4
110 00 Prague 1
Czech Republic
Phone: 42-2-24-22-8866
Fax: 42-2-24-21-0324

Civic Trust
17 Carlton House Terrace
London SW1Y 5AW
England

Conservation Information Network
Canadian Heritage Information Network
15 Eddy Street, 4th Floor
Hull, Quebec K1A 0M5
Canada
Phone: (819) 994-1200
Fax: (819) 994-9555
URL: <http://www.chin.gc.ca>

Europa Nostra-International Federation of Associations for the Protection of Europe's
   Cultural, Architectural and Natural Heritage
86 Vincent Square
London SW1P 2PG
England

Getty Conservation Institute
1200 Getty Center Drive, Suite 700
Los Angeles, CA 90049-1684
USA
Phone: (310) 440-7325
Fax: (310) 440-7325
URL: <http://www.getty.edu/gci>

International Center for the Study of the Conservation and Restoration of Cultural
   Property (ICCROM)
Via di San Michele, 13
00153 Rome
Italy

International Council on Monuments and Sites (ICOMOS)
International Secretariat
49–51 rue de la Fèdèration
75015 Paris
France
Phone: 33-14-567-6770
Fax: 33-14-566-0622
URL: <http://www.icomos.org>

International Council on Monuments and Sites (ICOMOS) United States
401 F Street #331
Washington, DC 20001
USA
Phone: (202) 842-1866
Fax: (202) 842-1861
URL: <http://www.icomos.org/usicomos>

International Institute for Conservation
6 Buckingham Street
London WC2N 6BA
England

L'Inspection Generale des Monuments Historiques
Direction du Patrimoine
Ministére de la Culture
3 rue de Valois
75042 Paris Cedex 01
France
URL: <http://www.culture.fr>

National Park Service
Heritage Preservation Services Program
P.O. Box 37127
Washington, DC 20031-7127
USA
Phone: (202) 343-9573
Fax: (202) 343-3803
URL: <http://www.cr.nps.gov>

The National Trust (England, Wales, Northern Ireland)
36 Queen Anne's Gate
London SW1H 9AS
England
Phone: 44-171-222-9251
Fax: 44-171-222-5097
URL: <http://www.UKindex._CO._UK/National Trust>

National Trust for Historic Preservation
Department of Public Policy
1785 Massachusetts Avenue NW
Washington, DC 20036
USA
Phone: (202) 588-6255
Fax: (202) 588-6038

National Trust for Scotland
5 Charlotte Square
Edinburgh EH2 4DU
Scotland
Phone: 44-131-226-5922
Fax: 44-131-243-9302

Shalu Association for Tibetan Cultural Heritage
127 rue de Sevres
75006 Paris
France
Fax: 33-14-567-9503

Tokyo National Research Institute for the Conservation of Cultural Properties
13-27 Ueno Park, Taito-ku
Tokyo 110
Japan

United Nations Educational, Scientific, and Cultural Organization (UNESCO)
The World Heritage Center
7 place de Fontenoy
75372 Paris
France
Phone: 33-14-568-1000
Fax: 33-14-567-1690

UNESCO Asian Cultural Center
c/o Nihon Shuppan Kaikan
6 Fukuromachi, Chinjuku-ku
Tokyo 162
Japan

Upper Silesia Cultural Heritage Centre
ul. Jagiellonska 25
40-032 Katowice
Poland
Phone: 48-32-517-104
Fax: 48-32-517-104

World Bank
1818 H Street NW
Washington, DC 20433
USA
Phone: (202) 477-1234
Fax: (202) 477-6391
URL: <http://www.worldbank.org>

World Conservation Monitoring Centre
Information Officer
219 Huntingdon Rd.
Cambridge CB30DL
England
Fax: 44-122-327-7136
E-mail: <info@wcmc.org.uk>

World Monuments Fund
949 Park Avenue
New York, NY 10028
USA
Phone: (212) 517-9367
Fax: (212) 517-9494

The Salzburg Seminar

For a half-century, the Salzburg Seminar has provided an international forum for bringing together women and men committed to making a difference in their professions and in their societies. The Seminar has over 16,000 alumni from more than 120 countries around the world, many of them in positions of national and international leadership.

Founded in 1947 by three Harvard University students, the Salzburg Seminar was initially established to promote dialogue among the young people of war-torn Europe and America. That first summer nearly one hundred young intellectuals from Europe and the United States gathered for six weeks at Schloss Leopoldskron in Salzburg, Austria, to study American politics, economics, and culture. Today the Seminar's mission remains much the same, but its thematic focus and geographic scope have expanded dramatically. Annually the Seminar conducts ten one-week sessions in its Core Program, ten workshops and conferences in its Center for the Study of American Culture and Language (CSACL), and a number of special sessions devoted to an issue of pressing social, political, economic, or cultural importance.

The Facility

Seminar activities are conducted at Schloss Leopoldskron, situated on seventeen acres overlooking a picturesque lake with a dramatic view of the Austrian Alps, minutes from the center of Salzburg. Built between 1736 and 1744 for Archbishop Leopold Firmian, the Schloss was restored in the twentieth century by Max Reinhardt, the renowned theater director and cofounder of the Salzburg Festival. The adjacent Meierhof building, dating from the seventeenth century, houses the new Center for the Study of American Culture and Language, the main lecture hall (Parker Hall), the reception area, and modern living accommodations for Fellows.

The Seminar prides itself on promoting American informality in a setting of European elegance. Faculty and Fellows live and work together in the Schloss and Meierhof for the duration of the session. A magnificent rococo library houses the Seminar's collection, consisting of some 10,000 books and over 130 journals and periodicals. Open twenty-four hours a day during sessions, the library is equipped with computers that provide access to an online catalog, CD-ROMs, and the Internet. A separate computer room with word processing capabilities is also available to session participants. Owned by the Salzburg Seminar and administered by the Schloss Leopoldskron Conference Center, the Schloss and Meierhof are available to other organizations throughout the year as a venue for symposia and conferences.

The Salzburg Seminar on the Internet

The Salzburg Seminar is linked to the Internet and has established a World Wide Web site. Seminar publications—including the Program Brochure, the President's Report, Session Reports, and application forms—are available on the Seminar's homepage. Session descriptions and faculty listings are updated regularly, enabling users to obtain the most recent program information from any computer in the world that is linked to the Internet and the World Wide Web. The homepage may be viewed at <http://www.salsem.ac.at>, and questions about the Salzburg Seminar may be directed by e-mail to <info@fc.salsem.org>. Friends, alumni, and potential applicants are encouraged to take advantage of these innovations in the Seminar's international networking and communication capabilities.

Participants

Faculty

John de Monchaux (Co-Chair)
Professor of Architecture and Urban Planning,
Massachusetts Institute of Technology
Cambridge, Mass., USA
General Manager,
Aga Khan Trust for Culture
Geneva, Switzerland

J. Mark Schuster (Co-Chair)
Associate Professor of Urban Studies and
    Planning,
Massachusetts Institute of Technology
Cambridge, Mass., USA

Stefano Bianca
Director,
Historic Cities Support Program
Aga Khan Trust for Culture
Geneva, Switzerland

Lester Borley
Secretary General,
Europa Nostra
Chairman,
ICOMOS Cultural Tourism Committee
Edinburgh, Scotland

John Costonis
Dean and Milton Underwood Professor of
    Free Enterprise,
Vanderbilt Law School
Vanderbilt University
Nashville, Tenn., USA

Dasha Havel
Director,
Civic Forum Foundation
Prague, Czech Republic

Franz Neuwirth
Senior Advisor,
Department of Monument Protection
Federal Ministry for Education and Cultural
    Affairs
Vienna, Austria

David Throsby
Professor of Economics,
Macquarie University
Sydney, Australia

Fellows

Adel Essa Mohammed Al-Hadi
Senior Architect,
Minstry of Housing, Municipality and the
    Environment
Manama, Bahrain

Isam Al-Rawas
Assistant Professor of History,
Sultan Qaboos University
Al-Khod, Oman

Selma Arnautovic Harrington
Principal Architect,
ANIMA Design
Harare, Zimbabwe

Cynthia Atherton
Assistant Professor of Art History,
Middlebury College
Middlebury, Vt., USA

221

Alexandra Bitušíková
Director,
Institute of Regional Research
Assistant Professor of Cultural Anthropology,
Metej Bel University
Banská Bystrica, Slovak Republic

Chris Campbell
United States Peace Corps
Hortobágyi National Park
Debrecen, Hungary

Juris Dambis
Head of State Heritage Protection Office
Riga, Latvia

Adeeb Daoud
Architect
Nazareth, Israel

Chris Dawes
Head of Heritage,
Department of National Heritage
London, England

Vikas Dilawari
Architect and conservation consultant
Bombay, India

Igor Doukhan
Dean of Arts Faculty,
European Humanities University
Minsk, Belarus

Arlene Fleming
Cultural resource management consultant,
Great Falls, Va., USA

Abdullah Hadrami
Director of Technical Cooperation,
General Organization for the Preservation of
    Historic Cities
Sana'a, Yemen

Claudia Hamill
Head of Europe and Overseas Relations,
The National Trust
London, England

Mikuláš Hulec
Architect,
Prague, Czech Republic

Khalid El Adli Imam
Assistant Professor of Urban and Regional
    Planning,
Cairo University
Cairo, Egypt

Mart Kalm
Assistant Professor of Art History,
Tallinn Art University
Tallinn, Estonia

Atis Kampars
Vice-Rector of Education,
Latvian Academy of Arts
Riga, Latvia

Ammar Khammash
Architect
Amman, Jordan

Elizabeth Kovács
Assistant of NGO Relations,
National Board for the Protection of Historic
    Monuments
Budapest, Hungary

Andri Ksenofontov
Head of Harjumaa-Tallinn Heritage
    Inspection Office,
Central Board of Antiquities of the Estonian
    Republic
Tallinn, Estonia

Thomas Lollar
Director,
Lincoln Center Poster and Print Program
New York, N.Y., USA

Monica Lotreanu
Associate Lecturer in Art History and Theory,
Fine Arts Academy
Bucharest, Romania

Eric Luiten
Director,
LAVA Landscape Architecture Consultants
Barcelona, Spain

Godfrey Mahachi
Deputy Executive Director,
National Museums and Monuments
Harare, Zimbabwe

Miroslava Makarevych
Chief Expert and Press Coordinator,
National Commission on the Restitution of
   Cultural Treasures
Kiev, Ukraine

Luis Mateus
Professor of Architectural Design,
University of Minho
Braga, Portugal

Kamila Matousková
Director,
Department of Preservation of Cultural
   Heritage
Prague, Czech Republic

Gordon Metz
Special Projects Director,
Mayibuye Center for History and Culture
Bellville, South Africa

Dino Milinovic
Secretary General,
Croatian Commission for UNESCO
Zagreb, Croatia

Oksana Minaeva
Research Associate,
Institute of Art Studies, Bulgarian Academy
   of Sciences
Sofia, Bulgaria

Amr Mahmoud Mostafa
Assistant Lecturer in Architecture,
Tantra University
Cairo, Egypt

Mauritz Naudé
Senior Researcher,
Natural Cultural History Museum
Pretoria, South Africa

Pilar Navascues
Director,
Cerralbo Museum
Madrid, Spain

R. Sami Nawar
Head of Jeddah Historic Preservation
   Department
Jeddah, Saudi Arabia

Terry O'Regan
Landscape Horticulturist and Designer,
BHL Landscape Group
Cork, Ireland

Katalin Pallai
Special Counselor to the Mayor,
Budapest, Hungary

Amir Pašic
Senior Researcher,
Center for Islamic History at Yildiz Technical
   University
Istanbul, Turkey

Maridea Petrova
Architect and Urban Planner
Ohrid, FYR of Macedonia

Jacek Purchla
Director,
International Cultural Center
Krakow, Poland

Sulhinisso Rahmatullaeva
Senior Researcher,
Academy of Sciences of the Republic of
   Tajikistan
Dushanbe, Tajikistan

Purna Man Shakya
Assistant Professor of Law,
Tribhuvan University
Lalitpur, Nepal

Sunny Stastny
Executive Director,
Civic Forum Foundation
Prague, Czech Republic

Heather Stoddard
Associate Professor in Tibetan,
National Institute of Oriental Language and
   Civilization
Paris, France

Alicja Szmelter
Assistant Professor of Town Building
   History,
Warsaw University of Technology
Warsaw, Poland

Olga Taratynova
Deputy Director,
State Office of Inspection for the
    Protection and Restoration of Historic
    Monuments
St. Petersburg, Russia

Bohdana Urbanovych
Director,
Center for the Historical Preservation and De-
    velopment of Architecturally Significant
    Central City Business Districts in Ukraine
Kiev, Ukraine

Matko Vetma
Architect,
State Institute for the Protection of Cultural
    Monuments
Dubrovnik, Croatia

Linda Wilson
Deputy State Historic Preservation Officer,
Concord, N.H., USA

Gil Yaniv
District Director,
Ministry of the Environment
Jerusalem, Israel

Ahmed Yassin
Principal Administrative Officer and
    Coordinator,
Heritage Managment Programmes, National
    Museums of Kenya
Nairobi, Kenya

Sergei Zuev
Head of the Center for Cultural Technologies
Moscow, Russia

Contributors

Stefano Bianca

is the director of the Historic Cities Support Programme of the Aga Khan Trust for Culture (AKTC) in Geneva. His mandate there is to interconnect the conservation and revival of important historic structures and open spaces with related community development, socio-economic improvements, and institutional strengthening of local groups. Dr. Bianca joined AKTC in 1991 after many years of professional involvement in the conservation and rehabilitation of historic cities in the Arab world. From 1976 to 1990, he directed major town planning and conservation schemes in Fes, Aleppo, Baghdad, Madinah, and Riyadh.

Lester Borley

is secretary general of Europa Nostra, an association of over two hundred heritage organizations and one hundred local authorities in thirty European countries headquartered in The Hague. Mr. Borley was formerly the director of the National Trust for Scotland (N.T.S.), the leading voluntary conservation body in Scotland supporting the preservation and presentation of 120 properties in its care. Before joining the N.T.S., Mr. Borley worked for the British Travel Association in the United States, Australia, and Germany marketing tourism. He was subsequently involved in the development of tourism projects in the United Kingdom as the chief executive of the Scottish and English Tourist Boards. He chairs the U.K. Cultural Tourism Committee, and is a member of the ICOMOS International Cultural Tourism Committee.

John J. Costonis

is dean of the Vanderbilt University School of Law and Milton R. Underwood Professor of Free Enterprise. His research has focused on the elaboration of governmentally-administered incentive programs either to secure the preservation of historic buildings or to conserve environmentally sensitive areas threatened by private market development forces. He has been a visiting research fellow and professor in environmental and land use studies at the universities of Aix-en-Provence, Caen, and Siena. Dean Costonis was formerly Professor of Law at the University of Illinois, the University of California at Berkeley, and New York University. His publications include *Space Adrift: Landmark Preservation and the Marketplace* and *Icons and Aliens: Law, Aesthetics, and Environmental Change* (both University of Illinois Press).

John de Monchaux

is professor of architecture and urban planning at the Massachusetts Institute of Technology. From 1981 to 1992 he served as dean of the M.I.T. School of Architecture and Planning. Professor de Monchaux was previously a principal planner with Kinhill, a planning design and engineering firm in Australia, and a partner in the Llewelyn-Davies architectural and planning firms in the United Kingdom and the United States. His current teaching focuses on the development and implementation of plans and policies with regard to urban design issues including historic preservation and reuse. He also has served as general manager of the Aga Khan Trust for Culture, a foundation concerned with the quality of architecture and the built environment in the Muslim world. He served as co-chair of Salzburg Seminar 332, "Preserving the National Heritage: Policies, Partnerships and Actions."

Dasha Havel

chairs the board of directors of the Civic Forum Foundation, an organization dedicated to cultural preservation and one of the first foundations established in the former Czechoslovakia after the Velvet Revolution. The foundation awards grants for the repair and restoration of historic monuments and organizes training sessions and seminars on historic preservation. She has participated in planning charettes for the chateaux of Lednice and Valtice conducted by the World Monuments Fund. She is also a board member of the Information Center for Foundations and Other Non-Profit Organizations in Prague; Eurocentres in Switzerland; and the European Cultural Foundation in the Netherlands.

Katherine Mangle

graduated from the Department of Urban Studies and Planning at M.I.T. with a Master in City Planning degree in June 1996. She researched the impact of intensive urban restructuring in Olympic host cities, the relationship between public policy and historic preservation, and the implementation of growth management strategies through intergovernmental cooperation in Colorado. Ms. Mangle served as a research assistant for Salzburg Seminar 332, "Preserving the National Heritage: Policies, Partnerships, and Actions."

Charles A. Riley II

is associate professor of business journalism at Baruch College, City University of New York as well as a freelance arts journalist. He is the author of *Color Codes* (University Press of New England) as well as *Small Business, Big Politics* (Peterson's), and editor, with Olin Robison and Robert Freeman, of *The Arts in the World Economy* (University Press of New England), a book based on Salzburg Seminar 309 "Economics of The Arts."

J. Mark Schuster

is associate professor of urban studies and planning at M.I.T., where he specializes in the analysis of government policies and intervention with respect to the arts, culture, and environmental design. He spent the 1992–1993 academic year as a visiting professor in the Division of Legal, Economic, and Social Sciences at the University of Barcelona, where he was affiliated with the Centre d'estudis de planificació and the Centre d'estudis i recursos culturals and continued his research on comparative cultural policy. He is the author of numerous books, articles, and reports on comparative cultural policy, and urban design policy, including: *Patrons Despite Themselves: Taxpayers and Arts Policy* (New York University Press) [with Michael O'Hare and Alan Feld], *Supporting the Arts: An International Comparative Study* (U.S. Government Superintendent of Documents), *Who's to Pay for the Arts? The International Search for Models of Arts Support* (American Council for the Arts) [with Milton Cummings], and *The Audience for American Art Museums* (Seven Locks Press). He has extensive international consulting experience, primarily with governmental agencies and nonprofit organizations, and serves on the editorial boards of the *European Journal of Cultural Policy* and the *Journal of Planning Education and Research*. He served as co-chair of Salzburg Seminar 332, "Preserving the National Heritage: Policies, Partnerships, and Actions."

David Throsby

is professor of economics at Macquarie University in Sydney, Australia, since 1974. He is recognized internationally for his research on the economics of culture and the arts, including the interface between economic and cultural policy, the economics of heritage preservation, and culturally sustainable development. He is the author of *The Economics of the Performing Arts* (St.

Martin's Press) [with Glen Withers]. He has been a consultant to the World Commission on Culture and Development and the World Bank, and is currently president-elect of the Association for Cultural Economics International. Professor Throsby is a member of the editorial boards of the *Journal of Cultural Economics* and the *European Journal of Cultural Policy*. He is chair of the National Association for the Visual Arts in Australia and a board member of the Museum of Contemporary Art in Sydney.

Index

Almy, Richard, 78n
Alvarez, José Luis, 77n
Amsterdam, 66
Ancient Monuments and Archaeological
	Areas Act of 1979, 54
Andrews, Gregory, 77n, 78n, 152
Appleyard, Donald, 30n, 31
Arkansas, 145
Arkoun, Mohammed, 166
Arts Council of Great Britain, 69–70
Atlanta, 65
AT&T, 159
Austria, 55–56, 61, 67, 110
Axelrod, Robert, 194–96

Bacow, Adele Fleet, 122
Baden-Württemberg, 145
Baker, R. Lisle, 78n
Bardach, Eugene, 45n, 47n
Basler, Ernst, 31
Baumol, William J., 46n, 47
Beaumont, Constance, 152
Benhamou, Françoise, 47n
Bentham, Jeremy, 90
Berra, Yogi, 7
Bianca, Stefano, 13–31, 158
Bitušíková, Alexandra, 162
Bolla, Gerard, 117, 123
Bologna, 30n
Borley, Lester, 124, 131, 158, 164–84
Boston, 74
Bourdieu, Pierre, 193
Bouuaert, Ignace Claeys, 52, 75n, 78
Brazil, 66
Brenneman, Russell L., 77n, 78n
Buchanan, James, 46n, 47
Burra Charter, 35, 45n, 165

Caisse Nationale des Monuments His-
	toriques, 146
Campbell, Christopher, 162

Canada, 24, 59
Chicago Plan, 91–92, 98n
Chicago School of Economics, 37
Civic Forum Foundation, 186
Clean Air Act, 93–94
Clotfelter, Charles T., 77n
Coca-Cola, 159, 199
Commission of the European Communities,
	52
Communist countries, 24–25
Convention for the Protection of the Archi-
	tectural Heritage of Europe, 102
Costonis, John J., 81–99
Council of Europe, 109, 182
cultural heritage: definition of, 18, 165–66
Cultural Schilling Law, 145
cultural tourism, 174–75
Czech Republic, 185, 187–88

Dale, Anthony, 57, 73, 76n, 79
Damascus, 14
de Monchaux, John, 3–12
de Monchaux, Suzanne, 151
Denmark, 56, 71
development rights transfer, 85–97
disincentives, 69
Disney Corporation, 160
Doheny, David A., 99
Dubrovnik, 145
Duroselle, Jean Baptiste, 183

Economic Recovery Tax Act of 1981, 60–61
Europa Nostra, 170, 180

Feilden, Bernard M., 30n, 31
Fernandez-Armesto, Felipe, 171
financing, 42–44, 144–46, 180–81
Florida, 145
Ford Motor Company, 159
Fowler, John M., 76n
France, 54, 61, 66

Frey, Bruno, 41, 46n, 47

Gates, Bill, 159
Georgia Department of Natural Resources, 104
Germany, 61, 62, 71, 104
Ghirardelli Square, 84
Giardina, Emilio, 47
Glasgow, 108
Gleye, Paul H., 120n
government: role in conservation, 19–23, 89–91
Grampp, William D., 46n, 47, 162
Grand Central Terminal, 82–85, 90, 92, 97
grants, 53–57; matching, 53–57
Graz, 56

Haider, Donald, 50, 53, 75n, 76n
Hamill, Claudia, 161
Hardin, Garrett, 81, 98n, 99
Harrison, Richard, 183
Hausman, J. A., 48
Havel, Dasha, 158–59, 184–200
Havel, Václav, 185
heritage management, 17–19
Herr, Phil, 147
Hewison, Robert, 46n, 48
Hillman-Chartrand, Harry, 129, 151
Historic Area Development Corporations (HADC), 28, 44
Historic Cities Support Programme of the Aga Khan Trust for Culture, 113
Hood, Christopher, 3–4, 8n, 103, 120n, 122n, 126–27, 128, 147, 150, 152
Hutter, Michael, 45n, 48

incentives, 5–6, 49–80; design of, 71–72; direct, 53–57, 72–73; impact of, 73–75; income tax, 60–62; indirect, 57–66, 72–73; property tax, 62–64; tax-based, 58–65
information, 5–6, 100–123; media, 115–16, 166–68; roles of, 102–13
Inteco, 167
International Council on Monuments and Sites (ICOMOS), 35, 75n, 121n, 161, 165
Islam, 25

Italy, 38

Johnston, Chris, 46n
Jukka, Jokiletho, 30n

Kansas, 145
Keune, Russell V., 123
Kimpton Hotel Group, 160

Lass, Andrew, 194
listing of heritage properties, 103–8, 168–70
London, Tower of, 39
Lumley, Robert, 123
Lund, Michael, 64

Mangle, Katherine, 203
Marquis-Kyle, Peter, 45n, 48
Maryland, 62–63
Massachusetts Institute of Technology, 4, 118, 147
McCaughey, Claire, 129, 151n
McDaniel, Paul, 59, 76n
McGee, Joseph H., 78n
McHarg, Ian, 168
McLuhan, Marshall, 166
Metz, Gordon, 144, 160
Mexico City, 146
Microsoft, 159, 200
Milan, 38, 43
Morris, Marya, 51, 75n, 77n, 78
Muslim countries, 14, 25, 27, 30n

National Historic Preservation Act of 1966, 111
National Trust, England, 68
National Trust for Scotland, 171, 177–78
Nepal, 145
Netherlands, 56–57
Netzer, Dick, 43, 47n, 48
New York City Landmarks Commission, 85
New Zealand, 165
Nolan, John R., 79
Notre Dame, Paris, 39

Oates, Wallace E., 46n
Ogas, Anthony, 46n, 48
Oldham, Sally G., 79
Olivetti, 159

ownership and operation, 5–6, 13–31

Paris, 83
partnerships, 26–28, 50, 157–200
Passel, Peter, 193, 199n, 200
Peacock, Alan, 37, 45n, 46n, 48
Pearce, B. J., 152n, 153
Peters, James, 79
Poland, 55, 65, 66, 103, 171
pollution emission credits, 93–94
Powers, Lonnie, 76n, 78n
preservation assets, 17–19
Prince of Wales Business Leaders' Forum, 191–92, 197
property rights, 5–6, 81–99
public vs. private ownership, 23

regulation, 5–6, 32–48, 187–89; desirability of, 38–44; hard, 34; problems with, 35–38; soft, 34–35, 112, 116
Ricketts, Martin, 46n, 48
Riley, Charles A., 157–63
Rio Agreement, 166
Rizzo, Ilde, 45n, 47
Roddewig, Richard, 50, 75n, 79
Rome, 14, 38, 43
Roscoe, John, 167

Salamon, Lester, 3, 8n, 45n, 64, 76n, 79, 125, 127, 147, 149, 153, 190
Salzburg, 56
Saudi Arabia, 25
Schumacher, E. F., 182, 183n
Schuster, J. Mark, 3–12, 49–80, 100–153
Selznick, Philip, 45n, 48
Serageldin, Ismail, 31, 44, 46n, 48
Solow, Robert M., 192
Spanish Historic Heritage Act of 1985, 71
Split, 14
Stigler, George, 37, 46n, 48
Stipe, Robert, 8n, 73, 77n, 78n, 79–80, 121n, 123, 151n, 153
Suddards, Roger W., 45n, 48
Sutter, Keith D., 47n, 48
Swiss Society for the Conservation of Historical Art Monuments, 55
Switzerland, 55, 70, 76n
Sydney Opera House, 39

Szczerba, Waldemar, 120n

Tax Reform Act of 1976, 60
Tax Reform Act of 1981, 61
Tax Reform Act of 1986, 61
Throsby, David, 32–48, 112, 116, 122n
Tollison, Robert D., 48
Tools for Community Design, 196
tools of government action, 3–6; choice of, 124–53; constraints on, 138–44
Tullock, Gordon, 46n
Turkey, 64

United Kingdom, 54, 68, 69, 116, 168–69, 174
United Nations Educational Scientific and Cultural Organization (UNESCO), 30, 35, 100, 107–8, 113, 117–18, 121, 143, 166, 169, 186
United States, 24, 59, 60, 65, 68, 73, 83, 94, 109, 113, 116, 146

valuation, 41–42, 189
Vatican City, 38
Veljanovski, Cento, 46n, 48
Venice, 35, 43
Vienna, 145
Virginia Neighborhood Assistance Act, 67

Walker, Meredith, 45n
waqf system, 27–28
Wates, Nick, 200
Weber, Stephen R., 80
Western Europe, 23–24
Will, Margaret Thomas, 121n
World Bank, 8, 28, 192–93
World Heritage Convention, 43, 169
World Heritage Fund, 118, 186
World Heritage List, 117–18
World Tourist Organization, 174
World Wide Web, 116, 184

Yugoslavia, 107

Ziegler, Edward H., 98–99
zoning bonus, 95
Zurich, 145
Zuziak, Zbigniew, 30n, 31

University Press of New England publishes books under its own imprint and is the publisher for Brandeis University Press, Dartmouth College, Middlebury College Press, University of New Hampshire, Tufts University, Wesleyan University Press, and Salzburg Seminar.

Library of Congress Cataloging-In-Publication Data
Preserving the built heritage : tools for implementation
J. Mark Schuster with John de Monchaux and Charles A. Riley II, editors
   p.   cm.
Based on the Salzburg Seminar's session on the topic convened in December 1995.
   "Salzburg Seminar books."
   Includes bibliographical references and index.
   ISBN 0–87451–813–x (alk. paper). — ISBN 0–87451–831–8 (pbk. : alk. paper)
   1. Historic preservation—Government policy—Congresses.   2. Historic preservation—
Congresses.   3. Cultural property, Protection of—Congresses.   I. Schuster, J. Mark Davidson,
1950–   .   II. De Monchaux, John.   III. Riley, Charles A.   IV. Salzburg Seminar.
CC135.P73   1997
363.6'9—dc21   97–5520